Language Acquisition
and Linguistic Theory

Language Acquisition and Linguistic Theory

Edited by
Susan L. Tavakolian

The MIT Press
Cambridge, Massachusetts
London, England

This book was set in VIP Times Roman by Village Typographers, and printed and bound by Halliday Lithograph Corporation in the United States of America.

Library of Congress Cataloging in Publication Data

Main entry under title:

Language acquisition and linguistic theory.

An outgrowth of the Language Acquisition Workshop held at the University of Massachusetts, Amherst, in April 1978.
  Bibliography: p.
  Includes index.
  1. Language acquisition—Congresses. 2. Linguistics—Congresses.
I. Tavakolian, Susan L.
P118.L253   401′.9   80–28940
ISBN 0–262–20039–2

Contents

Preface

This collection brings together research on children's acquisition of language that is original in its content and unique in its focus. The relevance of language-acquisition studies to theoretical linguistics has long been acknowledged, but relatively few studies of child language have incorporated this perspective into an analysis of the data. This volume focuses on the significance of language-acquisition studies to the construction of theories of adult language. The purpose of the research is to present experimental results on children's acquisition of language, to reveal something about adult grammar, and to address current issues in linguistic theory. The contributors relate language-acquisition data to a wide variety of theoretical questions and discuss a number of acquisition phenomena that have not been examined previously.

Linguistic theory provides a general framework within which data from child language can be fruitfully analyzed. Theoretical considerations can unify otherwise disparate and seemingly unrelated data from language-acquisition studies to provide a uniform account of children's linguistic knowledge. Conversely, theories of language acquisition constrain proposals about adult grammars by requiring that adult grammars be learnable within a relatively short period of time, that theories of adult language be consistent with what is known about children's acquisition of language, and that the acquisition process not depend on impossible learning procedures.

The first chapter, by Edwin Williams, relates theoretical constructs to language acquisition in a unique way. Williams reanalyzes a theoretical construct, $\overline{X}$ notation, as a series of hypotheses made by an aggressive language-acquisition device. These hypotheses take the form of questions and answers concerning the component categories of the base and rely on the notion of markedness to draw out the categorial implications of each hypothesis. $\overline{\text{X}}$ notation has been proposed as a way of expressing regularities in the base component of an adult grammar. Williams argues that his "learning diagrams" allow even wider generalizations in an adult grammar and in addition provide predictions of children's acquisition of the base rules.

Roeper, Lapointe, Bing, and Tavakolian also deal with the structure of the base, adopting a particular version of the lexicon set forth by Bresnan (1978) and examining within that framework children's acquisition of two rules that interact in an adult grammar: Passive and Dative Movement. This analysis of language-acquisition data follows the general trend in linguistic theory to reanalyze transformational rules as lexical rules.

Lust, Solan, and Matthei each make an important contribution to theories of anaphora. Solan demonstrates that at an early age children use structural relationships (specifically Reinhart's c-command), complement type, and linear order in determining the anaphoric relationship between a pronoun and a possible antecedent. The analysis thus provides support for c-command as the relevant structural restriction in adult grammar as well.

Lust's chapter is important for the connection it makes between the directionality of recursion rules and children's interpretation of forward and backward anaphora. She argues that in the early stages of language development the direction of anaphora will be constrained leftward in a left-branching language and rightward in a right-branching language. Lust's finding that directionality constraints hold for both null and pronominal anaphora supports analyses of adult grammars that collapse them. She also presents evidence that children are sensitive to the subtle distinction between coreference and anaphoric relations.

Matthei's analysis of reciprocals presents a challenge to predictions of reciprocal acquisition made by proposed universal conditions such as the Tensed-S Condition and the Specified-Subject Condition. His finding that children make many errors in determining the antecedent of a reciprocal suggests that a reinterpretation of the role of such rules in restricting the child's grammar may be necessary.

Phinney presents her finding that the parameters important for an analysis of anaphoric systems, directionality and hierarchical relationships, are also crucial for children's interpretations of negatives in complex sentences. Her data indicate that children shift from using only directionality in determining the scope of a negative to utilizing hierarchical considerations as well. This parallels the findings of Lust

(1978), Solan (1978), and Tavakolian (1978a) for children's interpretations of anaphoric elements. Phinney's results provide further confirmation of the necessity for incorporating theoretical constructs such
as directionality and hierarchical relationships into analyses of child
grammars.

Goodluck and Tavakolian each analyze children's hypotheses about
the structure of complex sentences that contain verbal complements or
noun phrase complements. Goodluck provides experimental evidence
for the presence of two putative universals in children's grammar: the
c-command condition on control of missing subjects, which requires
that a specific structural configuration hold between a missing subject
and its controlling NP, and the application of control rules with reference to underlying rather than derived structure. The existence of
these universals in children's grammars strengthens arguments for their
existence in adult grammars.

In my chapter I argue that the child's first hypothesis about the
structure of sentences containing relative clauses or verbal complements is that they consist of conjoined rather than embedded clauses.
The implication of this finding is that children analyze strings into "flat"
structures and that such analyses limit the number of hypotheses a
child must initially consider in dealing with complex sentences.

Valian, Winzemer, and Erreich also deal with the role of hypotheses in
a child's grammar. They present a model of language learning in which
acquisition occurs as a hypothesis-testing procedure. As an example
evidence from children's errors on Subject-Auxiliary Inversion and
Tense-Hopping are interpreted as failures to apply certain basic operations necessary in adult formulations of the rules. They argue for a
differentiation of the content of language acquisition (a theoretical
model) from the mechanisms of learning (their hypothesis-testing procedure) as a necessary step toward adequately assessing the relationship of linguistic theory and acquisition theory.

This collection addresses a number of theoretical areas: anaphoric
interpretation, proposed universal constraints, the structure of the
base, and structural analyses of complex sentences. In each case, data
from language acquisition are relevant to the analyses proposed for
adult grammars, and a link between children's developing grammars
and the target adult grammar is established. This volume, then, provides a new perspective for relating language-acquisition data to theoretical issues.

Susan L. Tavakolian

Acknowledgments

This volume grew out of the Language Acquisition Workshop held at the University of Massachusetts, Amherst, in April 1978. The workshop was sponsored by a grant from the Five Colleges (Amherst College, Hampshire College, Mt. Holyoke College, Smith College, and the University of Massachusetts). We are grateful to Five Colleges, Inc., for providing that opportunity for a number of researchers engaged in language-acquisition research and its relationship to linguistic theory to meet and exchange ideas and commentary.

A number of people contributed to the success of the workshop: Tom Roeper, Alan Prince, Larry Solan, Helen Goodluck, Lynn Ballard, Kitty Axelson, Jan Bing, Ed Matthei, and the participants who spent an exhausting but stimulating weekend discussing language-acquisition material. Subsequently others were instrumental in launching the publication of this volume: Joan Bresnan, Emmon Bach, and Barbara Partee. A particular statement of gratitude goes to Helen Goodluck, Larry Solan, and Tom Roeper, who acted as collaborators and advisors.

But especially we thank all the children who contributed the data on which these papers are based.

Language Acquisition
and Linguistic Theory

Introduction

Thomas Roeper

This book may remind some readers of early work in language acquisition. It seeks to find the precise connection between linguistic theory and a theory of language acquisition. A brief look at the past may show us why many of the old questions can be seen in a new light.

In the early 1960s linguistic theory provided a specific hypothesis about language learning: that the universal features of adult languages are innate in the child. It was not initially clear what would serve as evidence for or against this view. It is a challenge in any new domain of inquiry to formulate hypotheses that are sufficiently precise to allow evidence that falsifies them. The most natural first move was to develop experiments that were perfect reflections of linguistic theory. One hypothesis that sprang to mind was the derivational theory of complexity;[1] not surprisingly, it failed. What should one make of the failure? Some researchers (mostly psychologists) interpreted the results as reason to reject linguistic theory, whereas others (mostly linguists) interpreted the results as reason to reject experimentation (as mired in the detritus of performance). A third view seems far more natural, in retrospect. The first versions of both linguistic theory and acquisition theory were wrong. Each was a crude model applied to an enormously intricate mechanism, and thus each has been, and is, in need of great refinement.

What then is the mark of refinement or progress? We cannot expect to have a preestablished and fixed linguistic theory from which to develop an acquisition theory. We must use current theories in designing experiments that can help refine both our theory of adult competence and our model of an acquisition mechanism. Progress in any science has typical characteristics: First, new theories have some basic principles that achieve generality; the concept of markedness in language acquisition is an example. Second, new theories provide an improved "fit" between theory and data; increasingly subtle data should be included. Third, new theories of dynamic processes cast their generalizations in terms of a mechanism. In linguistics the mechanism should simulate the creative use or acquisition of language. An acquisition device should therefore be cast in terms of a model that projects hypotheses, considers evidence, and makes revisions. The links between parts of a mechanism are important and often surprising discoveries. In the same fashion a mechanism like a car may have some intuitively odd-looking but important parts (like a carburetor).

The chapters in this volume illustrate these characteristics. Therefore, they mark significant progress in both linguistics and language acquisition. Goodluck, Matthei, and Solan each deal with a basic principle of grammar that appears in a subtle form in English. For instance, Solan shows that a principle of tree structure (c-command) explains why children assign coreference in different ways for the sentences *The horse hit him after the sheep ran around* and *The horse hit him in the sheep's yard*. Williams develops a decision tree, which functions as a part of an acquisition mechanism and explains how children know that a phrase like *proudly of his children* is ungrammatical.

Those properties of grammars that are subtle provide the greatest challenge to noninnatist theories of learning. Being subtle they are not salient. Therefore they should be difficult for an uninformed perceptual device to "see." However, if there exists an acquisition device that is informed by innate universals, then it should not be surprising that it can "see" subtleties.

The evolution of a theory causes an evolution in the role of data. There are no preordained limits on the domain of relevant data. In fact, both acquisition data and adult linguistic intuitions may contribute to either a theory of acquisition or a theory of adult competence. The field of acquisition has exhibited a healthy flexibility toward what counts as relevant data. There has been a shift from the examination of spontaneous speech to experiments that dealt with language comprehension and then to the interpretation by adults of the nonlinguistic contexts in which children talk.

There is, furthermore, a sense in which the ultimate flexibility toward data is called for: the recognition that some data that might be extremely important are completely inaccessible. This applies particularly to theories about complex syntax. There are few if any meanings that a child cannot express in simple sentences. Therefore, meaning alone does not compel a child to use complex sentences. Consequently a child may consider and reject many hypotheses silently—in other words, there may be silent stages in acquisition. We must be prepared to project a theory where some of a child's hypotheses are never manifested but play a role in a coherent account of language acquisition. In fact, later stages in acquisition are often marked by a sudden ability in children to move from no response to a correct response (in an experiment) with no evidence of intermediate trial hypotheses. Work by Wexler and Culicover, for instance, implies the existence of silent stages. Whenever such theories are proposed, the appropriate question becomes: Do we have evidence against them?

It is appropriate, therefore, that promising hypotheses go beyond the experimental evidence with which they are compatible. They are motivated jointly by data and their putative role in a theory. The chapters by Lust, Tavakolian, and Phinney involve powerful hypotheses about tree structures that are justified by more than the data of language acquistion. Furthermore, the "fit" between their data and a refined theory constitutes an argument for the principles they propose.

The last decade of research in language acquisition has broadened our perspective immensely. It has become clear that language involves more than what linguistic theory represents. All of mental life is involved in an interaction that produces language. There are two fundamental views of "interactions" with respect to language acquisition: that language reduces to an interaction of "general cognitive abilities" and pragmatics; and that language is structured by an autonomous grammar (a distinct level of generalization) that determines how other factors interact. The other factors may include pragmatic, cognitive, and perceptual factors, but the grammar guarantees that only a small subset of possible interactions actually occurs. The second view is taken in most of the chapters.

It is perhaps useful to illustrate the "autonomous" view of grammar with a metaphor. The force of gravity is a factor represented by a distinct number in every equation about motion (on earth). The force of gravity may, however, be overwhelmed by other factors (such as friction) that are important in life (stopping a car on time) but that are far less important in a theory of physics.

In several chapters it is evident that pragmatic judgments of meaning can overwhelm syntactic principles when they are placed in opposition to one another. In each case a careful analysis shows that the syntactic factors are present when the pragmatic biases are eliminated.[2] It is quite natural for a device to be able to tolerate the presence of strong pragmatic effects if it can automatically "see" the presence of basic syntactic principles.

Let us now take a closer look at how an acquisition device could make use of nonlinguistic or "auxiliary"[3] hypotheses. They may play a role in the hypothesis-formation process (see Roeper 1978 and Roeper et al., this volume). Specifically, a child may use independent inferences about meaning as a confirmation routine for projected hypotheses about syntax. It is reasonable to suppose that a child knows by inference (knowledge of the meaning of individual words) that the sentence *The milk was drunk by John* should have *milk* as the object of *drink*. He then projects a passive rule that maintains this meaning.[4] Note that the Passive transformation is not the content of the inference and is not derivable from the inference. An acquisition device must couple the inference with a syntactic hypothesis. Most of the constructions discussed in this book can be acquired by this method.

The use of inferences can enable children to understand many sentences long before they possess the grammatical rules to generate them. Thus, many 3–5-year-old children may appear to understand constructions that they will not genuinely control until they are 8–10 years old. The discussion of how children learn *-able* in the chapter of Roeper et al. illustrates the point.

The relationship between auxiliary hypotheses and syntactic hypotheses is not in principle complex; it can be regarded as a trigger relation.[5] This means that the internal structure of one system is unrelated to the internal structure of another system except at the point of contact. For instance, Bruner (in press) has shown that children develop rituals of communication with their mothers that allow them to focus mutually upon an object before they begin to talk. This communication ritual may be a necessary precursor to a child's discovery of nouns and then noun phrases. There is nothing, however, about the internal structure of a communication ritual (for example, use of eye contact) that is involved in the internal structure of a noun phrase.

One might now wish to ask: Where does the original concept of a language-acquisition device proposed in the early 1960s stand? It is clear that a full understanding of acquisition must show how auxiliary hypotheses develop and function as triggers to linguistic knowledge. What emerges then from current research is an acquisition device with both an internal and an external dimension. The internal dimension retains its traditional role: If an organism is exposed to sentences of the language, it must project candidate grammars, as permitted by linguistic universals, and then evaluate those grammars in terms of linguistic simplicity to determine which one meets explanatory criteria. The linguistic universals, though innate, may not function at every stage of acquisition. For example, language acquisition may be facilitated if unbounded rules are not, in the early stages, within the range of hypotheses available to the child. In the work below there is some evidence that the c-command constraint appears early (Goodluck), whereas the "island" constraint appears late (Matthei).

The external dimension of an acquisition device involves the system of triggers that relate linguistic and nonlinguistic principles. In other words, grammars must meet "the dual condition of compatibility with the structural principles of universal grammar and with relevant experience."[6] Some grammars that are logically within the power of universal principles may be excluded by their failure to be "feasible" in the real world.[7] This enriched view of a language acquisition device suggests that many of the different strains of research in the field of language acquisition are compatible.

A remark made one day in class by Noam Chomsky is perhaps a fitting conclusion to this brief introduction. He pointed out that in a mature field, with fairly exact systems, small and remote information may cause vast shifts in the model. Physics, for instance, revised basic principles in terms of minute observations about particles. Likewise, linguistic theory changed the concept of surface structure by a close examination of where *want to* appears but *wanna* does not. Acquisition research is no different. We can make significant progress through the persistent revision of fundamental ideas based on increasingly refined research.

Notes

1. See Brown and Hanlon 1970.

2. This is explicit in the chapter by Roeper et al. It is involved in the experimental design of a number of the other chapters as well.

3. See Koster 1978.

4. Wexler and Culicover (1980) make the same assumption from an entirely different perspective.

5. See Chomsky 1965, pp. 27–47.

6. Chomsky 1975b, p. 35.

7. See Chomsky 1965.

Language Acquisition, Markedness, and Phrase Structure

Edwin S. Williams

Markedness theory is the study of how languages can differ from each other. In general, one might say that in a given domain of linguistic theory there is an "unmarked case" and that languages differ from the unmarked case in that domain along such-and-such dimensions and to such-and-such a degree. A concrete proposal about the dimensions and degrees in a particular domain constitutes a "map" of how languages can differ from one another in that domain.

Such a map of variation can be given a much more interesting interpretation, however. It may be understood as a map of (part of) the language-acquisition device: The "unmarked case" can be understood as the child's initial hypothesis about language (in advance of any data), and a dimension of variation can be understood as an ordered set of hypotheses about a particular aspect of linguistic structure that the child successively submits to empirical test in learning a language. When such an identification is made, the theory of learning (including the concepts of evidence and hypothesis) will bear on the theory of linguistic variation, and vice versa.

This essay is an attempt to make such an identification in one linguistic domain: phrase-structure rules.

1 $\overline{X}$ Features

These remarks are a critique of a central thesis of $\overline{X}$ theory, the thesis that phrase names are nonatomic (that is, they are composed of feature complexes). The conclusion reached here is that this thesis is not well supported and could well be wrong. An alternative account of the facts that this thesis was meant to cover will be given.

I will take Jackendoff's (1977) lexicalist syntax (LS) as the most thoroughly worked out version of $\overline{X}$ theory. Most of the criticisms

directed against this work apply equally to all versions of $\overline{\text{X}}$ theory that
have appeared explicitly in the literature or that are implicit in linguistic
descriptions that have appeared in the literature (of which there are
dozens).

The discussion will proceed as follows. In this section I identify five
independent hypotheses that make up the $\overline{\text{X}}$ theory as Jackendoff formulates it. In sections 2 and 3 I examine the two theses that are the
concern of this paper. In section 2 I examine the claim that there are
"cross-categorial" transformations, that is, transformations that apply
to natural subsets of phrase types, as defined by feature systems; and I
will conclude that there are none. In section 3 I examine the claim that
there are "cross-categorial generalizations" (that is, similarities among
base rules in languages) that can be expressed most naturally in a
system with nonatomic phrase names; I conclude that the rule collapsing allowed by various feature systems (in particular, Jackendoff's)
does a poor job of expressing these generalizations, and I outline an
alternative account of them.

If the conclusions of sections 2 and 3 are correct—that is, if there are
no cross-categorial transformations and if rule collapse is not an appropriate means of evaluating base components, then feature decomposi-
tion of phrase names plays no role in linguistic theory.

I count five independent hypotheses that are used in formulations of
$\overline{\text{X}}$ theory. Jackendoff uses all five, although he gives little discussion to
cross-categorial transformations. Four of them are essential to all formulations of $\overline{\text{X}}$ theory that I know of; only the "uniform-level hypothesis" (subsection 1.2) is not adopted by all practitioners.

1.1 Every Phrase Has a Head
This thesis is actually two; the first takes the form of a schema for base
rules as shown in (1).

(1) $X^n \rightarrow \cdots X^{n-1} \cdots$

Any base rule that has this form defines a head, X^{n-1}. Some systems
have rules that do not meet this schema; in LS, for example, certain
recursive rules do not. The other part of this hypothesis is that X^0 is a
lexical item.

1.2 Uniform-Level Semantics
Jackendoff makes the hypothesis that semantic rules apply uniformly to
phrases of the same (superscript) level, without regard to category

type. This means, for example, that degree modifiers of V and A will be found at the same level in the respective categories; in Jackendoff, this is V^2 and A^2. I think this thesis is implicit in most $\overline{X}$ work.

1.3 Every Lexical Category Has a Major Phrasal Category

Jackendoff makes the claim that for every lexical category X there is a syntactic phrase of type X^3, and there is no syntactic phrase of degree greater than 3.

I will assume that hypotheses 1.1–1.3 are correct. The remaining two theses are based on a feature analysis of the names of lexical categories (and thus, by thesis 1, of syntactic categories). Rather than taking N, V, A, and P as atomic, Chomsky takes the features αN and αV as atomic, and defines N, V, A, and P (and hence NP, VP, AP, and PP) in terms of them as in (2).

(2) $N = [+N, -V]$
$\quad V = [-N, +V]$
$\quad A = [+N, +V]$
$\quad P = [-N, -V]$

Jackendoff defines them as in (3).

(3) $N = [+subj, -obj]$
$\quad V = [+subj, +obj]$
$\quad A = [-subj, -obj]$
$\quad P = [-subj, +obj]$

There are two kinds of evidence for this kind of proposal—they are the subject of the final two theses of $\overline{X}$ theory.

1.4 The Existence of Cross-Categorial Transformations (CCTs)

This thesis maintains that there are transformations that apply to natural classes of phrase types, as defined by the features; and also that such rules are greater generalizations than rules that apply to single categories. For example, Bresnan (1976a) writes the relative clause rule as

(4) $NP - \overline{s}[COMP - W_1 - (P) - \overline{\overline{x}}[W_2 - rel - W_3] - W_4]$
$\qquad\qquad\qquad\qquad\quad {}_{[-V]}$

where $[-V]$ represents the natural class shown in (5).

(5) $\begin{Bmatrix} NP \\ PP \end{Bmatrix}$

If such rules are true generalizations, then clearly linguistic theory must
provide the feature system αN, αV to write them.

1.5   Cross-Categorial Generalizations (CCGs)

This thesis amounts to saying that base rules that can be collapsed using
the feature system and some abbreviating conventions are more highly
valued than base rules that cannot be. For example, suppose the base
contains the two rules given in (6).

(6) P′ → P NP
    V′ → V NP

In Jackendoff's features, these could be written as in (7)

(7) [+obj, −subj]′ → [+obj, −subj] NP
    [+obj, +subj]′ → [+obj, +subj] NP

and collapsed into (8).

(8) [+obj, αsubj]′ → [+obj, αsubj] NP

A feature-counting evaluation will, for example, rate this higher than a
pair of rules that cannot be collapsed.

I hope the preceding discussion is sufficient to indicate that the CCT
and the CCG theses (1.4, 1.5) are independent of the other $\overline{\text{X}}$ theses
(1.1–1.3). In the next sections I will examine CCT and CCG toward an
evaluation of the role that the phrasal features, and notation generally,
play in theory and explanation.

2   Cross-Categorial Transformations

If one has two features A and B and four objects to be categorized, as in
(9),

(9)
	+B	−B
+A	W	X
−A	Y	Z

then there are four natural classes of items, as in (10).

(10) [+A]   W   X
     [−A]   Y   Z
     [+B]   W   Y
     [−B]   X   Z

Neither {N}, {X}, {Y}, {Z}, {W Z}, nor {X Y} forms a natural class, since it takes as many features to specify each of them as there are.

We may specify the class containing all of W, X, Y, and Z as

(11) ∅

Note that the sets

(12) W X Y, W X Z, W Y Z, Y X Z

are not natural classes either. To see this, consider how we would give a feature specification to WXY, as shown in (13).

(13) $\left\{ \begin{array}{l} [+A] \\ \left[\begin{array}{c} -A \\ +B \end{array} \right] \end{array} \right\}$

This takes more features than its complement (14),

(14) [+A, −B]

which contains only one member—hence, it would be foolish to consider this a natural class, for it is the most complicated specification in this system.

I would like to put forward the claim that there are no transformations that apply to classes of phrases defined by a single feature (the only real kind of natural class afforded by a feature system with two features). To this I would add that there are just two kinds of things that can be the constant term of a transformation—either the name of some major category or a variable that ranges over all categories.

I will support this by an examination of two rules as formulated by Bresnan (1976a) that have constant terms that refer to natural subclasses of phrases. First, however, we will consider her formulation of Comparative Deletion, which is consistent with our proposal.

2.1 Comparative Deletion

Bresnan (1976a) formulates Comparative Deletion (CD) as shown in (15).

(15) $\bar{\bar{x}}[\bar{x}[\bar{\bar{Q}}-W_1]-W_2]\ \bar{s}[W_3-\underbrace{\bar{x}[\bar{\bar{Q}}-W_4]}_{\emptyset}-W_5]$

The deleted term does not pick out a natural subclass of phrases, but rather deletes any major phrase—hence, if features were banished, we could still write this rule using the general category variable X''.

Bresnan lists the following examples of phrase types that can be deleted:

(16) QP, AP, AdvP, NP

To these she could have added PP:

(17) PP: John put it [further under the rug] than I put it $[\emptyset]_{PP}$.

Hence, CD deletes every major category except VP—and we can explain this omission by noting that VPs never have an initial QP, as the rule requires.

2.2 Relativization
Bresnan writes the moved term of relativization as in (18).

(18) $[_{\bar{\bar{X}}}W_2-rel-W_3]$
$_{[-V]}$

The moved term is a natural subclass, the $[-V^2]$ categories, namely NP and PP. The major categories not moved are AP and VP (see (19)).

(19) ??The man proud of whom we are
   *The man hitting whom we were

I will argue below that there is little to gain, and much to lose, in excluding VP and AP from the structural description of relativization. If this is true, then we may rewrite the moved term of relativization as

(20) $[W_1-rel-W_2]_{\bar{\bar{X}}}$

which is in conformity with our proposal, since it employs no features.

The first point is that the formulation of *rel* given by Bresnan cannot be collapsed with Q-formation, even though in gross detail these rules do the same thing. Q-formation is illustrated by (21).

(21) $Q-W_1-[W_2-wh-W_3]_{\bar{\bar{X}}}-W_4$

The moved term of Q-formation is X^2, whereas the corresponding term in *rel* is $[-V]^2$.

Let us look at Q-formation. The implicit claim is that Q moves every category (any $\bar{\bar{X}}$), but here we find the situation shown in (22).

(22) *hitting whom were you

Thus, Q actually moves only NP, PP, and AP—but this is not a natural class (see (23)).

(23) $\left\{\begin{matrix} [+N] \\ \begin{bmatrix} -N \\ -V \end{bmatrix} \end{matrix}\right\}$

Hence, if we want to preserve the formulation of Q given by Bresnan, we would need to attribute the ungrammaticality of (22) to something independent of the SD of Q-formation.

Suppose we have discovered that something. Suppose for concreteness it is the surface filter shown in (24).

(24) *$[[X \text{ wh } \cdots]_{X^n}]_{COMP}$
          unless $X = P$

Given this filter, we can preserve $\overline{\overline{X}}$ variable in the formulation of Q. But if this filter explains why VP is not moved in questions, it will also tell us why VP cannot be moved in relatives, making the exclusion of VP in the SD of *rel* (innocuously) redundant.

Thus, the only advantage of the $[-V]^2$ formulation of *rel* over the X^2 one is the exclusion of AP. Can this, too, be explained independently? In fact, filter (24) will automatically rule this out as well.

(25) $[[[proud]_X \text{ of whom}]_{X^2}]_{COMP}$

Hence, AP is also redundantly excluded by the SD of *rel* and hence we may replace the $[-V]^2$ specification by the preferred X^2, in accord with our proposal.

The exclusion of APs like (19) is needed in Qs as well as relatives, as shown in (26):

(26) *proud of whom are you?

NPs of the form given in (24) are excluded from both as well, as in (27).

(27) a. *The mother of whom did you meet?
     b. *The man the mother of whom I met.

Hence the difference between *rel*s and Qs with respect to the movement of APs has nothing to do with different specifications of the moved category—rather, it has to do with the fact that there is no AP, as shown by (28),

(28) *$[who \text{ proud}]_{AP}$

for relatives corresponding to (29)

(29) [how proud]

in questions—that is, for reasons having to do with the base, it is
impossible to generate an AP with "who" in it that will not be excluded
by (24).

There are exceptions to (24), which I will not treat seriously here
since (24) was only proposed "for concreteness" anyway. One exception is when X = P—we might rationalize this by limiting X to major (=
open) lexical categories. Another exception is a set of nouns like
"height" as in (30).

(30) the reports [the height of the lettering on the covers of which]

I do not understand why such examples are good, but I would propose
that is not the normal case; rather I would call NPs like (31)

(31) *[the mother of a friend of whom]

the normal case. At any rate, these exceptions do not bear on the
choice between the $[-V]^2$ and X^2 formulations, since NP will be moved
by either rule, and the discrimination between (30) and (31) must be
made independent of the SD of the rule anyway.

I present this lengthy discussion of relativization as a paradigm case
of a reanalysis that eliminates the need for features. The elimination
was successful in two ways: By adding filter (24) to Bresnan's rules, we
augmented the empirical accuracy of her system, and at the same time
allowed a generalization of *rel* from $[-V]^2$ to X''. One might imagine
that even if features were permitted, the child would learn the X''
formulation and filter (24) anyway.

In general, if we exclude features from rules we have a more restrictive theory. To see this, consider that with two features (and four
categories) there will be 9^n transformations with n constant terms, but
without them only 5^n.

I will conclude, then, with well-meant rashness, that there is no
evidence from transformations in favor of features.

3   The Feature System
This section treats the role the feature system plays in the expression of
cross-categorial generalizations via the collapsing of base rules. First
we will look at some proposals for the collapse of some base rules of
English, principally made by Jackendoff, which use features as an essential part of abbreviating conventions that effect the collapse. Then
I will outline an alternative means of expressing cross-categorial
generalizations.

3.1 Collapsing Base Rules

Collapsing rules via abbreviatory conventions has no significance whatever unless there is an evaluation measure (EM) that favors the collapsed rules over rules that will not collapse. As in phonology, in $\overline{X}$ theory the (entirely) implicit measure of a set of rules is their length, in terms of symbols—the fewer the symbols in a set of rules, the higher they are valued. For example, consider the two systems in (32).

(32) a. X Y Z   b. X Y Z
        X W Z   Z W X

Using braces, (32a) can be reduced to four symbols, as in (33),

$$(33) \quad X \begin{Bmatrix} W \\ Y \end{Bmatrix} Z$$

but (32b) cannot be reduced. A symbol-counting EM will prefer (32a) to (32b).

Since the category features stand for natural classes, we may use them to abbreviate rules. Suppose, for example, we have the two rules shown in (34).

$$(34) \quad \begin{bmatrix} +subj \\ +obj \end{bmatrix}' \rightarrow \begin{bmatrix} +subj \\ +obj \end{bmatrix} NP$$

$$\begin{bmatrix} -subj \\ +obj \end{bmatrix}' \rightarrow \begin{bmatrix} -subj \\ +obj \end{bmatrix} NP$$

We can collapse them as in (35).

(35) $[+obj]' \rightarrow [+obj]$ NP

A "shortness-evaluation measure" (SEM) will prefer (34) to a pair of rules that cannot be collapsed. The claim made by an SEM is that shortness of rules corresponds to magnitude of linguistic generalization.

For the purposes of the rest of this section we will assume that the EM is an SEM. I know of no explicit statement to this effect in the $\overline{X}$ literature, but it is hard to imagine any other kind of EM that would be appropriate for the conventions of rule collapse.

By examining a number of cases, I intend to support the position that, in general, SEM with collapsing allowed by $\overline{X}$ features forces loss of generalizations or expresses arbitrary subgeneralizations. I will examine in detail Jackendoff's rule $\overline{N}/\overline{V}$ with respect to a number of generalizations of English and then look at some Greenberg universals with respect to the $\overline{X}$ feature-collapsing mechanisms.

Let us examine Jackendoff's main instance of rule collapse $\bar{N}/\bar{V}$ in order to illustrate the logic of SEM and collapsing.

$$(36)\ \begin{bmatrix} +\text{subj} \\ \langle +\text{obj}\rangle_1 \\ \langle -\text{obj}\rangle_2 \\ +\text{comp} \end{bmatrix}' \rightarrow X\ \langle(\text{NP})\rangle_1\ (\text{Prt}''')\ \begin{bmatrix} \langle +\text{subj} \\ +\text{comp}/2 \\ -\text{obj} \\ -\text{det} \end{bmatrix}''' \ (\text{PP})\ \left(\begin{bmatrix} +\text{obj} \\ +\text{comp} \end{bmatrix}'''\right)$$

$$\qquad\qquad 1 \qquad\quad 2 \qquad\quad 3 \qquad\qquad 4 \qquad\qquad 5 \qquad\quad 6$$

In Jackendoff's system, we have (37).

$$(37)\quad V = \begin{bmatrix} +\text{subj} \\ +\text{obj} \\ +\text{comp} \end{bmatrix},\quad N = \begin{bmatrix} +\text{subj} \\ -\text{obj} \\ +\text{comp} \end{bmatrix}$$

The term on the left is a collapse of V and N; what appears on the right is a collapse of the base definitions of $\bar{V}$ and $\bar{N}$.

Term 1 is the head.
Term 2, only in $\bar{V}$, is NP (direct object).
Term 3 is particle, occurring in both categories.
Term 4 is an NP for $\bar{N}$; for $\bar{V}$, it is a second NP, or a QP, AP, or AdvP.
Terms 5 and 6 are PP and S, for both categories.

This single rule is shorter than the two rules shown in (38),

$$(38)\ \begin{bmatrix} +\text{subj} \\ +\text{obj} \end{bmatrix}' \rightarrow \begin{bmatrix} +\text{subj} \\ +\text{obj} \end{bmatrix} (\text{NP})\ (\text{Prt}) \begin{bmatrix} -\text{obj} \\ -\text{det} \end{bmatrix}^3 (\text{PP})\ (\text{S})$$

$$\qquad\ \begin{bmatrix} +\text{subj} \\ -\text{obj} \end{bmatrix}' \rightarrow \begin{bmatrix} +\text{subj} \\ -\text{obj} \end{bmatrix} (\text{Prt})\ (\text{NP})\ (\text{PP})\ (\text{S})$$

and collapsing the rules makes their similarity conspicuous. Because these two rules are collapsible, they are more highly valued than the two rules in (39), which are not collapsible.

(39) VP → V (S) (PP) (AdvP) (NP) (Prt)
      NP → N (Prt) (NP) (PP) (S)

In fact, however, any pair can be collapsed—these as (40)—

$$(40)\ \begin{bmatrix} +\text{subj} \\ \langle +\text{obj}\rangle_1 \\ \langle -\text{obj}\rangle_2 \end{bmatrix} \rightarrow X\ \langle\text{S}\rangle_1\ \langle\text{PP}\rangle_1\ \langle\text{AdvP}\rangle_1\ \langle\text{NP}\rangle_1\ (\text{Prt})\ (\text{NP})_2\ (\text{PP})_2\ (\text{S})_2$$

with some saving of features. The savings in this case must be negligible.

3.2 $\overline{\text{X}}$ Feature-Collapsing and the Implicit SEM Evaluation

3.2.1 *Subject of NP.* Chomsky's original proposal of $\overline{\text{X}}$ theory was supported by a parallelism between NP and S illustrated by the tree diagram (41).

(41)

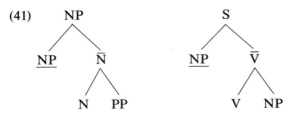

If we take both of the underlined NPs as "subjects," the notion "subject of" can now be defined as (42),

$$(42) \left[\text{NP}, \begin{Bmatrix} \text{NP} \\ \text{S} \end{Bmatrix} \right]$$

or in Jackendoff's system as (43).

(43) $[\text{NP}, [+\text{subj}]^3]$

However, English is one of the few languages in the world that has prenominal subjects of NP. In most languages, like French, no NP may appear prenominally, and the subject appears in a prepositional phrase. In French, for example, only the pronouns *ton, mon, son,* and *leur,* and so on may appear prenominally, and these may well be adjectives, agreeing in person and number with the head as they do.

Hence, English is one of the very few languages that can collapse NP and S, as in (44) and (45).

(44) NP $\rightarrow$ NP N^2
     S $\rightarrow$ NP V^2

$$(45) \begin{bmatrix} +\text{subj} \\ \alpha\,\text{obj} \end{bmatrix}^3 \rightarrow \begin{bmatrix} +\text{subj} \\ -\text{obj} \end{bmatrix}^3 \begin{bmatrix} +\text{subj} \\ \alpha\,\text{obj} \end{bmatrix}^2$$

In most languages, the rule will have to be (46)—a rule equivalent to the English rule by SEM.

$$(46) \begin{bmatrix} +\text{subj} \\ \langle+\text{obj}\rangle_1 \end{bmatrix}^3 \rightarrow \left\langle \begin{bmatrix} +\text{subj} \\ -\text{obj} \end{bmatrix}^3 \right\rangle_1 \begin{bmatrix} +\text{subj} \\ \langle+\text{obj}\rangle_1 \end{bmatrix}^2$$

SEM is incapable of telling us that the English construction occurs far less frequently than the French construction. One might hypothesize that the English construction is more marked, less natural, and harder to learn than the French construction. One might then expect the EM to rank the English grammar somewhat lower than normal, but SEM will not do this. In fact, the English construction was part of the original support for the $\overline{\text{X}}$ collapse (and SEM).

3.2.2 *Adverbs and Adjectives*. The S has adverbs at all levels, as (47) shows.

(47) a. V^1: word the letter carefully
    b. V^2: run quickly
    c. V^3: eat probably

NPs have AdjP generated on both sides of the verb, as shown by (48).

(48) the proud man
    the man proud of his children

If we accept the "uniform semantics" thesis, then we must assign APs to all levels of NP, because APs play roles parallel to the role of AdvP in S, as in (49).

(49) N^1: the careful wording
    N^2: the quick running
    N^3: the probable victory

Hence, the rule for $\overline{\overline{\overline{\text{N}}}}$, $\overline{\overline{\text{N}}}$, and $\overline{\text{N}}$ will be (50).

(50) $N^3 \rightarrow A^3 \ N^2 \ A^3$
    $N^2 \rightarrow A^3 \ N^1 \ A^3$
    $N^1 \rightarrow A^3 \ N \ A^3$

The rule for V^3, V^2, and V^1 might be (51).

(51) $V^3 \rightarrow Adv^3 \ V^2 \ Adv^3$
    $V^2 \rightarrow Adv^3 \ V^1 \ Adv^3$
    $V^1 \rightarrow Adv^3 \ V \ Adv^3$

We may collapse these rules as in (52) and (53).

(52) N/V   Ad(v)

$$\begin{bmatrix} +\text{subj} \\ \alpha\text{obj} \end{bmatrix} \rightarrow \begin{bmatrix} -\text{subj} \\ -\text{obj} \\ -\alpha\text{comp} \end{bmatrix}^3 \ldots$$

(53) $N/V^3 \rightarrow Ad(v)\ N/V^2\ Ad(v)$
$\quad\quad N/V^2 \rightarrow Ad(v)\ N/V^1\ Ad(v)$
$\quad\quad N/V^1 \rightarrow Ad(v)\ N/V^0\ Ad(v)$

Here, collapsing captures some generalization—at each level, there are corresponding adjective/adverb pairs. However, it only gets part of the generalization. Just as simple as (53) is a grammar in which N^3 and V^3 both had AdvP, N^2 had AP and V^2 had AdvP, and N^1 and V^1 both had AP, as shown in (54).

(54)
$$\begin{bmatrix} +\text{subj} \\ \alpha\text{obj} \end{bmatrix}^3 \rightarrow \begin{bmatrix} -\text{subj} \\ -\text{obj} \\ -\text{comp} \end{bmatrix}^3 \begin{bmatrix} +\text{subj} \\ \alpha\text{obj} \end{bmatrix}^2 \begin{bmatrix} -\text{subj} \\ -\text{obj} \\ -\text{comp} \end{bmatrix}^3$$

$$\begin{bmatrix} +\text{subj} \\ \alpha\text{obj} \end{bmatrix}^2 \rightarrow \begin{bmatrix} -\text{subj} \\ -\text{obj} \\ -\alpha\text{comp} \end{bmatrix}^3 \begin{bmatrix} +\text{subj} \\ \alpha\text{obj} \end{bmatrix}^1 \begin{bmatrix} -\text{subj} \\ -\text{obj} \\ -\alpha\text{comp} \end{bmatrix}^3$$

$$\begin{bmatrix} +\text{subj} \\ \alpha\text{obj} \end{bmatrix}^1 \rightarrow \begin{bmatrix} -\text{subj} \\ -\text{obj} \\ +\text{comp} \end{bmatrix}^3 \begin{bmatrix} +\text{subj} \\ \alpha\text{obj} \end{bmatrix} \begin{bmatrix} -\text{subj} \\ -\text{obj} \\ +\text{comp} \end{bmatrix}^3$$

The reason SEM cannot prefer (53) over (54) is that collapsing cannot take place "over bars"; that is, there is no way to collapse rules defining different levels of phrase—no way to collapse the rules for V''', V'', and V'.

The real generalization here is that in English, as in many languages, nominal phrases, of whatever level, contain only APs; verbal phrases, of whatever level, contain only AdvPs (with the exception of AP arguments).

Another example of a partial generalization captured by $\overline{X}$ collapsing is the rules of English, such as Jackendoff's rule for NP/S, which have S in final position. Collapsing is able to express the generalization that if S is final in N^3, then in V^3; if in N^2, then in V^2; if in V^1, then in A^1. However, it is totally unable to capture the (super)generalization that S is final in every category that contains an S, no matter what level. In fact, it is probably the case that every rule in English that has any complements at all has the form shown in (55).

(55) $X^n \rightarrow \cdots X^{n-1} \cdots PP\ S$

Jackendoff captures a small corner of this generalization in his $\overline{N}/\overline{V}$ rule, but his system is not capable of the full generality that is called for.

3.2.3 *NP Versus S.* One of the striking features of NP is the absence of direct NPs in the complement structure; Ss, on the other hand, have two.

Jackendoff deals with this lack of parallelism in two ways. His rule for complement structure is shown in (56).

$$(56) \begin{bmatrix} +\text{subj} \\ \langle +\text{obj} \rangle_1 \end{bmatrix}^1 \rightarrow \begin{bmatrix} +\text{subj} \\ \langle +\text{obj} \rangle_1 \end{bmatrix} \langle (\text{NP}) \rangle_1 \text{ Prt (NP)}$$

Since NP is [−obj], only one NP will be provided for $\bar{\text{N}}$. This is still one too many. The other one is gotten rid of by the surface by a rule of *of*-Insertion—in an NP like (57),

(57) $_{\bar{\text{N}}}$[destruction the city]$_{\bar{\text{N}}}$

an *of* is inserted between N and NP as in (58).

(58) the destruction of the city

There are several objections to this. First, it can be shown that *of* and the NP that follows it is a constituent. Heavy constituent shift in NP shows this, as in (59).

(59) a.   The destruction yesterday of the city
     b.   *The destruction of yesterday the city

The insertion rule does not predict this—it predicts the opposite.

Given this, one wonders why the rule should provide any NPs in the deep complement structure of $\bar{\text{N}}$. Why, for example, not write the rule as in (60)?

$$(60) \begin{bmatrix} +\text{subj} \\ \langle +\text{obj} \rangle_2 \\ \langle -\text{obj} \rangle_1 \end{bmatrix}^1 \rightarrow \begin{bmatrix} +\text{subj} \\ \langle +\text{obj} \rangle_2 \\ \langle -\text{obj} \rangle_1 \end{bmatrix}^0 \langle (\text{NP}) \rangle_2 \text{ (Prt) } \langle (\text{NP}) \rangle_2 \text{ PP S}$$
$$\qquad\qquad\qquad\qquad\quad 1 \qquad\quad 2 \qquad 3 \qquad 4 \quad 5\ 6$$

This rule is no more complex (by SEM) than Jackendoff's. It provides NPs for S and PPs for $\bar{\text{N}}$ complement structure.

This possibility is not acceptable because of an unstated assumption of $\bar{\text{X}}$ theory and because of the desire to give a unique definition of grammatical relations.

The unstated assumption is that when two rules are collapsed, the collapse must "preserve grammatical relations." In the $\bar{\text{V}}$ *destroy the city* the direct object *city* is an instance of term 4; but in the NP *de-*

struction of the city, the city is an instance of term 5. This is an intolerable result by this assumption.

Also, $\overline{\text{X}}$ theorists would like to have a single definition of "object of." Jackendoff's for English is (61),

(61) $[[+\text{subj}]^1, \text{NP}]$

but under the present theory it would be (62).

$$(62) \left[\left[\begin{array}{c} +\text{subj} \\ \langle -\text{obj} \rangle_1 \end{array} \right]^1 \langle \text{of} \rangle_1 \text{ NP} \right]$$

My rule is somewhat more complex.

We might be willing to tolerate this additional complexity for several reasons; first, the theory requiring *of*-Insertion is factually inadequate; second, the theory behind our rules says directly that NP contains no direct arguments in its complement; third, since the situation represented by English is extremely prevalent, if not universal, one would expect the language-acquisition device (LAD) to provide the definitions of the grammatical relations at little cost.

3.2.4 *Measure Phrases.* Measure phrases of the form *32 miles* are indubitably NPs; we note their distribution in the major categories listed in (63).

(63) a. PP: [into the woods] 20 miles
     b. AP: 20 miles farther than Jack
     c. VP: to jog 20 miles
     d. NP: *jog (of) 20 miles
               *20-miles jog

We see that no two categories show the same distribution of these phrases.

From what does this distribution follow? It is certainly not from rule collapse, which would lead us to expect uniform distribution across categories.

To begin with, consider S. Why is this phrase not preverbal as it is preadjectival? If we look at the items that can occur in front of the verb and after the subject, we find mainly auxiliary verbs and -*ly* adverbs—non -*ly* adverbs, for example, are not permitted, as (64) shows.

(64) a. *John yesterday left
     b. John $\left\{ \begin{array}{c} \text{carefully} \\ \text{*well} \end{array} \right\}$ worded the letter

Call this law the auxiliary verb intervention law (AVIL). Given this restriction, one would not expect these phrases to appear preverbally.

Next consider NP. I have already pointed out in general that NP allows no NP in $\overline{N}$ complement structure; one can generalize this and say that NP does not contain direct NPs anywhere except in the possessive determiner (call this no NP). If this is so, we would not expect these NPs to appear anywhere in NP.

Note that the explanation of the NP distribution has nothing to do with the S distribution. Two independent laws, AVIL and NO–NP, one dealing with S and the other with NP, give us the distribution. Each of these laws has motivation independent of the distribution of measure phrases, but each law has as its domain a single category. If $\overline{X}$ collapsing plays any role at all it is only a very weak one when compared to these two.

3.2.5 *Summary of Laws.* In the past few sections we have discovered some cases where real generalizations are at odds with those expressible in (and expected by) $\overline{X}$-rule collapsing. According to $\overline{X}$ the following statements are true:

• No language would be more complex than it is if its NPs had full NP "subjects" parallel to sentence subjects.
• English would be no more complex if the various N^n phrases differed in whether they were modified by adjectives in some cases, by adverbs in others.
• English would be simpler if NPs took direct objects.
• English would be simpler if measure phrases occurred in the same position in each category.
• English would be no more complex if $V^1 \to V \cdots PP\ S$ and $V^2 \to V^1 \cdots S\ PP$.

But we have seen that these expectations are at odds with some real generalizations:

• NPs never have adverbs, or direct NPs, except in the determiner; the auxiliary verbs permit only *-ly* adverbs to intervene.
• S always follows PP in a phrase.

At this point, an $\overline{X}$ theorist might say that $\overline{X}$ collapsing (and SEM) is simply a component of the evaluation of the base, and that these "real generalizations" reflect another component, which together with $\overline{X}$ collapsing and SEM yield a composite evaluation.

This may be so; I certainly have not presented a case that $\overline{X}$ collapsing has no role to play in evaluation, and there are a number of cases that $\overline{X}$ collapsing seems suitable for. In section 3.4 I will present an alternative approach to these cases.

3.3 Greenberg's Universals

If we look at a number of Greenberg's (1963) universals (numbers 13, 16, 17, 20, 24), we can make the same observation as for the previous examples: Either $\overline{X}$ collapsing predicts that the universal should not exist, or it does not predict that it does exist, or it captures an arbitrarily drawn subuniversal. Greenberg's universals will be translated into base-rule notation.

Universal 13 can be written as (65).

(65) $VP \rightarrow NP\ V \supset VP \rightarrow S\ V$

Even if we find a collapse of this rule with N^1, such as (66),

(66) $[+\text{subj}]^1 \rightarrow NP\ S\ [+\text{subj}]$

there is no reason that this system is to be preferred over (67)

(67) $[+\text{subj}]^1 \rightarrow NP\ [+\text{subj}]\ S$

unless NP objects and S complements collapse out, as in (68).

(68) $[+\text{subj}]^1 \rightarrow [+\text{subj}]^3\ [+\text{subj}]$

But, in English at least, these two terms are distinct, according to Jackendoff's collapse of V^1 and N^1.

Universal 16 can be written as (69),

(69) $S \rightarrow V\ NP\ NP \supset S \rightarrow Aux\ V\ NP\ NP$

which is not predicted by $\overline{X}$ theory.

Universal 17 is given in (70).

(70) $V^3 \rightarrow V\ NP\ NP \supset N^2 \rightarrow N\ AP$

There is no way $\overline{X}$ theory can predict this, since it involves rules of different levels.

Universal 20 makes the statement given in (71).

(71) NPs in languages are all of the forms
    a. demonstrative QP AP N
    b. N AP QP demonstrative
    c. N demonstrative QP AP

This is not predicted by $\overline{X}$ theory, but the nature of the generalization is not clear.

Universal 24 can be written as (72).

(72)
$$N^2 \rightarrow S \quad N^1 \Rightarrow \begin{cases} N^2 \rightarrow AP \ N^1 \\ \text{or} \\ P^1 \rightarrow N^3 \ P^0 \end{cases}$$

There is no prediction by $\overline{X}$ theory, since the rules cannot be collapsed.

Although $\overline{X}$ theory predicts none of these universals, there is some clear generalization they instantiate. Greenberg's universals 13, 17, and 24 show a generalization about the head in VSO and SOV languages— in VSO, it is initial in all categories (with certain specifiable leaks, like Aux); in SOV it is final in all categories. This generalization about the head is not achieved by collapsing.

A more glaring failure of $\overline{X}$ theory is the fact that languages are all either VSO, SVO, or SOV—in other words, S precedes O. Rule collapse and SEM as the only evaluation of the base predicts all combinations—VSO, SVO, SOV, VOS, OVS, OSV. Again, $\overline{X}$ collapse seems to play no role.

Again, the generalizations concerning the position of heads in VSO and SOV languages and the fact that S precedes O may reflect a component of evaluation that works in conjunction with $\overline{X}$ collapsing. But the question must be asked: Is $\overline{X}$ collapsing needed at all when this component is sufficiently elaborated?

3.4 Alternative to Features and Collapsing

Before discussing three cases of explanation in an alternative to $\overline{X}$ feature-collapsing and SEM, it is important to clarify one point about how $\overline{X}$ participates in linguistic explanations. It is often said that grammars are to "express" generalizations. But it must be borne in mind that no grammar expresses any generalization apart from choice of an evaluation measure. In $\overline{X}$ theory, collapsing expresses generalization only through a particular choice of EM; namely, SEM.

$\overline{X}$ theory has proceeded essentially by holding choice of EM constant (at SEM—this is often a covert assumption) and revising notation to accommodate new data and new generalizations.

I have noted a number of generalizations for which there is no reasonable revision of notation in $\overline{X}$ theory. The alternative I am proposing involves postulating a more complex EM than SEM, one that embodies substantive universals, rather than the formal universal embodied in SEM. Although formal universals seem to usually have greater generality, in two of these cases (3.4.2 and 3.4.3) the substantive universal makes much wider predictions than $\overline{X}$ SEM is capable of.

3.4.1 *A Successful Case.* $\overline{X}$ has some success with the case in (73).

(73) a. P → P NP ⊃ V O
　　 b. P → NP P ⊃ O V

If these implications hold, then $\overline{X}$ can express them by collapsing, as in (74).

(74) a. $\begin{bmatrix} PP \\ VP \end{bmatrix} \rightarrow \begin{Bmatrix} P \\ V \end{Bmatrix}$ NP　　　　or　　　　NP $\begin{Bmatrix} P \\ V \end{Bmatrix}$

　　　or

　　 b. $[+obj]^1 \rightarrow [+obj]$ NP　　　or　　　NP $[+obj]$

On the other hand, we might suppose that (73a) and (73b) were substantive (implicational) universals and reflected the structure of LAD in the sense that, for example, if LAD learns that the language is prepositional, it can conclude, without further evidence, that it is a VO language. We could represent this as in diagram (75).

(75)

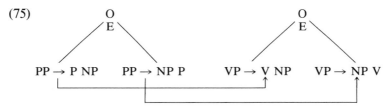

At the junctures labeled E, LAD needs evidence to decide between two possibilities. The arrows represent "free rides" by which LAD may short-circuit the need for evidence in one domain on the basis of conclusions in another domain.

In this particular case, the $\overline{X}$ theory is much to be preferred, since we must balance the great generality of SEM with the very particular universals embodied in the diagram. But this diagram is part of a much more general diagram whose power of generalization cannot be mirrored in $\overline{X}$ theory.

3.4.2 *The Structure of Universal Categories.* Returning to some problems that arose in connection with SEM and collapsing, we should first make a distinction between universal and nonuniversal categories.

Let us assume that there are four universal categories, one optionally realizable and the others obligatory (see (76)).

(76) N, (A), V, P = universal categories

Recall that, in English, every universal nonlexical category terminates in the sequence PP S. To capture this by feature-collapsing, it would be necessary to collapse all the base rules into one rule, with Boolean conditions on bars and features.

Suppose we were to say instead that there was a "unit" called "Comp," consisting of PP S, as in (77).

(77) Comp → {PP, S}

Now, what kind of rule is (77)? There is no evidence in English for a node Comp, which dominates some, or all of, the complement structure of the various phrases.

We will thus take Comp to be a metavariable used by the LAD to project base rules. Thus, it is one of the functions of LAD to discover the structure of Comp. Comp will be either of the structures shown in (78).

(78) a. PP S
     b. S PP

The braces in (77) indicate that the order of PP and S must be fixed by LAD, and that evidence will be required to do this.

Clearly, the evidence needed is rather simple—in fact, a single sentence will serve. Pursuing this approach, we may set up the representation of LAD base schema shown in (79).

(79) Universal Category Schema (UCS)
     a. Comp → {PP, A(x)P, S}
     b. X^n → {X^{n-1}, Comp, $Spec_x$}
     c. X^1 → {X, C^*, Comp}

In Comp, a node has been added for adverb phrases. I have inserted $Spec_x$, a specifier metavariable, in the general definition of the metavariable for the structure of the universal categories. Again, the braces mean that the order of elements must be fixed to project actual rules.

Rule (79c) is added to allow the interpolation of constituents between the head and Comp for phrases whose immediate head is lexical. Taking Jackendoff's expansion for $\overline{V}$ to be essentially correct, we may illustrate the correspondences between the metavariables and positions of the rule as in (80).

(80) $\overline{V} \rightarrow \underbrace{V}_{X^0} \underbrace{NP \ Prt \ NP \ AP}_{C^*} \underbrace{AdvP \ PP \ S}_{Comp}$

As can be seen, a large part of the language-particular structure of the base can be reduced to a small number of very simple questions, such as: In what order do such-and-such elements occur? In this sense, UCS (79) allows us to assess the "information content" of language-particular base components.

I have not really provided a picture of the acquisition of C*, nor will I. I assume its structure is learnable from a few simple positive examples.

In the unmarked case (which is all that concerns us), the order of elements $Spec_x$, X^{n-1}, and Comp, once fixed for one category, will be the same for all categories, and this aspect of the structure of the other categories can be inferred without evidence.

3.4.3 *The Structure of Nonuniversal Categories (NUCs).* Such categories as modal and adverb are not universal. But they are "related" to universal categories: modal to verb, and adverb to adjective.

A child exposed to English will begin to construct the verbal paradigm. The fact that modals fit this paradigm only sketchily serves to identify them as a distinct, but nevertheless verbal, class. I suggest that such verbs are simply tagged with a morphological diacritic, say x, that distinguishes them from fully paradigmatic verbs. So modals will belong to the class V_x.

V_x is probably unique to English—no other language is likely to give exactly the same interpretation to the morphological diacritic x.

It is my belief that the low-level induction of paradigms and morphology is capable of discovering "language-particular" regularities that could not be anticipated by an LAD in any detail.

In this way the lexicon serves as a "creative" input to the base, with respect to learning. Low-level induction is creative in this way and is appropriate to the learning of the lexicon. It is not appropriate to the learning of the base.

In English, the suffix *-ly* serves to produce adverbs from adjectives. Again, I propose that a morphological diacritic, x, distinguishes adjectives from adverbs;

(81) A = adjective
    A_x = adverb

The interpretation of this diacritic is the suffix -*ly* itself—in fact, we
may identify x with this suffix, and write adverb as in (82).

(82) $A_{[+ly]}$

The importance of this identification will become clear later.

Once the lexicon has supplied a NUC, the LAD must learn the
structure of the phrases that have that NUC for its head. My theory of
the learning of the structure of NUCs may be represented in a diagram
such as (83).

(83) Structure of NUCs

   a. C_x b. V_x (=M)   c. A_x (=Adv)

     $\downarrow$E $\downarrow$E $\downarrow$E

   i. $C_x^n \rightarrow C_x^{n-1}$ i. $V_x^n \rightarrow V_x^{n-1}$ i. $A_x^n \rightarrow A_x^{n-1}$

     $\downarrow$E $\downarrow$E

   ii. $C_x^n \rightarrow \{C_x^{n-1}, \text{Spec}_c\}$ ii. $A_x^n \rightarrow \{A_x^{n-1}, \text{Spec}_A\}$

     $\downarrow$E

   iii. $C_x^n \rightarrow \{C_x^{n-1}, \text{Spec}_c, \text{Comp}\}$

(83a) is an ordered set of hypotheses. The "unmarked" hypothesis is
(84).

(84) $C_x^n \rightarrow C_x^{n-1}$

That is, that the NUC phrase has no specifier or complement. The
reason that this is the unmarked, or initial, hypothesis is that it is the
most easily disconfirmed.

Suppose that the child hears evidence that the phrase in question has
specifiers, then hypothesis (i) is disconfirmed (by "evidence," indicated
by "E"), and the LAD advances to hypothesis (ii) and stays there until
it is disconfirmed, and so on.

(83b) represents the learning of the English modal: there is no evidence for an advance beyond hypothesis (i), so the modal has no Spec
or Comp.

(83c) represents the learning of adverb phrase. Evidence warrants an
advance from (i) to (ii), but no evidence warrants a further advance.

In the narrow sense of markedness adopted here (a measure of the amount of evidence needed to arrive at a language-particular feature of a grammar) I would say that in English adverbs are more marked than modals.

Note that the evidence that warrants an advance is "disconfirma-tory" in nature. It is not evidence in favor of the "next" hypothesis except insofar as it can be taken as disconfirmatory of the previous hypothesis.

Certain other imaginable hypothesis chains would not allow the evidence to be purely disconfirmatory. For example, suppose the un-marked case was for NUCs to have Spec, and a marked hypothesis (one requiring evidence to arrive at) was that the NUC phrase had neither Comp nor Spec. Now, suppose LAD is exposed to a Spec-less NUC language. There is no sentence in that language that will dis-confirm the hypothesis that some NUC has a Spec.

To learn this, it will be necessary to collect a large number of examples and notice that in all cases a particular NUC is Spec-less.

Although this is conceivable, certainly (83a) represents an "easier" learning strategy.

Thus we can give a partial ordering to the hypotheses on a particular dimension of linguistic variation by considerations of "ease of falsifi-ability." We may call this the principle of minimal falsifiability (PMF).

PMF is not a principle of linguistic theory. It is a general considera-tion that can guide us in our first approximations of linguistic theory.

PMF does not fully order a set of hypotheses. For example, it will not tell us that (83ai) is before (83aii) in (83a). This ordering was made for strictly empirical reasons.

The English adverb phrase has a Spec but no Comp. If the LAD scheme was as shown in (85) this would be impossible.

(85) $C_x^n \rightarrow C_x^{n-1}$

$\quad\quad \downarrow E$

$\quad C_x^n \rightarrow \{C_x^{n-1}, \text{Comp}\}$

$\quad\quad \downarrow E$

$\quad\quad ...$

So, this model predicts that a nonuniversal category will never have Comp but not Spec. It predicts that the presence of Comp entails Spec, but not vice versa.

Note that these hypotheses in (83a) are not full rules. They are under-determined by the fixing of the order of the elements on the right-hand side. But this order (at least in the unmarked case) will be fixed for all categories including NUCs, when it is fixed for the general case X^n. This predicts that Comp and Spec will be distributed identically in the universal and nonuniversal categories.

Finally, note that the Spec of a NUC is identical to the Spec of the universal category from which it is derived—hence, no new specifier system must be learned for a NUC. And Comp will be the same as in universal categories.

Hence, all that need be learned to learn the structure of a nonuniversal category is, first, that it has a Spec (if it does), and second, that it has a Comp (if it does). All other details are given universally, or decided on independently.

It is my hope that distributional information will not be criterial for the establishment of a nonuniversal category, that only the lexicon will serve this function. But once a NUC exists, its distribution must be determined—that is, it must be determined by LAD where the NUC appears on the right-hand sides of rules. I have only a few sketchy remarks on this topic.

• *Modals* have a distinct distribution from verbs. This is partly due to the absence of tenseless forms for modals—since they must bear tense, they must appear first in an S. Also, the rule of SAI refers specifically to modals.

• *Adverbs:* given the two categories A and A_x, how are they distributed? A is strictly a nominal modifier; A_x modifies everything else. How this is determined we do not know. The general scheme in English is shown in (86).

(86) $N^n \rightarrow A^n \cdots N^{n-1} \cdots A^n$
$\quad\;\; V^n \rightarrow A_x^n \cdots V^{n-1} \cdots A^n$
$\quad\;\; A^n \rightarrow A_x \cdots A^{n-1} \cdots A_x$
$\quad\;\; P^n \rightarrow A_x \cdots P^{n-1} \cdots A_x$

Now, consider the identification of *-ly* and x. It is well known that *-ly* adverbs, and few others, can appear in the Aux system, as in (87).

(87)
$\quad$ John $\begin{Bmatrix} \text{cleverly} \\ \text{carefully} \\ \text{*well} \end{Bmatrix}$ worded the letter.

If the distribution of syntactic categories is determined exclusively by the label on the outer brackets, then this suggests that the adverb phrases with *-ly* adverbs as heads are marked as in (88).

(88)

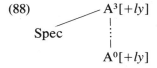

In other words, the morphological source of the NUC adverb is reflected in the syntactic category name, A^3 [$+ly$], and this "category" has a distribution distinct even from other adverbs.

• *Mapping into universal categories:* the importance of morphology in creating NUCs can be seen in some simple observations about morphology in general. Suffixes such as *-ion, -ness, -ity,* and so on create nouns, and *-ize, -en, re-,* and so on create verbs. The nouns and verbs created by such suffixes do not have a distribution distinct from nouns and verbs in general. It is imaginable, for example, that only *-ion* nominals could be objects of a certain preposition (just as only *-ly* adverbs can appear in Aux). But this is not the case, since these suffixes create members of (or actually belong to) universal categories.

3.4.4 *Summary and Comment.* In the past few sections I have outlined a "learning theory" for the structure of the universal and nonuniversal categories of the base. Here I will summarize the content of the theory and comment on it as an alternative to SEM and collapsing as a means of evaluating base components.

I have proposed that there are four universal categories and an (essentially infinite) supply of morphologically derivative nonuniversal categories (see (89)).

(89) N, V, P, (A)
   N_x, V_x, P_x, A_x

The structure of the universal categories is given by (90a), and that of NUCs by (90b).

(90) a. $X^n \rightarrow \{$Comp, X^n, Spec$_x\}$
       $X^1 \rightarrow \{X^n, C^*, $Comp$\}$
       Comp $\rightarrow \{$PP, A(x), S$\}$

b. C_x^n

$\quad \downarrow E$

$C_x^n \rightarrow C_x^{n-1}$

$\quad \downarrow$

$C_x^n \rightarrow \{C_x^{n-1}, \text{Spec}_c\}$

$\quad \downarrow$

$C_x^n \rightarrow \{C_x^{n-1}, \text{Spec}_c, \text{Comp}\}$

Although I have mentioned a certain amount of notation (brackets, abstract LAD metavariables), it is not my concern to invent a new notation; rather, I am mainly interested in the substantive interpretation given to these diagrams in 3.4.

To learn the rough outline of the English base system, one must follow the rules given in (91).

(91) a. Fix the order of X^{n-1}, Spec_x, and Comp for X^n.

b. Fix the order of $A(x)$, PP, S for Comp.

c. Learn that English has modals and adverbs (this will be learned by mechanisms not under consideration here).

d. Learn that adverbs have Spec.

If this learning takes place, the rules given in (92) can be projected.

(92) $V^1 \rightarrow V \ C^* \ PP \ AdvP \ S$

$\quad V^n \rightarrow V \ PP \ AdvP \ S$

$\quad A^n \rightarrow \text{Spec}_A \ A^{n-1} \ PP \ Adv \ S$

$\quad N^n \rightarrow \text{Spec}_N \ N^{n-1} \ AP \ PP \ S$

$\quad Adv^n \rightarrow \text{Spec}_A \ Adv^{n-1}$

$\quad M^n \rightarrow M^{n-1}$

Twelve rules can be projected in enough detail to be recognizable as the English base, from answering three relatively simple questions ((91c) being admittedly still an unsolved problem).

We might call (92) the "unmarked" portion of the English base. Questions (91a) and (91b) taken together allow only 36 base components. Although there is an infinite supply of NUCs, from morphology, there are only two binary questions (see (93)) that must be answered to discover the rough outline of their structure.

(93) a. Does it have a Spec?
     b. If so, does it have a Comp?

Thus given that the answers to (91a) and (91b) are fixed for some language, its NUCs can have only one of three possible shapes.

The "learning diagrams" theory of the base embodies very substantive universals. SEM and rule collapsing is a "formal" or "notational" theory. It is generally the case that a "formal" theory makes much more general predictions.

However in this case, the substantive theory makes equally wide and sometimes wider predictions. It does, for example, make predictions that could only be met in $\overline{X}$ theory by collapsing "across bars," and in effect collapsing the entire base into one rule.

The substantive theory of section 3.4 has been presented as a means of evaluating base components by reducing variation in base components to a small number of questions with simple answers. It can also be interpreted as a map of (part of) an aggressive acquisition device. It can also be interpreted as a map of variation of languages of the world. But there are some caveats.

I have specified the "unmarked" base components—in a sense of markedness that is exclusively related to learning: These are the base components that require the least amount of evidence to acquire.

It is natural to assume that languages will spontaneously tend toward unmarked states. But their progress toward these states may be impeded by a number of factors. For example, certain unmarked base configurations may pose unsolvable parsing problems. Hence, languages will shy away from these in order to remain useful.

So, the frequency of various configurations will not directly reflect their markedness. German for example, verb-final, but prepositional— a marked configuration, according to the theory presented here. If this theory is essentially correct, then it remains to be discovered why German is stable in this marked configuration.

Note

I have profited greatly from the opportunity to present material in this article at the GLOW conference in Amsterdam, 1977; at the University of Massachusetts Conference on Language Acquisition, 1977; and at the Friday Colloquium, University of Massachusetts, 1976. I am especially indebted to Emmon Bach, Henk van Riemsdijk, and Joe Emonds.

A Lexical Approach to Language Acquisition

Thomas Roeper, Steven Lapointe, Janet Bing, Susan Tavakolian

Recent work in linguistic theory proposes a significant shift in the location of rules. A number of formerly syntactic rules (such as Passive and Dative Movement) can be more precisely defined as lexical rules (Vergnaud 1973; Jackendoff 1975; Aronoff 1976; Bresnan 1976, 1978; Wasow 1977; Lapointe 1977; Brame 1978). The theory continues to undergo refinement, but some important implications for acquisition theory are already clear. In what follows we shall argue that the child's initial hypothesis is that rules are lexical. We shall characterize this hypothesis as the lexical approach to language acquisition. Two consequences follow from this claim: first, a lexical approach significantly decreases the total number of grammars available to the child, and second, a lexical approach offers an explanation for the often-overlooked fact of undergeneralization; children's rules are not as general as syntactic formulations predict.

We begin our discussion with an overview of lexical theory, then develop an acquisition theory, and finally examine pertinent experiments. In brief, our acquisition theory (Roeper 1978) contains two principles of hypothesis-formation that are reflected in the temporal sequence of rule acquisition. First, a construction that requires the interaction of two rules will be acquired after each of the rules is acquired individually.[1] Second, a hypothesis confirmed by the child initiates a chain of formally related hypotheses (following markedness theory, see the preceding chapter). The first principle receives support in the evidence we provide that dative precedes dative passive in acquisition. The second principle receives support from the fact that two formally similar lexical rules are acquired in a fixed order. The *-able* rule that relates *push the dog* to *the dog is pushable* precedes the dative passive that relates *I gave the boy the ball* to *The boy was given the ball* *by me*. Both verbs affect the first sister of the verb. Other factors contribute to the explanation of why *-able* occurs first, but they are insufficient to explain why the relationship between *-able* and passive dative is invariant across individual children. More careful research on this point is underway.

1 Overview of the Lexicon

The lexicon has traditionally been the locus of idiosyncratic information and morphological rules. Lexical rules have three crucial properties: they add derivational suffixes (*-able, -ment, -ical,* and so on) and syntactic rules do not; they change syntactic categories (*blue*$_{Adj}$ + *ness* = noun), and syntactic rules do not (Chomsky 1970); and they can limit productivity to particular semantic classes or particular lexical items (*civility, *evility*), whereas syntactic structural descriptions refer only to syntactic categories (N, V, Det, and so forth).

Chomsky (1965) made a proposal whereby lexical items had a set of subcategorization frames that specify the phrase structure contexts in which those items may appear. These frames allow us to represent a new set of facts in the lexicon. For instance, some verbs allow dative movement and others do not: *I gave a book to John* ⟹ *I gave John a book,* but *I announced the weather to Bill* ⟹ **I announced Bill the weather.* The fact that some verbs do not allow dative movement must be expressed with reference to particular words, and therefore it is impossible to express it just in terms of syntactic category symbols.

Bresnan (1978) introduced the suggestion that all rules are lexical except those that operate over long distances (over an essential variable). Thus *wh*-movement must be syntactic because it may operate over an indefinite number of clauses, as in (1).

(1) $_S$[Where did you say $_S$[I thought $_S$[John put the rice ——]$_S$]$_S$]$_S$

This view entails an important claim about lexical rules: They are bounded because they do not operate over a variable. This constraint simplifies acquisition because it eliminates many potential hypotheses for the child. The child never needs to consider the hypothesis that *John* in *I gave John the bread* could have been moved from three clauses away:

*I gave John the bread that Bill said Fred bought ——.

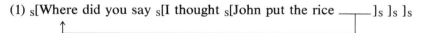

He knows it must come from another subcategorized position of the first verb. Similarly, -*ment* in *establishment* is interpreted locally; thus the boundedness constraint holds for all of morphology. Since the number of hypotheses is reduced, the lexical theory has intrinsic superiority over any syntactic theory that lacks an explanation for boundedness.

Three lexical rules in English show a remarkable similarity, and they have been the focus of a great deal of theoretical work (Aronoff 1976; Vergnaud 1973; Wasow 1977; Roeper and Siegel 1978). We chose them therefore as the basis for our experiments. The exact notation used to represent them is currently a matter of debate. Our theory and experiments do not bear on this question and therefore we choose for convenience the following formulation of Roeper and Siegel.

(2) First-Sister Rules
  a. The following rules form a lexical class because they each affect the first sister of the verb:
     (someone) *wash* $_{NP}$(the car)   i. the car is washable (-*able*)
                                        ii. the car is washed (passive)
                                       iii. car washing (compound)
  b. Rule: V (NP) $\Rightarrow$ (NP) *be* V $\emptyset$
           1   2   2   1

         or (NP – verb) $\emptyset$
              2   1
  c. Rule excludes: i. *the car is washable the Ford
                     ii. *the car is washed the Ford
                    iii. *car washing the Ford

The first-sister rule prevents the object position from being filled (see (2c)). It also prevents constituents that are not in first-sister position from being moved. Thus from *make the boat quickly* we can generate *boat making* but not **quickmaking* since there is no **John makes quickly*. Because it is possible to say *think quickly* (no object is required), we can generate *quick-thinking* by this rule. The compound experiments will not be discussed here but in a subsequent article.

2 A Partial Model of Acquisition

We can now ask where lexical rules should fit into a theoretical model of language acquisition. First, as mentioned, they simplify the problem of hypothesis formation through the elimination of potential grammars. Second, they allow in principle a solution to the "negative evidence" problem. Baker (1978) has observed that a special problem arises with optional rules: There is no counterevidence to a wrong rule. If a child hears *give the ball to Bill* it does not mean that *give Bill the ball* is incorrect. Therefore, if he generalizes *give* to *announce* and says *I announced him the answer,* the existence of *I announced the answer to him* does not show that the former sentence is incorrect. This problem does not arise with obligatory rules; the child who says *goed* can correct himself when he hears *gone,* because each verb has only one past participle.

The lexical approach offers a solution to this problem under the assumption that the child uses only positive evidence. For example, he does not generalize the dative double object from *give* to *announce* unless he hears examples of *announce* with a double object ("I announced him the answer"). He allows the double-object construction to occur for *give* just when he hears it used. Thus the child knows that Dative Movement constructions are linked to specific verbs or verb classes in the lexicon. We will return to this issue.

We may now turn to the question of how lexical rules affect an ontogenetic model of acquisition. The questions shown in (3) arise.

(3) a. How are first-sister rules acquired with respect to one another?
b. How are first-sister rules acquired with respect to other lexical rules?
c. How are lexical rules acquired with respect to syntactic rules? Is there any relationship?

To address these questions let us begin with a model of hypothesis formation. We assume the presence of a hypothesis generator constrained by universal grammar (Roeper 1978; Chomsky 1975). What controls the order in which a child makes hypotheses? We suggest there are three factors: input data, current grammar, and auxiliary (extralinguistic) hypotheses. Each merits discussion.

The input data are not every sentence a child hears. The child accepts into his hypothesis generator just those sentences that are relevant to his current hypotheses. The hypotheses that a child entertains at a given time are dictated by his current grammar. Thus if one lexical first-sister rule has been learned, the acquisition of that rule serves as the basis for a chain of hypotheses about other first-sister rules.[2] This view of the hypothesis generator predicts that we will find a particular temporal relationship in the order of acquisition of lexical rules that is constant for different children. What is that order?

2.1   Order of Acquisition of First-Sister Rules

Of the three first-sister rules we have discussed, we expect the Passive rule to be acquired first and to be the basis for the acquisition of the others. We have two reasons for this expectation. First, numerous unrelated languages have passive forms. Passive can therefore be thought of as an unmarked rule, which in our terms means that it is the natural first hypothesis in a chain of hypotheses about first-sister rules. Second, the acquisition of agentless passives by young children has been reported in a variety of studies (Maratsos and Abramovitch 1975; Beilin 1975). This result was confirmed in our own pilot experiments with agentless passive, passive, and *-able*. We shall describe those results briefly (for details see Roeper et al. (in preparation)).

The basic experimental paradigm is identical to the one described below in which we compared preschool, second grade, and fourth grade children in their ability to succeed in toy-moving tasks. The children were given four agentless passive sentences like *The rock was thrown* and four agentive passives like *The pig was chased by the horse*. The same children were given a series of questions about *-able* (such as *Is the fence jumpable?* or *Is the boy jumpable?*). In brief, all groups performed almost perfectly on the passive sentences: The preschoolers gave 87 percent (34 of 39) correct on agentless passives, and 95 percent (36 of 38) correct on agentive passives. The same children performed substantially less well on the *-able* sentences: They got 40 percent correct, and some of those correct answers may have been due to correct guesses using semantic information (see auxiliary hypotheses below). When we examined the children individually, we found that none of eight preschoolers were able to meet our criterion of answering six out of eight questions correctly. However, four of ten second-graders and ten of twelve fourth-graders met our criterion, which suggests that *-able* is acquired by most children between second and fourth grade. We seem to have found very precise evidence that Passive is the first first-sister rule to appear.

There is one line of criticism, however, that must be met. It has been argued by Maratsos and Abramovitch that early passives are indistinguishable from predicate adjectives. We believe (see Wasow 1977) that there is a distinction between a verbal passive and an adjectival passive although both may be generated in the lexicon. The adjective reading is stative and designates a property of the subject. Thus, in (4), *fat* and *hurt* both designate properties of the subject.

(4) a. John was fat.
    b. John was hurt.

Wasow notes that a form like *The door was closed* has two readings: a stative reading (*The door was not open*) and an active reading (*Someone closed the door*). We take the common view that the stative reading corresponds to an adjectival passive and the active reading to be a verbal passive. To be a verbal passive means that the speaker knows that the subject functions as the object of the activity. In other words, the speaker understands that the verb *close* has undergone the first-sister rule in the creation of *closed*. Which form, then, do the children use? There is reason to believe that the youngest children (2½ to 3½ years) use the adjectival forms. Wattman (1977) performed an informal experiment in which she sought to discover whether children understood the active reading. She gave children sentences like *She saw the broken toy* and *She saw the toy broken*. The latter takes the active reading in adult grammar, but children between 3 and·4 years persistently gave it a stative reading (= the broken toy) in a picture-selection task. This question deserves further investigation.

Nevertheless, our sentences in both the pilot study and the experiments to be discussed here differ in a crucial way from adjectival passives: The passives we used do not function in all adjectival contexts. We do not say *the kicked horse, *the cut knife*, or *the thrown rock*, because *kicked, cut,* and *thrown* cannot designate a result or a timeless property of a noun, and therefore these passives are verbal passives. Consequently, we believe that the children must have understood that the passive forms in our experiments have undergone the Passive first-sister rule.

Thus, we claim that Passive is the first rule of the first-sister chain. It should therefore precede both *-able* and verbal compound. In a forthcoming paper we show that the Passive rule also precedes the Verbal Compound rule (Roeper et al., in preparation).

2.2 The Interaction Relation
The second relationship of temporal ordering by our hypothesis generator is a reflection of intrinsic ordering in adult grammars.

(5) Acquisition of Interacting Rules
    A construction that requires the interaction of two rules will be acquired after each of the rules is acquired individually.

In adult grammar the dative passive is formed from the output of the Dative Movement rule. The Dative Movement rule puts the indirect object in first-sister position, where it may undergo Passive Transformation.

(6) I gave the ball to John $\Rightarrow$ I gave John the ball $\Rightarrow$ John was given the ball by me

Therefore, Dative Movement should precede Dative Passive.

Our predictions about the temporal ordering for the acquisition of two constructions does not involve predictions about whether the acquisition of these constructions is acquired early or late for any given child. We do assert that for any given child dative constructions will be acquired before dative passive constructions.

There is independent evidence that children acquire rules independently before they learn the interaction of rules. Thus children learn Subject-Auxiliary Inversion (*Can I sing?*) and *wh*-Movement (*What I can sing?*) before they learn their interaction (*What can I sing?*). This provides further grounds for the prediction that Dative Passive will follow Dative Movement.

2.3 Interaction Between First-Sister and Non-First-Sister Rules

Now we can pose another question: Can we make a prediction about the relation between Dative Passive and *-able*? If we can, this relation is important for any theory that argues that *-able* is a rule of morphology and Dative Passive is a rule of syntax. A clear temporal relation that holds constant across children, such as the ordering between *-able* and simple passive constructions, argues for the lexical approach to bounded rules in general. A theory that puts *-able* and Dative Passive in separate components of the grammar makes no prediction whatsoever. The *-able* is part of the first-sister hypothesis chain but not part of a rule interaction. If a clear temporal relationship exists between *-able* and dative passive in different children, it is unlikely that it is accidental. As we shall see below, such an interaction does exist between *-able* and dative passive; we will discuss possible explanations for the particular ordering there.

2.4 Auxiliary Hypotheses

What happens to those sentences that a child hears but that his hypothesis generator is not able to accept? They are not necessarily lost; a number of auxiliary mechanisms are available with which a child may determine their meaning. The best-known example of an auxiliary hypothesis is the use of the strategy NVN = SVO (Bever 1970). This strategy is not structurally defined and therefore cannot be part of a generative grammar. There are three other auxiliary hypotheses that deserve mention with respect to lexical rules.

A. *Item by item learning.* A child may learn the meaning of individual items without understanding the rule that creates them. Thus a child might learn *pushable* and *capable* in the same fashion without realizing that *pushable* (but not *capable*) can be divided into *push* and *able*. The acquisition of a lexical rule, like a syntactic rule, requires that a child be able to compose or decompose novel forms.

B. *Thematic analysis.* A child may use the intrinsic content of the elements *milk, drink,* and *-able* to correctly infer the meaning of *Milk is drinkable* since it would be implausible for milk to drink something.

C. *Contextual interpretation.* A child may infer from context or knowledge of the world that in *The boy is pushable* the boy could be either the subject or the object of *push,* depending on the context. Until the child has a uniform interpretation for *-able* words, we would not attribute knowledge of the rule to him. In the experiment we report below, where we controlled for contextual interpretation, we have evidence that children use a thematic analysis to interpret sentences with double-NP constructions before they acquire the Dative Movement rule.

The auxiliary hypotheses also play a role within acquisition theory that they do not play within adult competence. Roeper (1978) and Wexler and Culicover (1980) argue from different perspectives that a child may use a definition of meaning derived from context to trigger formal rules. We may examine Dative Movement from this perspective. A child may be unaware of the linguistic origin of a double-object construction (*John gave Bill the milk*) but he may be aware that there is only one plausible reading for the sentence. (*Bill* is the indirect object, and *milk* is the direct object). The child can then see that the meaning of the double-object construction is identical to the meaning of its prepositional alternate (*John gave the milk to Bill*). He then projects a transformation whose output preserves meaning across the two constructions. We can compare Passive and *-able* within this perspective. These rules are formally identical because they both add an affix and move the first sister. The passive, however, refers to actual situations, whereas the *-able* refers to a possible or potential situation. We can observe the fact that John is pushed more easily than the potential that John is pushable. In a sense the meaning of *-able* contains the meaning of passive if we paraphrase it as "able to be pushed." Therefore, in terms of an auxiliary procedure (which itself is not understood) the meaning of passive is more accessible. Thus, an auxiliary hypothesis that by nonformal capacities determines meaning triggers the formal analysis that is consistent with that meaning.

This leads to the prediction that children will exhibit the presence of auxiliary hypotheses before they have acquired the relevant formal rule. It is in general a significant task for the theory of acquisition to separate auxiliary hypotheses from rules of grammar. Failure to perceive the difference has led most of us to attribute knowledge of rules to children prematurely in some cases and to incorrectly underestimate the child's knowledge in other cases. Once the auxiliary hypotheses are understood, we discover that children acquire some rules surprisingly late and others rather early.

In summary, we can state the acquisition sequence derived from our theory in two ways. From the perspective of adult grammar, children will learn lexical items and their subcategorization frames (for instance, *be* + [Adj]) before they learn rules such as Passive. They will then learn lexical rules that change subcategorization frames (that is, Passive), and they will learn rule interactions after they have learned individual rules (such as Dative Passive). From the perspective of an acquisition model, children will acquire new structures by determining meaning through auxiliary hypotheses, then developing chains of formal hypotheses, and finally projecting rule interactions. The flow chart in figure 2.1 shows how these rules and constructions are acquired.

3 Experiments

We begin with an elaboration of the auxiliary hypothesis that applies to dative sentences. In many languages animacy is the criterion of indirect-object status (see Fillmore 1968). It is therefore natural for a child to consider the hypothesis that indirect objects must be animate. In English this is true much of the time, but there is a formal definition of indirect object that the adult grammar follows. Thus, we understand *I gave the car a kick* without difficulty. A child's grammar in English is mature when he accepts the formal definition of indirect object.

The child's auxiliary hypothesis can be stated as in (7).

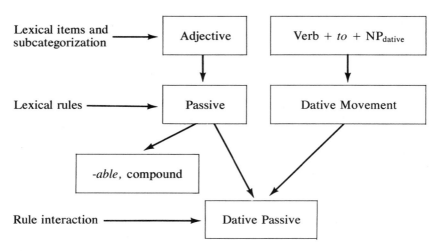

Figure 2.1
Acquisition of rules and constructions.

(7) If there are two postverbal NPs,
    a. the inanimate NP is the direct object, and
    b. the animate NP is the indirect object.

We exposed children to sentences where these strategies work (as in (8a)) and where they do not work (as in (8b)).

(8) a. Jim gave the cow the rock.
    b. Jim gave the rock the cow.

Our evidence shows that a significant group of children use animacy as a strategy.

The animacy/inanimacy distinction is also relevant to children's interpretation of first-sister rules such as *-able*. It is generally the case (see Fillmore 1968) that subjects of transitive verbs are animate. Therefore a child might develop the strategy "animate = subject" and "inanimate = object" in the absence of first-sister rules. We show that there is a stage where children correctly interpret (9a) but misconstrue (9b) with the cat interpreted as the washer.

(9) a. The wagon is washable.
    b. The cat is washable.

These results provide further support for animacy as an auxiliary hypothesis.

There is another strategy that children use that has an interesting connection to universal grammar. We call it the unmoved interpretation. A number of children not only acted as if the preposition *to* were present in sentences like *I gave the cow the horse,* but often repeated the sentence with *to: The dog gave the cow to the horse.* The only direct method to formulate this rule is by positing a comprehension strategy of *to*-Deletion. However, there is absolutely no adult evidence in behalf of such a strategy. Every adult sentence will have the first noun as the natural recipient and not the second (**Give the dollar the boy*).

The problem is to explain why children would prefer a *to*-Deletion analysis over the use of an NP-Movement rule. It is this kind of dilemma that a system of marked rules in universal grammar should explain. Maling (1973) has argued that the unmarked order puts the verb next to the direct object and not the indirect object. The *to*-Deletion strategy preserves this relationship, whereas the NP-Movement rule destroys it. Since our experiments were not designed to test this question, further research is needed. If the analysis holds, however, it will provide an excellent example of the direct reflection of universal grammar in child language.[3]

3.1 Dative-Passive Interaction
The experiment was designed to determine how Dative Movement and Dative Passive enter children's grammar. There are three logical possibilities: Outcome A—Children acquire Dative Movement and then Dative Passive. Outcome B—Children acquire Dative Passive and then Dative Movement. Outcome C—Children acquire both Dative Movement and Dative Passive at once. The relevant examples are (10)–(12).

(10) a. Bill gave the book to John.
     b. Bill gave John the book.
(11) John was given the book.
(12) A book was given to John.

Under all interpretations we expect children to understand (12), because there is no interaction between the Passive and Dative Movement rules in this S, although it contains an indirect object and a passive V form. Our hypothesis predicts that in outcome A Dative Movement precedes Dative Passive (the appearance of (10b) precedes that of (11)). When B holds, then Dative Passive appears before Dative Movement ((11) appears before (10b)); such a situation would require a completely different concept of how an acquisition mechanism works.[4] If C holds, then both appear at once ((10b) and (11) appear together). Then despite the fact that the Dative Movement rule precedes the appearance of Dative Passive logically, this fact is not reflected in the temporal sequence of acquisition. Both outcomes B and C would require a revision of our hypothesis generator.

Ten subjects were drawn from each of three grade levels (kindergarten, second grade, and fourth grade). These children were all native speakers of English and without any special impairments that might have influenced the results. All the children were regularly enrolled students at public grade schools in western Massachusetts.[5]

Subjects were required to pass a pretest in order to participate in the experiment. Each child was given the pretest shown in (13) and required to act out all of the sentences correctly. Any child who did not respond correctly to all six sentences was eliminated from further participation in the experiment.

(13) a. The pig gives the dog to the rock.
    b. The knife was cut.
    c. The sheep gives the chicken to the horse.
    d. The horse was kicked.
    e. The dog was kicked by the rock.
    f. The paper was eaten by the book.

The pretest was designed to ensure that only children who had mastered the unmoved dative constructions and the Passive rule were tested with respect to their knowledge of the Dative Movement rule and its interaction with the Passive rule.

A number of possible misinterpretations of passive constructions were controlled for. Sentences (13b) and (13d) are agentless passives in which the noun phrase is semantically plausible as either the subject or the object of the verb. Semantic cues will not aid the child in providing an interpretation for the sentence. Two passive sentences that were semantically implausible were also included. Sentences (13e) and (13f) both have inanimate agents in contexts that require an animate NP in the *by* phrase. We used these implausible passives to ensure that children have completely mastered the Passive rule and are not influenced by the implausible semantics. We were confident that children who passed the pretest had mastered the syntax of passive constructions.

The pretest also tested children's knowledge of sentences containing unmoved datives. Sentences (13a) and (13c) contain dative *to* phrases. Since indirect objects are most commonly animate, we controlled for animacy by having one sentence contain an animate indirect object (IO) and the other an inanimate IO. To pass the pretest a child could not be sensitive only to animacy in interpreting datives.

The questionnaire itself contained four sentence types to test children's knowledge of datives and to determine the extent of interaction between Passive and Dative Movement in the child's grammar. These are shown in (14)–(17).

(14) Dative movement

$$\text{The dog gave} \begin{Bmatrix} \text{the cow} \\ \text{the spoon} \end{Bmatrix} \begin{Bmatrix} \text{the horse} \\ \text{the rock} \end{Bmatrix}.$$

(15) Passivized dative

$$\begin{Bmatrix} \text{The dog} \\ \text{The spoon} \end{Bmatrix} \text{was given} \begin{Bmatrix} \text{the horse} \\ \text{the rock} \end{Bmatrix}.$$

(16) Passivized direct object

$$\begin{Bmatrix} \text{The dog} \\ \text{The spoon} \end{Bmatrix} \text{was given to} \begin{Bmatrix} \text{the horse} \\ \text{the rock} \end{Bmatrix}.$$

(17) Passive subject only

$$\begin{Bmatrix} \text{The dog} \\ \text{The spoon} \end{Bmatrix} \text{was given.}$$

To examine the auxiliary hypothesis sensitive to animacy (7), we systematically varied the animacy of the indirect and direct objects. A child could not correctly rely on animacy as a cue to the identification of indirect objects in all the sentences.

We also used sentences in which there was only a passive subject, such as (17). These sentences are rather odd and may not be fully grammatical in an adult grammar. They were included to supplement any findings concerning the animacy/inanimacy distinction between indirect and direct objects. We wanted to determine whether children systematically interpreted the initial NP in such sentences as a direct or an indirect object on the basis of the animacy of the NP. This would be a natural consequence of outcome B whereby Dative Passive was learned before Dative Movement.

Since animacy was systematically varied, each sentence type consisted of several subtypes, given in (18)–(21) and assigned the abbreviations that follow.

(18) Dative movement
    a. The dog gave the cow the horse.   AA
    b. The dog gave the cow the spoon.   AI
    c. The dog gave the spoon the cow.   IA
    d. The dog gave the spoon the glass.   II
(19) Passivized dative
    a. The dog was given the cow.   AA
    b. The dog was given the spoon.   AI
    c. The spoon was given the dog.   IA
    d. The spoon was given the glass.   II
(20) Passivized direct object
    a. The dog was given to the horse.   AA
    b. The dog was given to the spoon.   AI
    c. The spoon was given to the horse.   IA
    d. The spoon was given to the rock.   II
(21) Passive subject only
    a. The dog was given.   A
    b. The spoon was given.   I

Each questionnaire contained three tokens of each subtype, for a total of 42 sentences. The questionnaires were constructed using the verb *gave* and the following animate and inanimate objects: *pig, dog, horse, turtle, sheep, cow, chicken, elephant, rock, book, knife, tractor, fence, spoon, fork, glass.* The sentences were constructed by randomly selecting the required animate or inanimate NP for the direct and indirect objects. In sentences such as (18) that contained an agent NP as well as a direct and an indirect object the agent NP was always animate. The only restriction on the choice of NP was that no NP be repeated within a sentence. The sentences thus constructed were then randomized on the questionnaire. Four different questionnaires were prepared following this method.

Each child was interviewed individually and acted out the sentences with toy animals. The animals were arranged facing the child, with the experimenter to one side. The child was told that the experimenter was going to say some sentences and that the child was to act out the sentences with the animals. None of the children had any difficulty understanding the task, and all enjoyed the experiment.

In the actual presentation of the sentences, an extra animal was used for each sentence. That is, an animal not mentioned in the sentence was put out along with all the animals mentioned in the sentence. A natural

Table 2.1
Distribution of Responses to Sentences with Dative Movement

	Sentence Type													
	AA			AI			IA			II			Total		
	C^a	U	O	C	U	O	C	U	O	C	U	O	C	U	O
Kindergarten	8	20	2	10	19	1	2	28	0	12	18	0	32	85	3
Second grade	19	11	0	24	5	1	10	20	0	11	18	1	64	54	2
Fourth grade	17	11	2	23	7	0	19	11	0	18	12	0	77	41	2
Total	44	42	4	57	31	2	31	59	0	41	48	1	173	180	7

a. C = correct response; U = unmoved response; O = other responses.

interpretation of many of the sentences required the use of an animal not mentioned. An animal was put out rather than having the child select one in order to minimize any distraction from having to select from the array of animals.

As expected, children at all three grade levels do very well on sentences with passivized direct objects such as (20). Of 360 possible correct answers, 340 were correct. The errors were distributed evenly throughout the four subtypes, so animacy does not appear to be a factor influencing children's interpretation of passivized direct objects. This indicates that by kindergarten children have mastered sentences containing both passive and unmoved dative constructions. In these sentences the Passive rule has applied, but Dative Movement has not; these sentences contain both constructions, but there is no rule interaction.

The sentences with dative movement such as (18) also contain no rule interaction. However, the results for these sentences are quite different from those obtained for passivized direct objects. Unlike the nearly uniform correct responses to passivized direct objects, table 2.1 shows that even by fourth grade many children have not mastered the syntax of dative movement.

Overall the results suggest that animacy is relied on most heavily by second-graders as an indicator of the indirect object, that kindergartners rely more on the linear order of the noun phrases, and that fourth-graders have mastered more of the syntax of the dative construction.

Kindergartners interpret sentences with dative movement as though it had not occurred. That is, they interpret a sentence such as

Table 2.2
Response Percentages for Sentences with Dative Movement, for All
Sentence Types Combined

	C[a]	U	O
Kindergarten	27	71	2
Second grade	53	45	2
Fourth grade	64	34	2

a. C = correct response; U = unmoved response; O = other responses.

(22) The cow gave the dog the pig.

as though it were

(23) The cow gave the dog to the pig.

Seventy-one percent of the kindergarten responses to sentences with
dative movement were as in (23) (see table 2.2). In contrast, 45 percent
of the second-graders' responses were unmoved responses, and only 34
percent of the fourth-graders' responses were of this type. Most kindergartners seem to assume that the direct object precedes the indirect
object, and they interpret the two postverbal NPs in accordance with
that assumption.

Animacy does not seem to play an important role in the kindergarten
responses. The number of correct responses was fairly uniform across
the four subtypes; similarly, the number of unmoved responses was
nearly the same for all combinations of animate and inanimate indirect
and direct objects. The only exceptions to this uniformity were the IA
sentences such as (24).

(24) The dog gave the spoon the cow.

These sentences have a reversal of the expected semantic features for
direct and indirect objects: The indirect object is inanimate, and the
direct object is animate. Kindergartners gave more unmoved responses
to these sentences than to the other three subtypes.

Second-graders appear to be utilizing animacy as an indicator of
indirect objects. Seventy-two percent of the responses were correct
when the indirect object was animate, compared with 35 percent correct when it was inanimate (see table 2.3). They do best when these two
features occur in the expected way: 80 percent of the responses (24 of

Table 2.3

Response Percentages for Sentences with Dative Movement
According to Animacy/Inanimacy of Indirect Object

	Animate Indirect Object (AA + AI)			Inanimate Indirect Object (IA + II)		
	C[a]	U	O	C	U	O
Kindergarten	30	65	5	23	77	0
Second grade	72	26	2	35	63	2
Fourth grade	67	30	3	62	38	0

a. C = correct response; U = unmoved response; O = other responses.

30) were correct to AI sentences such as (25), in which the indirect object is animate and the direct object is inanimate.

(25) The dog gave the cow the spoon.

In contrast, fourth-graders do equally well on all four subtypes regardless of the animacy of the indirect object. Overall, they responded correctly to 64 percent of the sentences (table 2.2), with a range from 56 percent correct for AA sentences to 76 percent correct for AI sentences. Although it is clear that many fourth-graders have not mastered Dative Movement constructions, they seem as a group to rely more on their knowledge of the interaction of the Passive and Dative Movement rules and to be less influenced by semantic features of the NPs than the second-graders.

On the whole there is a progression in the number of correct responses as one moves from kindergarten to fourth grade. This pattern is to be expected, but there are individual children who are not typical of their grade level. There are some kindergartners who give responses more typical of second- or fourth-graders, and, conversely, there are second- and fourth-graders who give responses more like those of many kindergartners. It is revealing to consider the individual response patterns in examining the responses to passivized datives such as (26).

(26) The dog was given the spoon.

Table 2.4 shows the individual response patterns to sentences with Dative Movement, such as (18), and to sentences with passivized datives, such as (19). There are four logical possibilities for grouping the children: (1) children who correctly interpret both passive and dative-

Table 2.4
Individual Response Patterns to Dative Movement and Passivized Dative

	Grade	Number Correct (12 possible for each type)	
		Dative Movement	Passivized Dative
Group A[a]			
Sheila	K	9	2
Corinne	K	7	0
Stephanie	2	9	0
Melissa	2	8	3
Louis	4	9	5
Group B			
Billy	2	3	7
Group C			
Catherine	K	8	8
Amy	2	10	11
Ellen	2	5	6
Steven	2	6	8
Wayne	2	9	11
Butch	2	11	12
Daryl	4	12	12
Jeff	4	12	9
Joanne	4	7	4
Gary	4	11	8
Tabatha	4	7	7
Scott	4	8	6
Karl	4	11	9
Group D			
Michael	K	2	0
Jessica	K	2	1
Scott[b]	K	4	2
Raymond	K	0	0
Cheryl	K	0	1
Brodie	K	0	0
Kara	K	0	2
Lisa	2	2	0
Jeff	2	1	2
Michael	4	0	0
E. J.	4	0	0

a. Group A: Children who are acquiring Dative faster than Passivized Dative. These children had at least four more datives correct than passivized datives.
Group B: Children who are acquiring Passivized Dative faster than Dative Movement. They had at least four more passivized datives correct than dative movements.

Table 2.4 (continued)
Group C: Children who are acquiring both constructions together. They had three or more correct for both dative movement and passivized dative, and the gap between the number correct for each type is 3 or less.
Group D: Children who are not acquiring either construction very well. They had less than 3 correct for each type.

b. This child does not quite fit into this group because he has more than three dative-movement sentences correct, but he comes very close to fitting and so he has been included.

movement constructions, but who do not correctly interpret passivized datives (outcome A, earlier in this section); (2) children who correctly interpret passivized datives, but who do not correctly interpret dative-movement constructions (outcome B); (3) children who correctly interpret passive, dative-movement, and passivized dative-movement constructions (outcome C); and (4) children who correctly interpret passive but neither dative-movement constructions nor passivized datives. The last group of children does not have either of the rules involved in rule-interaction hypotheses; therefore the data from them do not bear on our hypotheses. Only one child out of 30 was in category (2). The other children were divided among the other categories.

Children were categorized according to two criteria: the number of correct responses for each construction and the difference between the number correct for each.

Group D consists of children who were not acquiring either construction very well yet. They had mastered the Passive by itself, since they passed the pretest, but they gave three or fewer correct responses to both sentence types, and the difference between the number correct for each was three or less. Because they had not mastered Dative Movement, it is not surprising that they did poorly on sentences such as passivized datives that require an understanding of it. This group was composed primarily of kindergarten children: seven of the ten kindergartners were in this group. However, there were also two children from the second grade and two from the fourth who followed this response pattern. There seems to be a great deal of individual variation in the acquisition of datives.[6]

Group A is composed of children who were acquiring dative-movement constructions faster than passivized datives. They correctly responded to four or more of the sentences containing dative-moved

NPs. Moreover, for them the difference between the number of correct responses to dative-moved sentences and the number correct to passivized datives was four or more. These children had a fairly good grasp of Dative Movement, but did less well on passivized datives. The reason for their poor performance on passivized datives cannot be a lack of knowledge about the passive, since they all had passed the pretest, which required fairly complete understanding of the syntax of passive constructions. We propose that these children's responses indicate that rule interaction between Passive and Dative Movement had not occurred in their grammars. Again we see a great deal of individual variation, with two kindergartners, two second-graders, and one fourth-grader in this group.

Group C consists of children who did equally well on datives and passivized datives. They correctly responded to three or more sentences with dative movement and to three or more sentences with passivized datives. The gap between the number correct for each sentence type is three or less. Passive and dative movement were allowed to interact to produce passivized datives. There are two possible ways in which these children may have arrived at this stage. It may be that at an earlier time these children had noninteracting rules of Passive and Dative Movement, but that at the time of our interviewing they had already changed their grammars to allow the rules to interact. Another possibility is that for some children rule interaction takes place immediately; as soon as the child acquires a lexical rule, it interacts with other lexical rules that are already part of the child's grammar. Our data do not decide between these two possibilities. However, our data do indicate that automatic rule interaction does not occur for all children. The children in group 1 utilize both Passive and Dative Movement, but do not have the two rules interacting in their grammars yet.

In group B there was only one child who did substantially better on passivized datives than on datives.

In sum there was exactly one of 30 children whose responses countered the hypothesis that Passive and Dative must be mastered separately before dative passive can be learned. This is strong evidence in favor of our hypothesis that rules must be learned individually before they can interact.

It is important to point out that children apparently do not use an auxiliary hypothesis for passivized datives that would give them a short-cut to correct interpretations. In particular, children do not use

Table 2.5
Acquired Constructions

Number of Children	Constructions
6	Passivized dative and *-able*
9	Neither
14	*-able* only
1	Passivized dative only

Table 2.6
Acquired Constructions

Number of Children	Constructions
16	Passivized dative and *-able*
15	Neither
27	*-able* only
3	Passivized dative only

a strategy that says, "Interpret the initial NP in passive sentences such as (27) as an indirect object."

(27) The dog was given.

Of the 180 responses to such sentences, 88 percent interpreted the NP as the direct object regardless of the animacy/inanimacy of the initial NP. This interpretation stands in contrast to the children's use of animacy as an auxiliary hypothesis in the comprehension of double-object sentences. It seems therefore that children rely exclusively on the interaction of grammatical rules in the interpretation of passivized datives.

4   Interaction of Dative Passive and *-able*
We return now to the question raised in 2.3: Are those children who know dative passive the same ones who know *-able?* The same 30 children were asked 20 questions that involved *-able*. The animacy/inanimacy of the NPs and the transitivity/intransitivity of the Vs were varied systematically in these questions. Typical sentences were *Can you show me: the stick is breakable* and *Can you show me: the boy is hittable*.

The combined results for the three age levels are shown in table 2.5.[7] If we supplement these results with those from 31 kindergartners, second-graders, and fourth-graders in a similarly constructed pilot experiment,[8] we have the data shown in table 2.6. In other words, the responses of 58 out of 61 children were consistent with the hypothesis that children do not acquire passive dative until they have acquired *-able*.

It is worth reconsidering how far apart these two constructions might at first seem to be. One is a relatively infrequent syntactic form and the other is a relatively infrequent morphological form. From this perspective we have no reason to expect any consistent order in their acquisition across children. One might expect one child to acquire *-able* before passivized dative and another to acquire *-able* after passivized dative. Nonetheless, we found virtually total consistency in the order of acquisition of these constructions. For all but three children acquisition of *-able* preceded passivized dative.

We can speculate on an explanation for this acquisition order. We have proposed that a rule like *-able* is part of a chain of lexical rules. Its acquisition is facilitated by the acquisition of another first-sister rule, namely Passive. The Dative Movement rule is not in the first-sister chain. We advance the following hypothesis: Rules within a hypothesis chain are acquired before there is an interaction of those rules with other rules outside the chain. We hope to explore this theoretical hypothesis in future research.

5 Conclusions and Implications

Our results lend clear support to each of the three mechanisms in our hypothesis generator. There is evidence that children use auxiliary hypotheses, hypothesis chains (for first-sister rules), and rules that interact. The fact that these mechanisms are expressed in terms of a temporal sequence of acquisition suggests that each stage requires genuine mental reorganization. In other words, our claims involve more than formal aspects of psychological reality; real-time mechanisms are involved.

We can contrast our theory of hypothesis generation with other theories that are plausible in principle. One might imagine that our claim about temporal ordering is wrong, and that all structures that are formally similar could be acquired simultaneously. Alternatively, one might imagine that different structures are acquired in random order on the basis of particular heard sentences (see Fodor 1966). Under this approach, passivized dative could be acquired before dative. Our evidence clearly supports the hypothesis generator we have proposed and neither of these alternatives.

In the opening discussion we stated that one virtue of the lexical approach was its capacity to solve the problem of "negative" evidence. We have not addressed the issue directly in these experiments, but we are aware of pertinent information. Melissa Bowerman reports to us that her children have said things like "I said him nothing." Examples like this seem to challenge the fundamental principles of a lexical approach. They reveal exactly the kind of generalization for which lexical theory denies the need.

Neither a pure overgeneralization theory nor a pure lexical theory can account for these facts. The overgeneralization theory says that a child generalizes wherever he can; the lexical theory says that a child makes generalizations only on the basis of heard sentences. How can we resolve this problem? Kenneth Wexler (personal communication) offered an ingenious solution. He suggested that children assume that there is one structure (syntactic or morphological) for each semantic notion like dative or past tense. The child hears the form *John told him the answer* and may generalize the construction to include *John said him the answer* on the assumption that all verbs of talking allow double-object constructions. If he does make this generalization, then when he hears *John told the answer to him* and *John said the answer to him* he eliminates both of the double-object constructions, following the principle that there should be one structure for one semantic notion. However, he hears *told him the answer* (but never hears *said him the answer*), and therefore he is forced to accept the fact that, contrary to his last assumption, some semantic notions are coupled with two different structures. The overgeneralization of past tense works in the same way. Initially the child has irregular forms like *came* and *ran*. When he hears forms like *talked* and *walked* he eliminates the irregular past tense forms in favor of forms like *comed* and *runned*. He persistently hears *came* (and not *comed*), which forces him to change back to the original irregular form. We can enrich the lexical approach to acquisition to account for these patterns of generalization in child language.

Our method has been one in which we both assume and test the theory that we espouse. The lexical approach to adult competence was assumed as the basis for experimentation; the fact that the results are consistent with our hypotheses supports the lexical theory upon which they were based. This of course does not prove that the data are inconsistent with other theories. An insightful model of language acquisition develops from using data from a combination of sources rather than attempting to devise "independent" proofs of either a linguistic or an acquisition theory.

Notes

1. This view contrasts with Fodor's (1966) suggestion that a construction such as passivized dative could be learned independent of other constructions. When a child learns a large number of constructions that are unrelated in his grammar, he replaces them with a simple phrase structure component and transformational rules. If this view were correct, children could learn passivized dative before passive sentences and/or dative-moved sentences, and the order of acquisition of these constructions could vary from child to child.

2. It is also possible that the chain might include rules that move material into first-sister position, such as dative.

3. We know from our pretest (see below) that children control the prepositional indirect object (*to* + NP) before they master the double-NP construction. Therefore they may try to convert the double-object construction into the prepositional form that they learned earlier. The fact that they learn the prepositional form earlier may also be due to the universal unmarked order.

4. See Fodor 1966.

5. We express our gratitude to Hugh Haydon, principal of the Four Corners School in Greenfield, Massachusetts, and to John Byron, principal of the Federal Street Schools, also in Greenfield. We are also indebted to the teachers in these schools who allowed us to interrupt their schedules to gather data from the children and to their students, who patiently acted out our often peculiar sentences.

6. This variability contrasts with children's acquisition of other constructions, such as pronoun interpretation. C. Chomsky (1969) reports that children acquired certain facts of pronominal reference fairly uniformly at about 5½ years.

7. The children who acquired these constructions met our criteria (six of eight correct for *-able* sentences and nine of 12 for passivized dative).

8. Particular thanks go to Greg Carlson, who did much of the planning and experimentation for the pilot experiment.

3 The Acquisition of Structural Restrictions on Anaphora

Lawrence Solan

Although considerable debate continues among linguists around the issue of how some of the generalizations about language should be formulated, there seems to be a general confidence that formulations in many cases are possible, and that one such formulation will be the "right one." What it means for a particular formulation to be right depends crucially on what the native speaker of the language actually has in his head. That is, the formulation must be both empirically adequate and a reflection of the speaker/hearer's psychology. This formulation will reflect both linguistic universals (the innate organizing principles that govern the structure of all languages) and what the speaker has learned about his particular language during the language-acquisition process (see Chomsky 1965, 1975b). Given an empirically adequate description of part of a grammar for a particular language, part of that description will follow automatically from universal grammar, and part will be language-specific. Exactly which subparts of the grammar fit into which category is also subject to debate. Generally, those generalizations that are present in many of the world's languages and that cannot be easily "learned" from the data are considered candidates for linguistic universals.

In this chapter a particular part of the grammar of English will be considered: the restrictions on anaphora. An analysis of the relevant constructions will first be presented and shown to be empirically adequate. After a brief discussion of relevant literature on the acquisition of the restrictions on anaphora, a series of experiments expressly designed for testing the acquisition of the restrictions posited in this chapter will be described. In particular, the experiments address the question of whether those aspects of the restrictions that can be assumed to be universal are indeed acquired rapidly by children, in spite of sparse evidence, as the general theory of language development just outlined would predict. Finally, a discussion of the significance of this approach to language-acquisition research both to the study of language development and to the study of linguistic theory will be offered.

Structural Restrictions on Anaphora

For the past decade, linguists have been discussing the structural restrictions that prevent anaphora from occurring in sentences such as (1).

(1) *He* promised John that *Bill* would not be there.

He and *Bill* cannot be coreferential. Writers such as Langacker (1969), Wasow (1972), Lasnik (1975), and Reinhart (1976) have all attempted to capture the correct generalization with structural accounts that claim that a pronoun cannot be "higher on the tree" than its antecedent. Whether the relative order of the pronoun and antecedent is a part of this restriction has been a matter of controversy, as has been the definition of "higher on the tree."

That the direction of anaphora is a part of the restriction becomes clear when we look at languages other than English. In Thai, for instance, there is an absolute prohibition against anaphora just in case the pronoun precedes the intended antecedent. In Japanese the same holds for certain types of anaphora, in spite of the fact that it is a left-branching language, and "higher" elements on the tree are sometimes on the right (see Nakai 1976). English also has pairs such as (2).

(2) a.   John spoke with *Bill's* wife about *him*.
    b. *John spoke about *him* with *Bill's* wife.

These sentences differ minimally by the order of the PPs in the verb phrase, although only (2a) allows anaphora. The restriction, then, should rule out only "backward" anaphora, that is, anaphora in which the pronoun precedes the intended antecedent.[1]

The structural definitions of hierarchical relations given in (3) have been proposed as relevant to the restrictions on anaphora.

(3) Node A $\begin{cases} \text{commands} \\ \text{governs} \\ c\text{-commands} \end{cases}$ node B if neither dominates the other

and the first $\begin{cases} \text{S node} \\ \text{cyclic node} \\ \text{branching node} \end{cases}$ dominating A also dominates B

(NP,S = cyclic nodes).[2]

In the structure (4), for example,

(4)

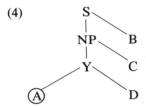

node A commands node B; commands and governs node C; and commands, governs, and c-commands node D, if we assume that node Y does not represent a cyclic category.

In (5) is my own version of the structural restriction on anaphora, which draws heavily on earlier statements by Lasnik and Reinhart in particular.

(5) Backward Anaphora Restriction (BAR):
    Backward anaphora (Pro$_i$ ... NP$_i$) is impossible if
    (a) Pro and NP are clausemates and Pro governs NP;
    or
    (b) Pro and NP are not clausemates, and Pro c-commands NP.

The BAR consists of a number of different statements. First, it makes the claim that word order is important. Only anaphora between a pronoun and a full NP to its right is ruled out. Second, both the structural definitions "govern" and "c-command" play a role, specifying what it means for a pronoun to be "higher on the tree" than an antecedent under different circumstances. Finally, it is more difficult to get anaphora when the two elements to be related are in the same clause. In my dialect, anaphora is allowed in (6a), but not (6b).

(6) a. Bill watched *him* while *John* ran.
    b. *Bill watched *him* during *John's* run.

At least for my dialect of English, Lasnik's restriction, which uses only "govern," is too strong, and Reinhart's, which uses only "c-command," is too weak to account for the data in (6). However, it should be recognized that speakers do vary slightly in the statements of their individual restrictions (see Solan 1978b). The stronger restriction against intraclausal anaphora is also needed to rule out anaphora in (2b), in which the pronoun does not c-command the intended antecedent, since there is an intervening PP node. The BAR, as it is stated, is intended to apply only in cases of definite pronoun anaphora. For pronouns bound to quantifiers, a somewhat different restriction is needed.[3]

As one would expect, it makes sense to claim that certain aspects of the BAR are language-specific, whereas others follow directly from linguistic universals. Specifically, the notions "c-command" and "govern" themselves may be part of universal grammar, because they play a broad role in linguistic theory (see Reinhart 1976) and because they are relationships that might be difficult for a child to compute solely on the basis of data. It thus seems plausible to consider that the child learning language automatically considers some phrases "hierarchically superior" to others, and that this ranking is more or less accurately described by the relationships being discussed. In addition, the use of word order and a sensitivity to the difference between clausemates and nonclausemates may be part of universal grammar, but it is unlikely that the particular use of them that the BAR makes is. The general theory of acquisition I have outlined briefly makes the prediction that those aspects of the BAR that can plausibly be claimed to be universal should present children with little trouble, while other aspects might. This should hold regardless of which aspects seem intuitively more complex to the linguist.

A series of experiments was conducted to determine how children acquire the BAR. Earlier work by Lust (1977a) and Tavakolian (1977) indicates that children at first have a restriction that simply bans all backward anaphora, regardless of structural considerations.[4] The question asked here is whether children, once they know that backward anaphora is possible in English, adopt the correct notions of "c-command," "govern," and directionality, and whether they distinguish between intra- and interclausal anaphora. Consider (7), in which anaphora is allowed, and which is a structural description of (6a).

(7)

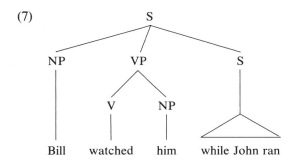

Given a sentence of the form NP – V – NP – Complement, the possibility of anaphora can be changed in three ways: by adjusting the position of the pronoun, as illustrated in (8), the pronoun can be made to *c*-command the antecedent, rendering anaphora impossible.

(8) **He* watched Bill while *John* ran.

Second, as (9) shows, anaphora becomes impossible when the complement is attached to the VP instead of the S.

(9) **Bill told *him* that *John* would not be here on time.

Since *tell* strictly subcategorizes for a *that* complement, the subordinate clause is attached to the verb phrase. Anaphora is ruled out because the direct object *c*-commands other nodes in the verb phrase. Finally, by adjusting the complement type (noun-phrasal or clausal), it is possible to alter anaphora possibilities, as we have already seen in (6b), since intraclausal anaphora is allowed less than interclausal anaphora.

Experiment 1: Acquisition of Restrictions on Anaphora
In experiment 1, all three of the factors discussed so far—pronoun position, complement attachment, and complement type—were varied systematically. The sentence types used are listed in (10).

(10) a. He told the horse that the sheep would run around.
    b. The horse told him that the sheep would run around.
    c. He hit the horse in the sheep's yard.
    d. The horse hit him in the sheep's yard.
    e. He hit the horse after the sheep ran around.
    f. The horse hit him after the sheep ran around.
    g. He hit the horse after the sheep's run.
    h. The horse hit him after the sheep's run.

Table 3.1
Experimental Conditions

Sentence Type	Attachment	Complement	Pronoun
10a	VP	S	Sub
10b	VP	S	Obj
10c	VP	NP	Sub
10d	VP	NP	Obj
10e	S	S	Sub
10f	S	S	Obj
10g	S	NP	Sub
10h	S	NP	Obj

Table 3.2
Independent Effect of Each Variable on Anaphoric Possibility

Sentence Type	Attachment	Complement	Pronoun
10a	x		x
10b	x		
10c	x	x	x
10d	x	x	
10e			x
10f			
10g		x	x
10h		x	

As can be seen in table 3.1, these sentences are organized in a factorial design, with each of the three factors varied. Table 3.2 shows how each factor independently rules out anaphora in certain cases. I follow Williams (1975) in claiming that temporal PPs are attached to the VP node. Note that attachment and pronoun position conspire to define the *c*-command relationships for each sentence. Complement type dictates whether the strong clause (5a) or the weak clause (5b) of the BAR is to be used.

Each child heard three cycles of the eight sentence types, each cycle of sentences presented in a different random order. Choices of verbs, animals, temporal and locative prepositions, and noun phrases were

Table 3.3
Percentage of Responses with Pronoun Interpreted Anaphorically

Sentence Type	Age			Total
	5 years	6 years	7 years	
10a	17	22	0	13
10b	17	17	6	13
10c	17	25	6	16
10d	14	44	22	27
10e	11	11	3	8
10f	39	25	28	31
10g	8	28	14	17
10h	42	42	33	39
Total	20	27	14	20

also randomized so that each child actually heard a unique set of 24 sentences.

We presented 36 children (12 each of 5-, 6-, and 7-year-olds) with three tokens of each of the eight sentence types. Each sentence contains the names of two animals and contains one pronoun. In the children's environment were four toy animals and a variety of props. The children were tested separately and were asked to act out the sentences using the toy animals and the props. During a short practice session that always preceded the experiment it would become clear that the child understood both the task and the relevant vocabulary and was not afraid to act out sentences using toys not mentioned in the sentences.

The results are first presented in table 3.3. Note that children have relatively few anaphoric responses (20 percent). They interpret the pronoun as referring to one of the two animals present in the environment but not mentioned in the sentence most of the time. This is consistent with the findings of Lust and Tavakolian, who both found that children between 2 and 5 years of age tend to avoid backward anaphora completely. While C. Chomsky (1969) found some children allowing anaphora on sentences such as (10a) some of the time, she also generally found children avoiding backward anaphora, especially the youngest children in her study (5 years old).

Anaphoric responses to sentence types other than (10f) and (10h) were considered to be errors (although anaphora is possible for adults

Table 3.4
Percentage of Responses with Pronoun Interpreted Anaphorically

	Attachment		Complement		Pronoun		
Age	VP	S	S	NP	Sub	Obj	Total
5	16	25	21	20	13	28	20
6	27	26	19	35	22	32	27
7	8	19	9	19	6	22	14
Total	17	24	16	24	13	27	20

in (10h) in some dialects). The 6-year-olds made significantly more errors than the 5-year-olds (4.5 versus 2.5) ($t_{22} = 1.92$, $P < 0.05$), while 7-year-olds made only 1.5 errors per child. Since there were 18 chances to commit an error, the error rate was relatively low, ranging from 8 percent to 25 percent for the different age groups. The surprisingly poor performance of the 6-year-olds will be discussed in greater detail below.

In table 3.4, the results are organized according to the three factors that are varied in the experiment: attachment of the complement, type of complement, and placement of the pronoun. Children, like adults, allow anaphora more frequently when the complement is attached to the S node (24 percent) than when it attached to the VP node (17 percent). This difference is significant, $F(1,33) = 5.04$, $P = 0.032$. Similarly, when the pronoun was in the object position, children responded anaphorically significantly more frequently (27 percent) than when the pronoun was in the subject position (13 percent), $F(1,33) = 12.02$, $P = 0.001$. The combination of these two facts, plus the fact that there is a significant interaction between attachment and pronoun position, indicates that children are using the notion "c-command" in determining anaphoric possibilities. Referring to table 3.3, one can see that anaphoric responses to sentence types (10f) and (10h) do exceed anaphoric responses to all of the other sentence types (31 percent and 39 percent, respectively), and these are precisely the conditions under which the pronoun does not c-command the potential antecedent.

If children were using either command or govern uniformly, then we would expect no differences in table 3.4, since the factors that were varied systematically have no effect on either of those relationships.[5] Even sentences (10f) and (10h), for which children had so many anaphoric responses, have pronouns that both command and govern their antecedents. To argue that children are using no structural principle at all would also be difficult, since it is not obvious that it is possible to account for adult distinctions without structural principles, and children are making the same distinctions here that adults make according to the BAR.

Children also take the complement type into account in determining anaphoric possibilities. This time, however, they do exactly the opposite of what adults do. They allow anaphora significantly more frequently when the antecedent is embedded in a noun phrase (24 percent) than when it is embedded within a subordinate clause (16 percent); $F(1,33) = 5.04, P = 0.013$. This indicates that while children know that complement type (that is, clausematedness) is a factor, they are unable to make correct use of this knowledge. Six-year-olds make a greater distinction between complement types than do 5-year-olds, accounting for at least some of the increased error rate for the older children.

Since they indicate that children make basic syntactic distinctions but misapply them, the results regarding complement type are particularly striking. This situation can be explained by the claim that children at 6—unsure of the restrictions on backward anaphora—begin, wrongly, to apply the restrictions on bound anaphora (reflexives and reciprocals) to cases of backward anaphora, which causes them to allow anaphora more frequently when the pronoun and antecedent are in the same clause (actually the same cyclic domain). In (11), for example, the reflexive must be bound to *Bill,* and cannot be bound to *John.*

(11) John said that Bill shaved himself.

The precise statement of the restrictions on bound anaphora has received much attention in the linguistic literature, with descriptions ranging from Postal's (1971) Clausemate Condition to Chomsky's (1973) Specified-Subject Condition and (1980) Opacity Condition. Regardless of the correct statement, the restriction has the effect of allowing anaphora across an NP boundary, but not across a clause boundary. As (12) illustrates, when the reflexive is embedded in a noun phrase, the antecedent for the reflexive pronoun can be found outside the noun phrase, just in case the NP has no subject.

(12) a. John told Bill a story about himself.
     b. John told Bill Max's story about himself.

In (12a), the reflexive can refer to either of the two individuals mentioned, in spite of the fact that neither is contained in the noun phrase *a story about himself*.

Looking again at test conditions (10f) and (10h), it becomes plausible that children are using the correct notion, but in the wrong way.

(10f) The horse hit him after the sheep ran around.
(10h) The horse hit him after the sheep's run.

In (10f), the embedded clause contains the potential antecedent to the pronoun, meaning that the child (or adult) must cross a clause boundary in order to allow anaphora. This is not the case for (10h), in which there is no clause boundary between *him* and *sheep's*. The situation is thus analogous to the difference between (11) and (12a). Overgeneralization of the restriction on bound anaphora is thus sufficient to account for children's preferring backward anaphora when the antecedent is embedded in a noun phrase rather than a clause. These differences are explored more in the experiments to be described.

Experiment 2: Preposed Complements
That children distinguish between NP and S complement types is also shown in experiment 2. For adults, anaphora is possible in both of the sentence types when the pronoun is embedded in a preposed structure. The test examples are shown in (13).

(13) a. After he ran around, the horse hit the sheep.
     b. After his run, the horse hit the sheep.

In neither case does the pronoun either *c*-command or govern anything in the main clause, as (14) illustrates.

(14)

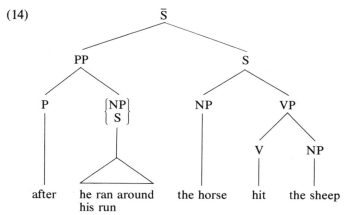

Table 3.5
Percentage of Responses with Pronoun Interpreted Anaphorically

Sentence Type	Age			
	5 years	6 years	7 years	Total
1	44	28	36	36
2	47	61	64	57
Total	46	44	50	47

Thus, backward anaphora is possible. However, if it is the case that children do generalize the restrictions on bound anaphora to include backward anaphora, then we would still expect them to allow anaphora significantly more frequently in (13b), where the pronoun and possible antecedents are not separated by a clause boundary.

The materials for this experiment were randomized in the same manner as those for experiment 1, and were presented to the children as part of the same questionnaire. The 36 subjects and the procedure were exactly the same.

As table 3.5 shows, children allow anaphora significantly more often when the pronoun is embedded in an NP (57 percent) than when it is embedded in an S (36 percent); $F(1,33) = 14.88$, $P = 0.001$.[6] In addition, the 6-year-olds made this distinction significantly more frequently than the 5-year-olds ($P = 0.031$). These results are completely consistent with those of the first experiment and support the claim that children begin around the age of 6 to overgeneralize the restrictions on bound anaphora to include backward anaphora in general. That children respond anaphorically more frequently in experiment 2 (47 percent) than they did in experiment 1 (20 percent) is attributable to their knowledge of the role that c-command plays in the restrictions on anaphora.

Note that it would be difficult to explain these results by arguing that children are misrepresenting the structure of these sentences, that they have the right restrictions but the wrong trees (or other structural representation of the sentences). First, the results of experiment 1, which show that children do pay attention to the c-command relationship, support the claim that the children's representations are very much like the adult ones. Second, any hypothesis intended to explain the results of experiment 2 on the basis of structural misrepresentation would necessarily claim that the older children know less about the structure than the younger ones, since it is the 6- and 7-year-olds who distinguish between sentence types in this experiment. Empirical support for this claim does not seem likely.

Experiment 3: Reflexives
To test the plausibility of the overgeneralization of bound anaphora restrictions as an explanation of the results of the two experiments, the 5- and 6-year-olds were given ten sentences each of the form shown by (15).

(15) The dog said that the horse kicked himself.

Work by Matthei (this volume) on reciprocals and by Read and Hare (1977) on reflexives has shown that children do sometimes interpret the pronoun as being bound to the main clause subject, in violation of the restrictions discussed above.

The claim here is that the 6-year-olds have begun to overgeneralize the restrictions on reflexives and reciprocals. But in order to do so, these children must at least know that these restrictions exist. Thus, if it is the case that the 5-year-olds make significantly fewer errors on sentence (15) than the 6-year-olds, this claim will be disconfirmed, since children cannot begin to overapply something that they do not know. In fact, such results would indicate that 6-year-olds have trouble with anaphora in general, independent of the particular restrictions discussed here. In addition, if both the 5- and 6-year-olds do poorly on reflexives (which is a possibility when one considers the literature cited above), then the claims I present would also not be supported, although it could not be said that the results fall into a pattern of 5-year-olds doing generally better than 6-year-olds.

Each child was presented with 10 tokens of the test condition. Both matrix and subordinate verbs were randomized, each child hearing a different set of sentences, with the provision that each child heard each verb only once. To prevent boredom, the sentences for this experiment were mixed with those from another experiment, which will not be discussed here.

Although the procedure of this experiment was the same as for the other two, the subjects were 11 each of the 5- and 6-year-olds who had participated in the other studies. Seven-year-olds were not tested, since the relevant hypotheses concerned only the younger children.

The 5-year-olds got 89 percent correct, while the 6-year-olds got 87 percent correct; the difference is trivial. Thus, although the 6-year-olds do significantly worse on backward anaphora than do the 5-year-olds, distinguishing incorrectly on the basis of complement type, this is not the case when it comes to reflexives. As was described above, had the 6-year-olds made significantly more errors on the reflexive sentences than the 5-year-olds, it would have been impossible to maintain the claim that they have begun to overapply the restrictions on reflexives. Since this did not happen, the overgeneralization hypothesis remains plausible, although it cannot be claimed that this overgeneralization is caused by the fact that the children have just learned this restriction, since the 5- and 6-year-olds do equally well.

Experiment 4: Forward Anaphora
The BAR claims that the direction of anaphora, the structural relationship between the pronoun and the potential antecedent, and the type of complement into which the potential antecedent is embedded are all factors that contribute to the restrictions on anaphora. Thus far I have discussed only the last two of these factors. In this experiment, it was asked whether the direction of anaphora in itself affects children's interpretations.

The same 36 children who participated in the first two experiments were also presented with the following four sentence types in another toy-moving experiment. The sentences used are given in (16).

(16) a. The pig told the horse that he would run around.
    b. The pig hit the horse in his yard.
    c. The pig hit the horse while he ran around.
    d. The pig hit the horse during his run.

Each sentence type corresponds to a syntactic structure from experiment 1. Children received only one token of each of the four types, although verbs, NPs, and so on were randomized as in the other experiments.

Among the three age groups, it was found that 94 percent of the responses were anaphoric. Comparing this number with the 20 percent of experiment 1 and the 47 percent of experiment 2, it can be seen that the relative order of the pronoun and intended antecedent does make a difference in children's restrictions on anaphora, which is consistent both with the results of Lust and Tavakolian and with the BAR. In particular, the results of experiments 2 and 4 should be compared, since there were two possible antecedents within each sentence in these two experiments. The results are still marked, with children allowing anaphora twice as often in experiment 4 as in experiment 2. From this it can only be concluded that children prefer forward anaphora to backward anaphora, which supports the view that the structural restrictions on anaphora are actually structural restrictions on backward anaphora.

Conclusion

Children are aware at a very young age of the various components of the BAR: structural relationships (that is, c-command), complement type (that is, noun-phrasal or clausal) and linear order of the pronoun and the intended antecedent. Given that linguists have been trying to capture the correct notions over a long period of time, it makes sense to claim that children's ability to acquire language makes these notions easily accessible to them.

With respect to the issues raised at the beginning of this chapter, the results of the studies reported here support the claim that those aspects of the grammar of English that follow directly from linguistic universals give children little difficulty in spite of their apparent complexity in some cases. Children's use of the c-command relationship is a striking example, and is supported in other work by Goodluck (in this volume) on the acquisition of other interpretive rules for English. It also seems reasonable to claim that restrictions on anaphora are universally unidirectional; I know of no language that restricts forward anaphora at all. Once again, work reported here as well as the work of Lust (1977a) and Tavakolian (1977) cited above indicates that children are well aware of the effect of directionality on the restrictions on anaphora. Finally, while languages seem universally to distinguish between noun phrases and clauses, and other literature (Roeper 1978) shows that children master this distinction very early and with apparent ease, the precise application of this distinction to the restrictions on anaphora cannot be claimed to be universal. In fact, many speakers of English do not make this distinction in their BARs. From these facts it follows naturally that children would demonstrate knowledge of the relevant distinction as a factor that might play a role in the application of rules of grammar, but might initially misapply it in an attempt to formulate a more unified theory of anaphora that includes both backward anaphora and bound anaphora.

Other work in language acquisition (for example, C. Chomsky 1969) does show this age group (around 6 years) to be one in which children are prone to overgeneralization. In Chomsky's results, children overextend the class of verbs that are subject to the Minimal Distance

Principle, so that they interpret *Bill* as the subject of *mow* in both sentences in (17), since *Bill* is the closest noun phrase to the missing complement subject.

(17) a. John promised Bill to mow the lawn.
     b. John told Bill to mow the lawn.

This principle works for almost every verb in English except *promise*. Similar cases of overgeneralization have been discussed recently by Goodluck and Roeper (1978) and Echeverria (1975).

In the experiments described here, it is also argued that children overgeneralize. However, the overgeneralization in this case involves not lexical classes of verbs, but entire structural principles. That children are able to make such creative use of these principles makes it less surprising that the components of the BAR are so accessible to the children, and do not take long to learn.

Notes

I have benefited from discussions with Emmon Bach, Carol Chomsky, Chuck Clifton, Helen Goodluck, Tom Roeper, and Edwin Williams, all of whom I wish to thank. The research for this paper was supported in part by NIH grant HD 09647 to S. Jay Keyser and Thomas Roeper.

1. Reinhart (1976) argues that directionality is not a part of the restriction, on the basis of sentences such as "*On *John's* bed he put Max." However, it is argued in Solan (1978a) that the restrictions on anaphora apply before the rule that preposes *on John's bed* in the sentence above, making such examples irrelevant.

2. The term "govern" is synonymous with Lasnik's (1976) "kommand."

3. See Partee 1975 for further discussion of the restrictions on pronouns bound to quantifiers.

4. However, Lust, in this volume, suggests that while children's initial hypotheses are directional in nature, which direction they choose may be determined by other factors in the structure of the language they are learning.

5. Actually some children may be using govern (as may some adults), but these children are not in the majority, and the statistical evidence still points to *c*-command being a factor for the overall group.

6. For this experiment, a child choosing either of the two noun phrases mentioned in the sentence was producing an anaphoric response.

4 **Constraint on Anaphora
in Child Language:
A Prediction for a Universal**

Barbara Lust

Anaphora refers to the natural language situation wherein a term must be interpreted by reference to another term in a sentence or discourse. For example, in (1), the pronoun *he* is interpreted by reference to the name *John* (under its most likely interpretation with neutral stress). Likewise, in (2) the null term ∅ must be interpreted by reference to the previous occurrence of this name.

(1) *John* read the play and *he* smoked a pipe.

   ↑_____|

(2) *John* read the play and ∅ smoked a pipe.

   ↑_____|

Anaphora refers to the interpretive relation (shown by the arrow) between a governing term (such as the name *John*) and an anaphor such as *he* or ∅. Sentence (1) exemplifies a relation of pronominal anaphora; sentence (2), a relation of null anaphora. Anaphora is a principal device for redundancy reduction in all natural languages. Although it is well known that some anaphora can be determined by extrasyntactic (pragmatic as well as discourse) factors (see, for example, Hammerton 1970; Kuno 1972; Hankamer and Sag 1977; Williams 1977a, b; Stenning 1978), this study is concerned with sentential anaphora, not with discourse or contextual anaphora.

It is generally considered now in linguistic theory that anaphoric relations must be determined at the surface-structure level of language (Wasow 1972; Lasnik 1976; Chomsky 1975b, 1977; see Bresnan 1978 for a review). Semantic interpretation rules (which refer to surface structures) or general principles of pragmatics must account for these relations (Wasow 1972; Chomsky 1975b, 1977; Hankamer and Sag 1976;

Reinhart 1976; Lasnik 1976). Certain known constraints on sentential anaphora interpretation, however, suggest that possible anaphora is at least partially determined by syntax. Both linear order and dominance (hierarchical constituent structure or "command") relations appear to be involved in these constraints (Langacker 1969; Lasnik 1976; Reinhart 1976). Anaphora then may be viewed as an aspect of natural language that lies at the intersection between syntax and semantics.

This chapter presents evidence of a constraint on pronominal anaphora in early child language. Comparing this constraint to a constraint previously found on null anaphora in early child language (Lust 1977b), I argue that one unique constraint on anaphora may be involved in both cases. I discuss the nature of this constraint, considering that it may reflect a general constraint on the acquisition of semantic interpretation rules in a first language. Finally, I formulate a prediction for a universal constraint on anaphora in child language.

Previous research on first-language acquisition of coordinative sentences with null anaphora by young children (2–3 years old) suggested that this acquisition was developmentally constrained in directionality (Lust, 1977b). Specifically, in an elicited imitation task, redundancy reduction was constrained in a forward direction in these sentences. That is, when the reduction site followed the unreduced term (forward reduction) (see (3)), children frequently reduced redundancy; that is, they converted (3a) to (3b). When the reduction site preceded the unreduced term (backward reduction) (see (4)), children rarely if ever reduced redundancy; that is, converted (4a) to (4b). Although development of sentences with redundancy, such as (3a) and (4a), was generally primary to development of sentences with null anaphora such as (3b) and (4b), when reduced coordinations had a forward direction as in (3b) they were as easy for children as unreduced sentences such as (3a). Youngest children, in addition, found forward-reduced coordinations, such as (3b), significantly easier than backward-reduced coordinations, such as (4b).

(3) Forward Reduction
    SV + $V
    a. *Kittens* hop and *kittens* run.
    b. *Kittens* hop and ∅ run.

(4) Backward Reduction

   SV̸ + SV

   a. Kittens *hide* and dogs *hide*.

   b. Kittens ∅ and dogs *hide*.

Similar results were found for VO coordinative sentences (simple imperatives) as well as for SVO sentences. For example, children frequently reduced redundancy in sentences like (5) (forward direction), but never in sentences like (6) (backward direction).

(5) Forward Reduction

   SVO + $VO

   a. *Mary* cooked the meal and *Mary* ate the bread.

   b. *Mary* cooked the meal and ∅ ate the bread.

(6) Backward Reduction

   SV∅ + SVO

   a. Mary baked *the bread* and Sarah ate *the bread*.

   b. Mary baked ∅ and Sarah ate *the bread*.

Similar results were also found for VS sentences (with permuted order, that is, sentences with "existential *there,*" as in *There are trees and there are flowers*).

Further research on the development of coordination in natural speech (Lust and Mervis 1980) suggested that the developmental constraints on redundancy reduction observed through the elicited imitation task were also evident in young children's natural speech, thus suggesting that the effects were not artifacts of the imitation task.

As explanation for these results it was proposed that language development might reflect sensitivity to a syntactic constraint on the universal transformational schema of conjunction reduction by which coordinate redundancy is syntactically reduced in a forward direction (Hankamer 1971; Maling 1972; cf. Lust 1977b).

As we saw above, however, the putative transformational schema of coordination reduction derives structures characterized by null anaphora, as in (2b), (3b), and (4b). Since it is clear that semantic interpretation rules of anaphora must be structurally constrained (see the references in the first paragraphs of this chapter), constraints on these general rules of anaphora would obviate those on specific transformations that derive them grammatically. Correspondingly, first-language acquisition of anaphora might need only be sensitive to general constraints on the semantic interpretation of such anaphoric structures.

Specifically, if the forward-directionality constraint previously observed on coordination reduction in child language is grammatically
determined, it may be determined by sensitivity to general constraints
on semantic interpretation of such anaphoric structures. It may not be
determined by sensitivity to specific constraints on the specific transformational schema of coordination reduction.

If this is the case, then this same constraint on acquisition would be
expected to hold for other forms of anaphora that are not derived by a
conjunction reduction schema. Specifically, if this same acquisition
constraint also holds for pronominal anaphora, then the constraint must
correspond to a constraint on semantic interpretive rules, not to a
constraint on transformational rules, since it is now believed that pronouns are not transformationally derived (see references in the first
paragraphs). This argument would be particularly cogent if the constraint would hold for forms of pronominal anaphora that do not occur
in coordinate sentences. Moreover, we may inquire if the constraint
would hold equivalently over different types of subordination (some
more coordinative than others).

1 Experiment on Pronominal Anaphora

This study was designed to discover whether children's use of pronominal anaphora would be characterized by a constraint in a forward
direction similar to that found for coordination reduction. Pronominalization may occur in either coordinative sentences, such as (1), or
subordinative sentences, such as (7) and (8). Like coordination reduction, pronominalization in subordinate sentences may work either forward, as in (7), or backward, as in (8).

(7) Forward Reduction
    b. *John* read the play while *he* smoked a pipe.

(8) Backward Reduction
    b. While *he* smoked a pipe, *John* read the play.

That is, the pronoun may either follow the governing term as in (7)
(forward reduction) or precede it as in (8) (backward reduction), just
as in coordination reduction the null site may either follow or precede
its governing term.

The study inquired whether, with pronominal anaphora, children
would reduce redundancy preferentially in a forward direction, and not
in a backward direction; whether they would find forward-pronominalized sentences significantly easier than backward-pronominalized sen-

Table 4.1
Sentence Types used to Elicit Imitation in Study of Pronominalization, and Examples

---

NP – NP

I. NP – NP$_s$

Jane was sad, because *Jane* dropped the ice cream cone.
Mary was sad while *Mary* was playing ball.

II. NP$_s$ – NP

Because *Sam* was thirsty, *Sam* drank some soda.
While *Dad* was driving the car, *Dad* bumped a truck.

NP – Pro

III. NP – Pro$_s$

Tommy ran fast because *he* heard a lion.
Jenna drank some juice while *she* was having lunch.

IV. Pro$_s$ – NP

Because *she* was tired, *Mommy* was sleeping.
While *he* was outside, *John* saw a fire truck.

V. NP$_s$ – Pro

Because *Jenna* saw a mouse, *she* ran away.
While *Tom* was riding the horse, *he* looked around.

Note: NP specifies noun phrase; Pro specifies pronoun; s specifies subordinate clause. NP$_s$ specifies NP occurs in subordinate clause.

tences; and, finally, whether although children might prefer not to reduce redundancy by pronominalization in early development, this developmental effect would be modulated by directionality of pronominalization. That is, would children find forward-pronominalized sentences with forward anaphora as easy as unpronominalized sentences with redundancy? Thus a set of results parallel to those in the previous study of coordination reduction with null anaphora was sought.

In addition the study inquired whether a directionality effect would hold equivalently over sentences with both a clearly subordinative connective (*while*) and those with a connective that was structurally and semantically ambiguous between a subordinative and a coordinative function (*because*) (see Williams 1970, 1974 on the structural ambiguity of the *because* connective versus the *while* connective).

Imitation was elicited from children of a set of 20 complex (subordinative) sentences exemplified in table 4.1. The sentences varied as to whether redundancy was reduced or not, that is, whether pronominal-

ization occurred or not. (In types I and II on table 4.1 pronominalization does not occur; in types III and IV it does.) Sentences also varied
in pronominalization direction. Sentences of type III on the table represent forward pronominalization; sentences of type IV backward
pronominalization. Sentence type I corresponds to (that is, allows) forward pronominalization; type II corresponds to backward pronominalization (although forward pronominalization is also allowed in this
case). Sentence connectives were *while* or *because* within each type.

Notably, sentence type V is essentially a control. Sentences with
backward pronominalization, such as type IV, differ in clause order
from sentences with forward pronominalization, such as type III. Type
IV backward-pronominalized sentences have preposed subordinate
clauses, whereas sentences with forward pronominalization (type III)
have standard order, with the subordinate clause following the main
clause. Psycholinguistic research with both adults and children has
found that sentences with preposed subordinate clauses are more difficult to process (Clark 1970; Levin and Kaplan 1970; Kornfeld 1973;
Fodor, Bever, and Garrett 1975). A difference between children's imitation of types III and IV therefore might be due to clause order rather
than to pronominalization direction. To test for this possibility, imitation of type V sentences was elicited. These had forward pronominalization but preposed subordinate clause. If clause order alone were
significant to a difference between III and IV (forward and backward
pronominalization) then differences between these should not be
significantly greater than differences between the cases where the subordinate clause followed or preceded the main clause when pronominalization direction did not vary (as in III and V).

There was one replication for each of the five sentence types and for
each of the connectives, giving a total of 20 sentences for imitation.

All sentences were 11 syllables in length. NPs that related to pronouns anaphorically were all proper names. Pronouns and names all
occurred in subject position. Pronominal and nominal stress was
noncontrastive.

Children were grouped as discussed below. The basic design was
thus factorial by four-factor analysis of variance (ANOVA): Group
× Pronominalization (+ or −) × Directionality (forward or backward)
× Connective (*because* or *while*). There were repeated measures on the
last three factors (sentence types I–IV). A separate analysis was performed on sentence types III, IV, and V, where difference between

Table 4.2
Subjects of Pronominalization Study

Young Children

	Subgroup		
	1	2	3
MLU range	2.0–3.75	3.76–4.75	4.76
N	7	8	9
Mean MLU	3.19	4.32	5.69
Mean age	2,9	2,11	3,2

Older Children

	Subgroup			
	1	2	3	4
Age range	3,6–3,11	4,0–4,5	4,6–4,11	5,0–5,7
N	14	13	9	9
Mean MLU	5.86	5.93	6.35	6.67
Mean age	3,8	4,2	4,8	5,3

performance on III and IV was evaluated in comparison to difference between performance on III and V. Score range in all cases was 0–2.

Ancillary imitation errors like inflection or tense changes were discounted in these analyses. A change of *while* connective to *when* (a frequent change) was also discounted.

The subjects were 69 children from Cambridge, Massachusetts and Ithaca, New York between the ages 2 years, 6 months and 5 years, 7 months (2,6–5,7). The subject sample is shown in table 4.2. Children were first grouped into a "young group" by MLU (mean length of utterance) (mean MLU 4.50, ages 2,6–3,5, mean age 3,0, $N = 24$) and an "older" group by age (ages 3,6–5,7, mean age 4,4, mean MLU 6.14, $N = 45$). Each group was analyzed separately by similar analyses.

Subgroups were established within each group as shown on table 4.2. Young children were grouped into three subgroups by MLU (1: 2.0–3.75; 2: 3.76–4.75; 3: ≥4.76). The rationale behind this subgrouping is the observation (Brown 1970) that at about MLU 3.50 children begin to demonstrate compound (coordinative) and then complex (subordinative) sentences in their natural speech. Older children were divided into four 6-month age groups. There were 12 males and 12 females in the

young group, and 27 males and 18 females in the older group. There
were no significant effects of sex in either group (as measured by
ANOVA on differences in total score correct on imitation, so the data
have been pooled.

Young children were tested in their homes, where a parent participated in the research. Older children were tested in nursery schools
where an experimenter (E) conducted the research.

A natural speech sample was first collected of the child in natural
conversation in a play situation with the parent (at home) or with E (in
school). E brought a few toys and a book to focus this conversation. A
minimum of 100 utterances was collected. (Mean number of utterances
collected was 132 for the young children, 102 for the older.)

The elicited-imitation task was then administered either by the parent (in the home) or by E (in the nursery school). The 20 sentences were
usually administered in two sessions of 10 sentences each. The task was
introduced with a command like: "I am going to tell you a little story.
Can you say this little story just the way I say it?"

All sessions were tape-recorded on a Sony Cassette-Corder TC-110.

There were 1,380 sentences for analysis. Mean numbers of correct
imitation for each sentence type are shown in table 4.3. ANOVA on
these data produced basically analogous results for both the young and
older children. For both groups the pronominalization factor was
highly significant ($F(1,21) = 17.92$, $P<0.001$ for the young children;
$F(1,41) = 46.18$, $P < 0.001$ for the older children). As can be seen from
figure 4.1, sentences with pronominalization (types III and IV) are
generally significantly easier than sentences without pronominalization
(types I and II). Mean numbers correct were 0.41 and 0.20, respectively, for the younger children, and 1.47 and 0.88 for the older children. However, with the young children, the pronominalization factor
interacted significantly with developmental level ($F(1,21) = 15.27$,
$P = 0.001$). As can be seen from figure 4.1, before developmental language level 3 (MLU ≤ 4.76), sentences with pronominalization and
those with redundant NP were nearly equivalent in difficulty.

Directionality was also highly significant for both the young and
older groups ($F(1,21) = 11.16$, $P = 0.003$ for the young; $F(1,41)$
$= 15.75$, $P \leq 0.001$ for the older), with forward forms clearly correct
more often than backward forms. However, in each group there was
also a significant interaction between the pronominalization factor and
the directionality factor, as shown in figure 4.2 ($F(1,21) = 4.87$, P
$= 0.04$ for the young; $F(1,41) = 18.27$, $P < 0.001$ for the older). As can

Table 4.3
Mean Number of Correct Imitations for each Sentence Type

| | Sentence Type | | | | |
	I (NP – NP$_s$)	II (NP$_s$ – NP)	III (NP – Pro$_s$)	IV (Pro$_s$ – NP)	V (NP$_s$ – Pro)
Young Children					
Subgroup					
1 (MLU 2.0–3.75)	0.143	0	0.071	0	0
2 (MLU 3.76–4.75)	0.188	0.250	0.438	0.063	0.313
3 (MLU ≥ 4.76)	0.333	0.222	1.167	0.50	1.056
Older Children					
Subgroup					
1 (age 3,6–3,11)	0.750	0.608	1.679	1.107	1.430
2 (age 4,0–4,5)	0.810	0.808	1.654	0.962	1.538
3 (age 4,6–4,11)	1.00	1.00	1.945	1.445	1.834
4 (age 5,0–5,7)	1.11	1.278	1.889	1.334	1.834

Note: Since there was no significant difference between sentences with different connectives (*because*, *while*), means for these sentences have been conflated. Score range = 0–2.

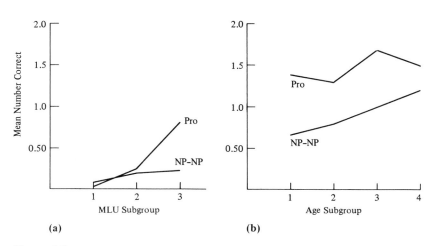

Figure 4.1
Success on pronominalization and on redundant NP sentences by developmental level. **a** Young children. **b** Older children.

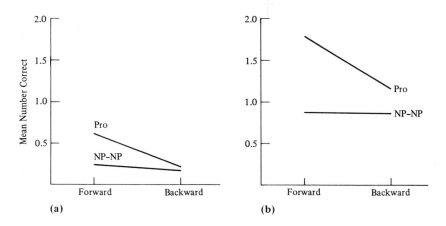

Figure 4.2
Success on forward and backward reduction direction (sentences with and without pronominalization). **a** Young children. **b** Older children.

Table 4.4
Sentence-Imitation Success, Based on Pronominalization and Clause Order

	Mean Number Correct	
Sentence Type	Young	Older
III. Forward pronominalization, standard clause order (NP – Pro$_s$)	0.61	1.77
IV. Backward pronominalization, reversed clause order (Pro$_s$ – NP)	0.21	1.18
V. Forward pronominalization, reversed clause order (NP$_s$ – Pro)	0.50	1.62

Test of significance of difference between III and IV and between III and V:
Young t (23) = 2.42, P = 0.02
Older t (44) = 5.34, P = 0.001

be seen in figure 4.2, the directionality factor is significant only for pronominalized sentences (types III and IV), not for redundant NP sentences (I and II). Sentences with forward pronominalization (type III) were significantly easier for children to imitate than sentences with backward pronominalization (type IV). Means were 0.61 and 0.21, respectively, for the young children and 1.77 and 1.18, respectively, for the older children. Redundant NP sentences types I and II did not differ significantly from each other, as can be seen in the figure.

The difference in children's success in imitation of forward and backward pronominalization was not due to the variation in clause order between them, but to pronominalization direction. This is shown by the fact that there was no significant difference in children's imitation of redundant NP sentences (types I and II), which varied in clause order alone. It is also shown by the fact that children (young or older) did not find the control sentence (type V), which had preposed subordinate clause and forward pronominalization, significantly more difficult than the sentence type III, which has standard clause order with similar forward pronominalization direction (see table 4.4).

For the young children, developmental level (MLU) was also a significant factor in overall imitation success ($F(2,21) = 4.99$, $P = 0.017$). Mean numbers correct at each of the three MLU levels were 0.054, 0.234, 0.556, respectively. For the older children, developmental level (age) was not a significant main effect (overall mean number correct 1.18).

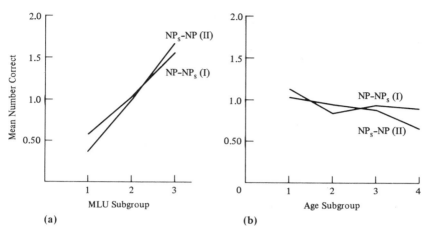

Figure 4.3
Spontaneous pronominalization of sentences with redundant NP. **a** Young children. **b** Older children.

Error analysis of children's imitation errors also showed significant effects of the pronominalization, directionality, and developmental factors. About 50 percent of sentences with redundant NP (types I and II) were spontaneously pronominalized by both young (54 percent) and older (47 percent) children. As can be seen in figure 4.3, the amount of this spontaneous pronominalization of redundancy increased significantly with developmental language level in the young children and then remained at a relatively constant rate with age in the older children. Notably, all of these spontaneous pronominalizations were forward in direction. That is, children always reduced the second redundant NP. There was not a single instance of backward pronominalization—even in type II sentences, where backward pronominalization would have been equally grammatical. As can be seen in figure 4.3, type I and type II sentences were spontaneously pronominalized (in a forward direction) to a nearly equivalent degree in both young and older children.

Fewer model pronominalized sentences (types III and IV) were spontaneously nominalized or pronominalized so as to change pronominalization in these sentences (22 percent in the younger group, 15 percent in the older group). Notably, almost all changes in pronominalization structure in these cases occurred on the backward-pronominalization (type IV) sentences. Only 1 percent and 4 percent (young and older children, respectively) of sentences with forward pronomi-

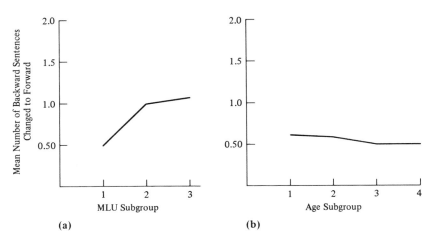

Figure 4.4
Conversion of backward pronominalization to forward pronominalization
(NP – Pro or Pro – Pro). **a** Young children. **b** Older children.

nalization (type III) were changed in pronominalization structure. As
can be seen in figure 4.4, 44 percent of backward-pronominalized sentences were changed in pronominalization structure in the young
group. Twenty-eight percent were changed in the older group. In all of
these cases of change in backward-pronominalization sentences, children reversed the pronominalization direction by positioning the name
first (where the pronoun had been) and the pronoun second (where the
name had been), as in conversion of (9a) to (9b), or, in a smaller number
of cases, by dropping the name altogether and putting a pronoun in
both positions, as in (9c). Young children elaborated another 2 percent
of these backward-pronominalization sentences to redundant NP, as in
conversion of (9a) to (9d); older children elaborated 6 percent of these
cases.

(9) a. While *he* was playing with blocks, *John* built a bridge.
    b. While *John* was playing with blocks, *he* built a bridge.
    c. While *he* was playing with blocks, *he* built a bridge.
    d. While *John* was playing with blocks, *John* built a bridge.

The last two types of change rarely occurred with sentences of either of
the other pronominalization types (III or V).

The main effect of connective type (*because* or *while*) was not
significant in either young or older children. In the older children,
however, connective type interacted significantly with the pronomi-

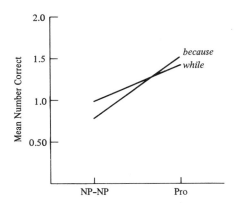

Figure 4.5
Effects of pronominalization on sentences with *because* and *while* in older
children.

nalization factor $(F(1,41) = 8.83, P = 0.005)$. For sentences with redundant NP, sentences with *while* were slightly easier than sentences
with *because,* although with pronominalization, sentences with *because* were slightly easier than sentences with *while* (see figure 4.5).
This result corresponded to the fact that the pronominalization factor
and connective type also interacted significantly to determine amount
of spontaneous pronominalization of redundant NP sentences and
amount of spontaneous pronominalization change in sentences with
pronouns $(F(1,41) = 5.30, P = 0.03)$. More redundant NP sentences
(I, II) with *because* were spontaneously pronominalized (50 percent)
than those with *while* (44 percent), although more pronominalized sentences (III, IV) with *while* than with *because* were changed in pronominal structure (17 percent versus 13 percent). It appears that the
older children find redundant NP sentences with *because* slightly more
unacceptable than those with *while*. They thus pronominalize these
more "coordinative" sentences more often and vary their pronominalized forms less often.
    In conclusion, then, children generally prefer sentences with redun-
dancy reduction by pronominalization to those without, except at early
developmental stages where these are equivalent in difficulty. In addition, children demonstrate a constraint on directionality of pronominalization. They resist backward pronominalization in their imitation.
They succeed in imitating sentences with forward pronominalization
more often than those with backward. They spontaneously pronomi-

nalize redundancy only in a forward direction, never in a backward direction. They convert backward pronominalization to forward pronominalization. Children come to differentiate more coordinative and more subordinative connectives (*because* and *while,* respectively) after age 3½, slightly favoring reduction of the more coordinative; but they continuously generalize the directionality constraint over both connectives.

2 Pronominalization and Coordination Reduction

If we compare these findings on pronominalization in child language with those on coordination reduction in child language, the two processes appear analogous.

In both cases, children demonstrate a capacity to map back and forth between sentences with redundancy and related sentences without redundancy. Most frequently they accomplish this mapping by reduction (either by pronominalization or deletion), converting one of the redundant terms to a pronoun or null site. In both cases, this reduction is constrained in a forward direction. That is, the full term must precede the null site or pronoun resulting from reduction, even when it is grammatically possible that the null site or pronoun precedes.

For both pronominalization and conjunction reduction, this directionality constraint is closely related to developmental language level. Both pronominalization and coordination reduction improve significantly with language development from 2 to 3 years of age, not after age 3½. For pronominalization, amount of redundancy reduction by pronominalization peaked (about 80 percent) at the third developmental language level (mean MLU 5.69; mean age 3,2), as did reversal of backward pronominalization to forward pronominalization. With older ages, these effects weaken. For coordination, reduction by deletion in SVO sentences had peaked at a similar developmental language level (mean MLU 5.91; mean age 3,0) and then dropped with age similarly.

The analogy between the constraints on pronominalization and coordination reduction is even more salient when we notice that development of complex sentences is mediated by coordination. That is, children develop complex sentences by first converting them from subordinative to coordinative (either with or without the connective *and*). In the foregoing study of pronominalization, at the second developmental language level 58 percent of the (subordinative) sentences were converted to coordinate sentences (see figure 4.6). Children's first con-

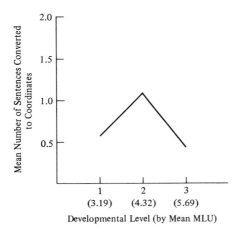

Figure 4.6
Conversion of subordinative sentences to coordinative sentences at each developmental level in young children.

versions to forward pronominalization occur in the context of such derived coordinate sentences, and are a type of coordination reduction.

As figure 4.5 illustrated, children differentiate a more coordinative (*because*) connective from a more subordinative connective (*while*) only at the older ages, after early stages of language acquisition are complete. At this time, children spontaneously reduce redundancy in sentences with the more coordinative connective (*because*) more often than that in sentences with a more subordinative connective (*while*), while obeying the forward-directionality constraint in each case. This again suggests a close relation between the directionality constraint on pronominal anaphora and that on coordination reduction.

Given these similarities between the directionality effect noted for both pronominalization and conjunction reduction, we might then conclude that one unique constraint is operating in child language in both cases.

2.1 A Constraint on Anaphora

Since both pronominalization and coordination reduction derive structures with anaphora, this unique constraint can be called a constraint on possible anaphora. Notably, since only one of these domains is thought to be derived transformationally, a unique constraint for both domains must be independent of this transformational component. Since anaphora is defined at the level of surface structure, a constraint on anaphora must be formulated in terms of properties of surface structure—that is, principally linear order or dominance (constituent structure). One might hypothesize that the constraint is based on linear order, and is independent of dominance (constituent structure), for the following reasons: My two studies show that the constraint appears to generalize over both coordinative and subordinative sentences, and in the study reported here children did not modify directionality of anaphora when hierarchical or command structure would have allowed this.

We thus might make a first attempt to state the unique constraint as in (10).

(10) Constraint on Anaphora in Young Children's Language (English)
     A governing term must precede an anaphor (pronoun or null site)
     in the linear order of surface structure, regardless of relations
     of hierarchical structure between these (coordinate, right-
     branching, or left-branching).

Below we will consider further evidence on the nature of this constraint which shows that, although the constraint as stated in (10) appears to be supported in part, it also appears insufficient or incorrect in part.

Further analyses of the results of the pronominalization study reported and of the previous coordination study confirm indirectly that the unique constraint should be formulated as a constraint on semantic interpretive rules of anaphora that are defined at the level of surface structure.

The directionality factor significantly interacted with coordination reduction, as it did with pronominalization. That is, the directionality effect did not hold for nonpronominalized sentences with redundant NP (that is, for types I and II, which corresponded to forward and backward pronominalization patterns), but only held for pronominalized sentences (types III–IV). Similarly, the directionality effect did not hold for sentential coordinations (which corresponded to forward and backward reduction patterns; for example, sentences (3a) and (4a) or (5a) and (6a) but only for phrasal or reduced coordinations (such as (3b) and (4b), or (5b) and (6b). In both studies, moreover, the directionality effect was most strongly demonstrated in children's spontaneous reductions of sentences with redundancy to those without it ((3a) to (3b), or (5a) to (5b), or reduction of types I and II to type III). In both studies, then, the directionality effect corresponded to surface struc-

tures where a null site or pronoun exists as an "anaphor" or copy of a
related term in a compound or complex sentence. These results suggest
that the directionality constraint in acquisition of both pronominalization and coordination relates to the surface structure of sentences.
Since semantic interpretation rules of anaphora apply to surface structure (see the references in the first paragraphs of this chapter), the
acquisition constraint appears to apply to the domain of semantic interpretation rules of anaphora in both cases.[1]

One of the substudies in Lust 1977b also suggested that surface
structure is critically involved in the directionality effect on coordination reduction in child language. There I showed that the directionality
effect was determined by the derived permuted order of sentence constituents, and thus by surface, not underlying order. As mentioned
above, in coordinate sentences with ostensible permuted VS + VS
order, such as (11), children reduced redundancy freely in a forward
direction in accord with surface order (VS + V̷S).

(11) VS + V̷S
    a. There are trees and there are flowers.
    b. There are trees and ∅ flowers.

The directionality effect did not accord with underlying order in these
reductions.[2] Since this underlying order corresponds to a backward
reduction pattern (SV̷ + SV), if the directionality effect was based on
underlying order it would have prevented redundancy reduction in
those cases, contrary to the facts.

That children treat pronominalization as not transformationally derived, in distinction from coordination reduction, is suggested by the
major difference between results of our pronominalization and coordination studies. Whereas children generally found nonreduced coordinations to be significantly easier than reduced coordinations, they
generally found pronominalized sentences to be significantly easier
than nonreduced sentences with redundant NP. It may be that the
developmental primacy of nonreduced over reduced structures holds
only in the case where these are related transformationally. If this is
true, the developmental data of this study corroborate the thesis that
pronominalized and redundant NP sentences are not transformationally related.[3]

A directionality constraint, such as stated in (10), is generally supported by other literature in the field of first-language acquisition. Solan
(1978a), for example, reports that children 5 to 8 years old generally

succeed at forward pronominalization more frequently than at backward pronominalization (in a comprehension task). Tavakolian (1977, 1978a) also found that children 3 to 7 years old imposed a linear precedence constraint, favoring foward pronominalization, in interpreting sentences with pronominalization. Moreover, Tavakolian found as I did, that this constraint appears to generalize over both null and pronominal anaphora.

In earlier literature, Roeper (1973) had reported that German-speaking children found imitation of sentences with certain forms of forward (null) anaphora to be significantly easier than those with backward anaphora. In a study of children 5–10 years old, C. Chomsky (1969) found errors on backward pronominalization (in a comprehension task) to persist almost to age 6, although this was not the case for forward pronominalization.

3   The Nature of the Constraint on Anaphora

Several problems remain for the characterization of the precise nature of the constraint tentatively formulated in (10).

3.1   Anaphora and Coreference

It is now known that an interpretive relation of anaphora is bipartite, at least (Hust and Brame 1976). We must ask which component of anaphora is affected by the constraint adumbrated in (10). Anaphora, as in (1) or (2), involves a grammatical relation between the two grammatical terms—that is, the governing name and the anaphor. By this relation, the two terms are construed as being in relation to each other and the semantic reading of the govening term is assigned to that of the anaphor. Second, anaphora in (1) or (2) involves a nongrammatical or cognitive judgment of coreference. In cases such as (1) or (2), where the governing term is referential, the object referred to by the governing term is picked out, and the judgment is made that the object referred to by the anaphor is the same as that referred to by the governing term.

The directionality factor that we have observed in child language clearly constrains the grammatical relation between anaphor and antecedent. For children, the governing term must precede the anaphor in linear order. Notably, this directionality factor does not appear to constrain the cognitive judgment of coreference *per se*. We saw that the constraint characterizes anaphora in coordination reduction where the governing term may not be referential, for example sentences with verb redundancy as in (4) or as in simple imperatives (with VO structure). In addition, in the pronominalization study reported, children appear to interpret the backward pronominalized sentences coreferentially, then to reverse the linear order of pronoun and name in uttering their imitation in accord with the directionality constraint. The constraint does not prevent the initial coreferential judgment in these cases. Moreover, we noted that children imposed forward pronominalization in type I sentences with redundant NP, thus signaling a coreferential judgment for the NP. These NPs are supposedly noncoreferential in adult grammar, as opposed to NPs in type II sentences, because of a "noncoreference constraint" that characterizes NPs in sentences with this type I hierarchical structure (Lasnik 1976). Children do not observe this constraint, as evidenced by their forward pronominalization in this sentence type. Children's judgment of coreference thus does not appear constrained in our data. The grammatical relation of anaphora (the construal relation) does appear constrained. Further research (Lust et al. 1980) has confirmed this distinction.

3.2   Linear Order and Dominance

Although I have tentatively formulated the observed constraint on anaphora in child language in terms of linear order alone in (10), recent research suggests that this may not be accurate. Both grammatical and empirical facts suggest that the constraint may critically involve dominance or "command" (hierarchical constituent structure).[4]

Differences in linear order of a governing expression and an anaphor are in fact fundamentally confounded to a degree with differences in dominance or "command" relations between governing term and anaphor. As has recently been observed by Reinhart (1976) with regard to pronominal anaphora, what precedes in English, also usually commands, because of the principally right-branching nature of the English language.[5] Elsewhere we have observed that in fact for both null anaphora (in coordination reduction) and pronominal anaphora, differences in directionality of anaphora typically confound linear-order differences and command-structure differences (Lust 1978).

The necessary involvement of the factor of "command" relations has led linguists to formulate constraints on well-formed pronominal anaphora in terms of the command relations between a governing expression and an anaphor as well as in terms of their linear-order relations (Langacker 1969; Lasnik 1976). The confounding between linear order and dominance relations in English led Reinhart (1974) to argue that "dominance" alone may be sufficient to characterize these constraints.

Because command structure and linear order are confounded in sentences with anaphora, the nature of the observed directionality constraint on child language is ambiguous. The foregoing formulation of this constraint may as well be restated in terms of the dominance factor.

More particularly, the directionality constraint observed may be explained by the fact that children generally may insist on a concordance of anaphora structure with the principal command structure of their language. Children learning English may prefer forward anaphora (rightward reduction), in concordance with the basic branching direction of their language (right branching). Children learning English may eschew backward anaphora (leftward reduction) because they resist modulating anaphora in cases where the basic branching direction of their language is reversed. Notably, it is not leftward-branching structures that children resist, as was shown above (see the control sentence type V), but backward anaphora in a backward-branching structure.

If this explanation of the directionality constraint on anaphora in child language is true, then the proper formulation of this constraint would not be as stated in (10) but, rather, as in (12).

(12) In early child language, direction of anaphora accords with the principal branching direction of the specific language being learned.

Notably, more recent research in English has attempted to unconfound linear order and command and has suggested that young children are indeed sensitive to dominance or command relations as well as to linear order in anaphora (Solan 1978a; Lust et al. 1980; Lust and Clifford (in preparation)). These results would support (for English) a reformulation of the constraint stated in (10), so as to involve command rather than simply linear order, as in (12).

4 Prediction for a Universal
If the revised statement of the constraint in (12) is true, it postulates a universal principle for first-language acquisition that must be interpreted specifically by the language learner for each specific language being learned. The principle lends itself to empirical test. It predicts that in both right- and left-branching languages direction of anaphora will be constrained in early child language; that is, directional modula-

tion of anaphora will not occur. But in different languages the direction
of early anaphora will vary with variation in the basic branching structure of the language. Principle (12) predicts that the early language of
children learning a left-branching language will be constrained leftward, while that of children learning right-branching languages will be
constrained rightward.[6]

I am currently testing this prediction in a cross-linguistic project on
first-language acquisition in several languages with different branching
directions (Lust 1978). Initial results in Japanese and Arabic have been
in accord with the prediction (Lust and Barazangi 1978; Lust and
Wakayama 1979).

5 Conclusion

In this chapter I have evidenced a directionality constraint on pronominal anaphora in early child language in English. This constraint
has been found to be unique and abstract because it holds for both
pronominal anaphora and null anaphora (in coordination reduction). I
have argued that the constraint may be best defined as a constraint on
semantic interpretive rules of grammatical anaphora (of grammatical
construal of a relation between a governing term and an anaphor,
which is determined by surface structure). I have attempted to state
this constraint (12) in terms of constituent structure dominance relations, and have suggested that an alternative formulation of this constraint in terms of linear order alone ((10)) may be incorrect.

I have postulated that this constraint may accord with recent grammatical description of constraint on anaphora in linguistic theory.
Thus, this description may represent a fundamental property of natural
language that provides constraint on the first-language acquisition process. I have stated predictions for further research based on (12) as a
possible universal principle of first-language acquisition.

Notes

I thank Kate Loveland, Cindy Mervis, Laura Beizer, John Keilp, Leah Becker-
dite, and Stephanie Reader for assistance in data collection. I appreciate also
the kindness of the following nursery schools in letting us interview their children: Cornell Nursery, North Campus Union, Fenzel's Nursery, South Hill
Day Care, and IAAC in Ithaca, New York; and Children's Village Nursery,
Newtowne School, and Christ Church Nursery in Cambridge, Massachusetts.

This research was supported in part by NIMH Postdoctoral Fellowship at MIT 1–F22–HD01226–01,02 and by Cornell University State College of Human Ecology grant 349–3376.

1. We need to study further exactly which aspects of surface structure are relevant to this constraint (see Chomsky and Lasnik 1977 for discussion of this issue).

2. Although there is considerable question as to whether sentences such as (11) are derived by a *there*-insertion transformation (cf. Milsark 1974; Langendoen 1973), the argument in this section would not be vitiated if the relationship of sentences (11a) and (11b) were described by semantic interpretation rules.

3. Notably, there are alternative explanations possible here. One is that null anaphora in coordination reduction reflects "obligatory" anaphora, whereas pronominal anaphora reflects "optional" anaphora, and that developmental ordering of full forms before reduced forms occurs only in the case of "obligatory" anaphora. Another explanation has been suggested by Elan Dresher (personal communication): It may be that the greater difficulty of reduced coordinations is due to the fact that they have a "gap" in surface structure corresponding to the null anaphor. Pronominalized sentences, although anaphoric, do not have a "gap," since their anaphors are not null. Processing difficulties such as accrue in sentences with gaps (cf. Wanner and Maratsos 1974) may not accrue in sentences with non-null anaphors. These processing differences may determine the developmental ordering of these two anaphoric structures.

4. Although the notion "command" has undergone several redefinitions in linguistic research, we use the term only in a general sense in this chapter to refer to any form of hierarchical dominance of one term over another that is displayed in tree structure analysis. (See Solan 1978a for a review of these redefinitions of the notion "command.")

5. By principal "branching direction" of the language, I refer to the principal direction in which major recursive devices of the language position complements (primarily relative clauses and predicate complements). A right-branching language positions principal recursive elements to the right of a non-null leftmost element; a left-branching language positions principal recursive elements to the left of a non-null rightmost term (see Chomsky 1964 and Kuno 1973, for example).

6. The precise developmental facts related to this constraint remain to be worked out in further research. As suggested in the study reported here, the constraint seems to hold at the earliest developmental stages we have measured, although it is most notable at MLU levels 5.5–6.0. Of course, since I have not studied children below about 2½ years or below a roughly "two-word" stage of language development, I still do not know certainly whether children actually "begin" the language-learning process with sensitivity to the language facts described in this constraint. This remains a possibility. Moreover, I still do not know the precise relation of this early constraint to later developmental levels and to adult grammar. This is now being studied.

5   Children's Interpretations of Sentences Containing Reciprocals

Edward H. Matthei

It seems that every discussion of constraints on linguistic theory either begins or ends with some reference to "the child" and the "learnability" of certain kinds of grammars. This should not be surprising, because at least part of the motivation for wanting to constrain linguistic theory comes from a desire to discover something about the biological endowment that makes language acquisition possible for human beings. It is Chomsky's view, put forward in almost every work of his since his *Aspects of the Theory of Syntax* (1965), that constraints on the rules of grammar are part of the language-acquisition device. Constraints on linguistic theory restrict the class of possible grammars for human languages. Their role in the language-acquisition process, then, is to reduce the number of possible grammars that children have to evaluate when they learn a language, thus making an otherwise difficult or impossible task a manageable one.

The experiment I will describe is part of an enterprise I have undertaken in order to see if and how constraints like those proposed by Chomsky (1973, 1975a, 1975b, 1977) may operate as children attempt to learn a language. Going a little bit beyond the scope of this essay, the questions I wish to consider are: How does a child learn a language? What kinds of "assumptions" about language do children bring with them when they start making guesses about the way the languages they are learning work? Is there some set of principles that seem to guide children's guessing about languages and grammars?

To begin, I will consider some of the specific constraints proposed by Chomsky, and I will illustrate how they operate in sentences containing reciprocal pronouns. After discussing an experiment involving children's interpretations of two-clause sentences containing reciprocal pronouns, I will touch on some of the basic reasons for the necessity to put constraints on the theory of grammar. A discussion of the general problem of language learning and of some of the results from the formal study of language learning will serve as the basis for this section. Finally, I will consider the implications of the results of the experiment in light of the preceding discussion of the problem of language learnability.

1   Chomsky's Recent Proposals

The person who has learned a language has constructed a system of rules and principles (a grammar, in other words) that determines the sound-meaning correspondences in the domain of that language. The grammar constructed by a linguist is a theory about what this system is like. The general theory of grammar, called "linguistic theory" or "universal grammar," is a system of principles that specifies what counts as a grammar (conditions on form) and how grammatical rules work to generate structural descriptions of sentences (conditions on function). Conditions on the form of grammars include specifications of the possible form of base structures, transformational rules, phonological rules, and so forth. Conditions on function include constraints on the operation of these rules such as the principle of the cycle, the A-over-A Condition (Chomsky 1965; Bresnan 1976a), or the Coordinate Structure Constraint (Ross 1967). The major problem in grammatical theory is to restrict the class of grammars that are available in principle to the learner. The clear intent behind this is to make some progress toward formulating a solution to the problem of how people are able to acquire a language. The construction of a theory of grammar can be viewed in part as an attempt to specify the properties of grammars that hold by necessity rather than as the accidental results of experience. As Chomsky is quick to point out, this "necessity" is intended to mean biological rather than logical necessity. We can look upon attempts to formulate some sort of restrictive theory of universal grammar as attempts to discover something about the biological endowment that makes language learning possible for human beings.

With this in mind, Chomsky has set out in recent years to formulate a very restrictive theory of grammar. He starts with the basic notion that a grammar is a mechanism that determines sound-meaning relations. He then assumes that this mechanism is a set of rules that associate (syntactic) transformational derivations with representations of sound and meaning. In his recent work, Chomsky has said very little about the system for representing sounds, assuming the basic framework of

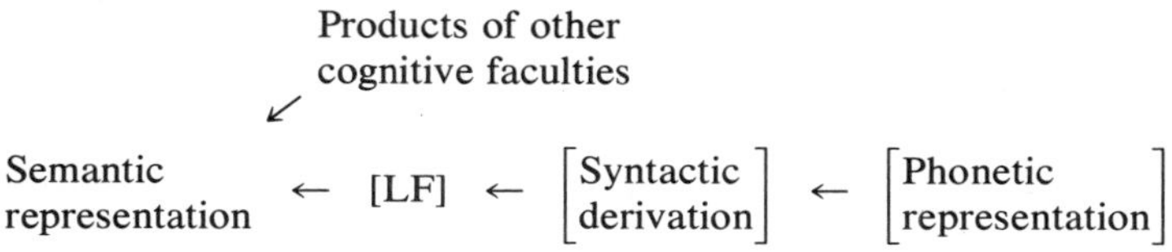

Products of other
cognitive faculties

Semantic   ←   [LF]   ← $\begin{bmatrix} \text{Syntactic} \\ \text{derivation} \end{bmatrix}$ ← $\begin{bmatrix} \text{Phonetic} \\ \text{representation} \end{bmatrix}$
representation

Figure 5.1
Chomsky's model of the sound-meaning relation.

The Sound Pattern of English (Chomsky and Halle 1968) with some modifications.[1]

Chomsky has been more concerned of late with the relation between a syntactic representation and some sort of semantic representation. In his model, a grammar contains a set of rules that associates syntactic derivations with representations in a system that he calls logical form (henceforth referred to as LF). A representation in LF is supposed to incorporate the features of syntactic structure that enter directly into semantic interpretation (such as scope relationships) and are strictly determined by the properties of sentence grammar (as opposed to those features that are determined by the rules governing the structure of discourses). He further assumes that there is another system of rules that takes representations in LF, along with the products of "other cognitive faculties," and associates them with some kind of "semantic" representation. These "semantic" representations may involve such things as beliefs and expectations, as well as properties of LF determined by grammatical rules; and these representations will contain all of the information needed for running inferences, determining the felicity or truth of utterances, and so on. Thus, the relation between sound and meaning in Chomsky's model can be illustrated as in figure 5.1. The grammar relates sounds to meanings through the medium of syntactic derivations.

This way of looking at things embodies a certain version of the "thesis of the autonomy of syntax" (see Chomsky 1973). Chomsky assumes that the rules of sentence grammar can be parceled out into two categories. The first category (the category of rules making up what Chomsky (1974) has called "formal grammar") determines representations on all levels of linguistic description except at the levels of LF and beyond. The second category of rules associates these representations with representations in LF. The whole network of assumptions and hypotheses has been called by Chomsky the "extended standard theory."

Within this extended standard theory, we can restrict the class of grammars by placing constraints in a number of different places. We can impose conditions on the base rules, thus restricting the variety of possible base structures that can enter into a derivation. We can limit the expressive power of transformational rules so that the things that transformations can do will be limited. Or we can place restrictions on the so-called interpretive rules that associate representations in LF with syntactic derivations.

In addition to these kinds of restrictions, we can add conditions on rule application that may not directly limit the variety of admissible grammars but may contribute indirectly to this end by enabling us to reduce the expressive power of certain kinds of rules. The discussion will center on restrictions on the expressive power of transformational and interpretive rules that Chomsky has proposed, as well as the conditions on the application of rules that become necessary within the restricted theory of transformations proposed by Chomsky in his recent works.

Chomsky has proposed that the expressive power of transformations be severely restricted to the point where the two rules in (1) make up the only transformations in the "core" of grammar.[2]

(1) a. Move NP
    b. Move *wh*

Many problems arise with such radical restrictions on the expressive power of transformations. It should be immediately obvious that a grammar that is limited to such rules as those in (1) will overgenerate tremendously. The intricate constraints on what can move and where it can go that we have become accustomed to seeing in the formulations of specific rules cannot be built into such rules. Chomsky has pursued two specific approaches to eliminating the problem of overgeneration: to impose general conditions on the application of rules, and to impose conditions on the outputs of rules (surface structure filters). The second kind of restriction has, in general, been related to the rules of semantic interpretation (Jackendoff 1972); but recently Chomsky and Lasnik (1977) have proposed a number of syntactic surface structure filters that make reference to specific properties of the complementizer system. We will be concerned with conditions of the first type and, more specifically, with conditions that apply both to transformational rules and to interpretive rules.

2   Chomsky's Conditions on Rules

Chomsky has suggested that we can eliminate many of the problems of overgeneration by introducing to the grammar a few general conditions on the functioning of rules. The two stated together in (2) interact with the rule of Reciprocal Interpretation.

(2) In a structure of the form
   ... X ... $_\alpha$[... Y ...]$_\alpha$ ... X ...
no rule can involve X and Y where
i. α is a tensed-S (the Tensed-S Condition) or
ii. α contains a subject distinct from Y and not controlled by X (the Specified-Subject Condition).

Now consider the sentences in (3).

(3) a.   The men like each other.
    b. *The men want John to like each other.
    c. *The candidates expected that each other would win.

Sentences like these have suggested to some, for example Postal (1974), that there is some sort of "clausemate" constraint on the rule that interprets *each other,* making it necessary for the referent of *each other* to be contained in the same clause in which the *each other* appears. Let us assume, following Chomsky (1974, 1977), that there is a rule called Reciprocal Interpretation that assigns an appropriate interpretation to sentences containing the sequence *NP . . . each other.*[3] This rule will say nothing about clausemate restrictions; it will simply say something like "Interpret *NP . . . each other* in such-and-such a manner." The rule can apply in sentence (3a), but it cannot apply in (3b) because the connection between the NP, *the men,* and *each other* will be blocked by the intervening specified subject, *John.* Similarly, the rule is also blocked in (3c), this time because the dependent clause, *that each other would win,* is a tensed S, and hence the Reciprocal rule cannot relate *the candidates* and *each other.* The interpretive rule acts as a "filter" in these cases, since uninterpretable strings will be marked ungrammatical and thrown out.

2.1   Possible Implications for Language Acquisition

The status of these conditions is not clear. What their role in the theory of grammar is—if they have any role at all—is an empirical matter. Nor is it clear what role in the language-learning process Chomsky sees these conditions playing. But, for the sake of argument, I shall take a strong (and, perhaps, too simplistic) view of the operation of these constraints in the language-learning process.

Let us, then, assume that every child comes into the world with constraints like those in (2) "wired in" as standard equipment. Whether these constraints are represented directly or indirectly as restrictions on the child's guessing procedure is not important; it is sufficient for the argument here that they exist in some form in the learner. I have done an experiment on children's interpretations of sentences containing reciprocals. Before going on to discuss the design and the results of the experiment, though, I would like to consider a number of general hypotheses about the outcome of the experiment if we take a strong interpretation of the role of Chomsky's constraints in language learning.

The experiment is an attempt to find out how children interpret reciprocals in two-clause sentences like (4).

(4) The demonstrators said that the National Guardsmen were hitting each other.

Notice that the only grammatical interpretation of this sentence involves the National Guardsmen hitting the National Guardsmen and not the demonstrators. Both the Specified-Subject Condition and the Tensed-S Condition will block the application of the Reciprocal rule to the sequence *The demonstrators . . . each other*. What should we expect to see if we look at children's interpretations of sentences like these? There are a number of hypotheses and families of hypotheses that we might consider.

Hypothesis A. It is possible that children will start out interpreting sentences like (4) in exactly the same way as adults. That is, once they discover the Reciprocal rule, the first hypothesis they will make is that it is a "clause-bound" rule because of the constraints that they innately possess.

Hypothesis B. Children may misinterpret sentences like (4) because they have not yet figured out how to apply the constraints. Specifically, children may have to figure out what the domain of application for the constraints is. We might, then, expect them to make mistakes until they have determined such things as where clauses begin and end in complex sentences. This suggests a couple of subhypotheses.

Subhypothesis B.1. The presence of a complement marker such as *that* or *to* may help children to apply constraints correctly since such markers "signal" the beginning of a new clause.

Subhypothesis B.2. Perhaps clauses containing tense markers (tensed Ss) will be easier to recognize as new clauses because they are more like simple one-clause sentences; hence, we may find children applying the constraints correctly in these cases sooner than in cases where the reciprocal is in a nonfinite clause of some sort.

Hypothesis C. Children may have to learn that the Reciprocal rule is subject to the constraints. They may treat *each other* just as they would any other pronoun. Ordinarily, anaphoric reference is not subject to the constraints, because much of the determination of the referents for pronouns is subject to discourse conditions. In other words, children's first guesses about the Reciprocal rule will be that it is not subject to the constraints.[4]

2.2 An Experiment

The experiment was specifically designed to test hypothesis B. Note that subhypotheses B.1 and B.2 both predict that we will find a difference in children's interpretations of reciprocals that depends on the type of complement that contains the *each other*. Four types of sentences, each of which contained a different kind of verb complement, were used in the study; examples of each sentence type are given in (5).

(5) a. *that* complements:
       The horses said that the cows jumped over each other.
    b. Deleted-*that* complements:
       The pigs said the chickens pecked each other.
    c. Infinitival complements:
       The cows want the lambs to kiss each other.
    d. Gerundive complements:
       The pigs noticed the boys patting each other.

This allows us to test to see if there is any difference in the interpretations children give to sentences that contain finite-clause complements ((5a) and (5b)) and nonfinite complements ((5c) and (5d)), or to those that contain complement markers ((5a) and (5c)) and those that do not ((5b) and (5d)).

While doing a pilot study I noticed that the children appeared to find simple sentences like those in (6) easier to understand when the subject was a conjoined NP, as in (6b), than when it was simply a plural NP, as in (6a).

(6) a. The cows were kicking each other.
   b. The pig and the lamb were kissing each other.

I decided to include a test of this intuition in the experiment. If children
somehow find it easier to understand reciprocals when there are clearly
two distinct individuals involved then perhaps this might influence
any tendency they might have to violate the "clausemate" constraints
on Reciprocal Interpretation. Therefore, I varied the subject NPs in
both the matrix sentences and the complements so that some were
simply plural NPs while others were conjoined NPs.

It was suggested to me in discussions with my colleagues that the
children might somehow be attaching *each other* to the highest S node
in a sentence if it turned out that they took the subject of the matrix
sentence as the referent for the reciprocal. In order to test this hypothesis, I attached a prepositional phrase to the end of some sentences that
could only be related to the verb in the complement, as in (7).

(7) The cows said that the boys tickled each other on the tummy.

This would effectively block attachment of *each other* to the highest S
node, since the branch of the tree attaching the PP to the VP of the
complement would "cut off" attachment of *each other* to the matrix-S
node, as shown in diagram (7').

(7')

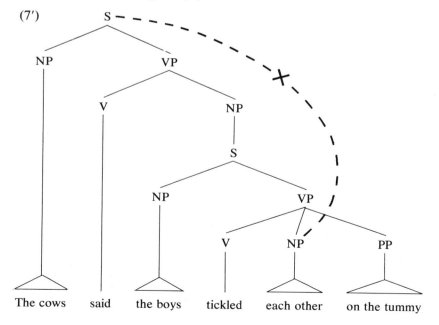

(See Solan and Roeper 1978 for a discussion of how this "highest-S attachment" phenomenon can be seen in the child's emerging grammar.)

Because the principal hypothesis being tested involved possible differences attributable to differences in sentence *type,* the experiment had to be designed to avoid the "language-as-fixed-effect fallacy" (Clark 1972). Verbs in both the matrix S and the complement were inserted randomly into sentence frames so that each child received a different set of sentences. This allows us to collapse any variance that might be due to the choice of a particular verb or verbs with the intersubject variance.

Two one-clause sentences that included two NPs and a reciprocal pronoun were also included; these are shown in (8).

(8) a. The boys bumped the cows into each other.

  b. The lamb and the dog pushed the horses to each other.

Both of these sentences are, or can be construed to be, ambiguous with respect to the referent of the reciprocal. These were included as a check to see if children had a preference for choosing the closest or the first NP as the referent for *each other.* In all, 34 sentences were included in the test. (See table 5.1 for a complete list of the verbs used in the experiment.)

During the experiment the child and the experimenter sat on the floor, facing each other. A row of toy animals and people (from a Fisher-Price set of barnyard creatures) was set up between the child and the experimenter. The child usually set up the array, so that each animal was within easy reach of the child. There were two of each animal, and the children usually arranged the animals in pairs.

After some preliminary discussion about the animals, the experimenter explained that he wanted to play a sort of game with the child in which he would read something to the child and then ask the child to show him "what happened" by taking the animals mentioned in the sentence and "making them do it." Every effort was made to allay any fears about being evaluated that the child might have by letting her or him know, in one way or another, that as far as the experimenter was concerned there were no right or wrong answers. All of the children, in fact, appeared to be perfectly willing to treat the whole affair simply as a game.

To begin, the experimenter read a number of simple declarative sentences like *The pig jumped over the lamb,* to acquaint the child with the task. Then the experimenter introduced between three and five one-

Table 5.1
Verbs Used in the Experiment

I. *that* complements and "deleted" *that* complements

say	know
think	pretend
claim	decide
dream	suggest
remember	prove

II. Infinitival complements

expect	force
like	remind
ask	dare
tell	coax
want	command

III. Gerundive complements

hate	pardon
notice	permit
prefer	discuss
remember	imagine
stop	suggest

IV. Verbs in complements

kick	bump into
pat	tickle
push	bite
touch	hit
kiss	jump over

clause sentences containing reciprocals, like those in (6). If the child appeared to understand these sentences correctly (that is, as adults do), the experimenter moved on to the actual test. No children who failed to understand the one-clause sentences with reciprocals were included in the test sample.[5]

Test sentences were read to the child as many times as it was necessary to ensure that the child remembered a sentence correctly. Most of the children spontaneously rehearsed the sentences aloud, so it was relatively easy to tell when they had remembered the sentences correctly. While rehearsing, the children gave the sentences normal intonation contours and gave no indication that they were just remembering strings of words instead of structured utterances.

Scoring was done by the experimenter, who recorded who did what to whom when the child acted out the sentences. Originally a tape recorder was also used, but in many cases it turned out to be a distraction for the children, and it was not used in most of the sessions.

The subjects were 17 children ranging in age from 4 years, 2 months to 6 years, 6 months. All of them were in preschool or day-care programs in the Amherst and Northampton, Massachusetts, area. They were all native speakers of English, and none of them had a history of hearing or language difficulties. They were tested individually in rooms away from the general noise and activity of the group. Most children were able to run through the test in a single 35–45-minute session; others were tested in two sessions of about 20–25 minutes on consecutive days.

We will now consider how each of the hypotheses sketched earlier fares in the light of the data from the experiment. Hypothesis A predicted that the children would not make the mistake of choosing the subject of the matrix clause as the referent for *each other*. The results of the experiment clearly show that the children did make this mistake; 64.4 percent of the total number of responses were ones in which the children chose the matrix clause subject as the referent for *each other*. (Table 5.2 summarizes the data.) That is, they would interpret a sentence like (9) as meaning that the pigs tickled the chickens, and vice versa.

(9) The chickens said that the pigs tickled each other.

Indeed, some of the children in the sample consistently chose the matrix clause subject over the subject of the complement as the referent for the reciprocal pronoun. Hypothesis A, therefore, appears to be wrong.

Hypothesis B predicted that we would find some differences in the children's responses that depended on the type of complement in which the *each other* was embedded. A one-way analysis of variance was carried out to see if there was any significant effect of complement type on the children's responses. The result of this analysis showed no significant effect, $F(3,48) < 1$; that is, neither the presence of a complement marker (*to* or *that*) nor the presence of a tensed verb in the complement sentence affected the children's tendencies to look outside of the embedded clause for a referent for *each other*. The general hypothesis, including the two subhypotheses B.1 and B.2, appears to be incorrect. Phinney (1977) has also found that complement type does not appear to affect children's misinterpretations of the scope of negation in two-clause sentences. To be more explicit, she found that chil-

Table 5.2
Summary of Data from Experiment

Sentence Type[a]	Total Errors[b]	Mean ($N = 13$)	Total Errors for Sentence Type
that			
2. c–c	8	0.615	62 (mean = 0.596)
8. c–c	9	0.692	
13. sg–pl	9	0.692	
14. c–pl	7	0.538	
19. pl–c/PP	5	0.385	
26. pl–pl/PP	9	0.692	
29. pl–pl	7	0.538	
33. c–pl/PP	8	0.615	
"deleted" *that*			
3. pl–pl	12	0.923	70 (mean = 0.673)
5. pl–sg	11	0.846	
9. c–pl	11	0.846	
10. c–c	8	0.615	
11. c–c/PP	7	0.538	
18. sg–pl	6	0.462	
17. pl–pl/PP	9	0.692	
24. pl–c/PP	6	0.462	
Infinitival			
4. pl–pl	11	0.846	64 (mean = 0.615)
6. c–c	12	0.923	
12. c–pl/PP	9	0.692	
22. pl–c	6	0.462	
23. pl–pl/PP	6	0.462	
30. sg–c	7	0.538	
32. pl–pl	8	0.615	
34. c–c/PP	5	0.385	
Gerundive			
1. c–pl/PP	10	0.769	72 (mean = 0.692)
7. c–c/PP	10	0.769	
15. pl–c	8	0.615	
16. sg–pl	8	0.615	
20. c–pl	9	0.692	
21. c–c	9	0.692	
25. pl–pl	10	0.769	
31. pl–pl/PP	8	0.615	

a. c indicates conjoined NP; pl indicates plural NP; c–pl indicates matrix subject NP was conjoined and complement subject was simply plural.

b. "Errors" refers to matrix-sentence subjects chosen as referents for *each other*. (Four children consistently made no errors; data on them are not included.)

dren interpreted sentences like those in (10) as if they contained
negatives in *both* clauses.

(10) a. Gertrude sees that Martin is not eating.
     b. Gertrude does not see that Martin is eating.

That is, the interpretations that the children gave to both of these
sentences involved Gertrude not seeing that Martin was not eating.
Phinney found that complement type had no effect on the children's
tendency to assign such interpretations to sentences like these. This
lack of an effect of complement type, therefore, appears to be quite
general.

A look at the data also shows that the children did not all of a sudden
start obeying one or both of the constraints, either. That is, there is no
sharp cutoff at which the children start to interpret the sentences as
adults do. This suggests that there are no sudden discoveries of the
domain of application for the constraints. Read and Hare (1977) have
found a similar gradual development toward adult grammar in children's interpretations of reflexive pronouns in English, where the rule
that interprets reflexives is also subject to "clausemate" constraints
like the Reciprocal rule.

This apparently gradual development of the clausemate restriction
also seems to provide evidence against hypothesis C. If children have
to learn that the rule of Reciprocal Interpretation is subject to the
constraints, we might expect them to suddenly start interpreting the
two-clause sentences correctly. However, I admit that this argument is
rather weak, and that the best way to see if children do actually gradually develop toward the adult interpretation of these sentences is
through a longitudinal rather than a cross-sectional study.

In describing the design of the experiment, I mentioned two other
hypotheses that this experiment was specifically designed to test: the
possible difference between conjoined and plural NPs as preferred referents for *each other* and the possibility of "highest-S attachment" of
each other. These hypotheses were tested by performing a two-way
analysis of variance with repeated measures on the data summarized in
the four-cell matrix in table 5.3. Because no effect of complement type
was found, the combining of the data from two sentence types in table
5.2 can be justified. The results of the analysis show no effect on the
choice of the matrix clause subject as the referent for *each other* due to
a sentence-final PP, $F(1,12) < 1$. This indicates that the children were
treating *each other* strictly as an anaphoric element. The fact that they

Table 5.3
Summary of Data Used in Two-Way Analysis of Variance to Test Effect
of Conjoined versus Plural NP and Sentence-Final Prepositional Phrase.

	c–pl	pl–c	
	that complement	Infinitival complement	Marginal mean
No PP	"Deleted" *that* complement	Gerundive complement	
	18	14	16
	Infinitival complement	*that* complement	
PP	Gerundive complement	"Deleted" *that* complement	
	19	12	15.5
Marginal mean	18.5	13	

also interpreted the grammatical role of the reciprocal in the complement correctly (as the object of the complement verb) also is an argument against highest-S attachment for *each other*. This finding should
not be considered as providing evidence against the highest-S attachment hypothesis in general, however. What it indicates is that the
errors that children made cannot be explained by saying that the children were simply attaching the *each other* to the wrong place in the
tree. The problem is strictly one of knowing where one can look for a
referent for the reciprocal pronoun.

The results do show a strong tendency for the children to choose
a conjoined NP as the referent for *each other*, $F(1,12) = 11.524$,
$P \leq 0.005$. Perhaps this is due to some sort of saliency effect. The
presence of two distinct referents in one NP position in a sentence may
bias the children toward choosing conjoined NPs as referents for reciprocals no matter where they occur in the sentence.

Results from the single-clause sentences containing two possible referents for *each other* show a tendency for the children to choose the
nearest NP as the referent for *each other* when the referent for *each
other* is ambiguous. In 85.3 percent of the responses the children picked
the second NP in the sentence as the referent for the reciprocal—the
NP closer to the reciprocal. Even the children who consistently chose
the matrix clause for the referent for *each other* appear to follow this

same strategy. Therefore, the predominance of matrix clause referents for *each other* in the two-clause sentences does not seem to be the result of a preference to take the first NP in a sentence as the referent for *each other*.

What can be learned from this experiment? We have seen that children will violate both the Specified-Subject Condition and the Tensed-S Condition. We have also seen that there seem to be no signals that the children pick up on in different kinds of complements that help them to apply the constraints earlier in some complements than in others or to apply one constraint correctly earlier than the other. Children apparently start out with the hypothesis that *each other* behaves just like any other anaphoric element in English. Tavakolian (1977) has found that children will search outside of a sentence to find a referent for ordinary pronouns like *he, she,* and *it* in cases of backward pronominalization (when a pronoun precedes its referent). This gives us a way to test to see if children really do treat reciprocals just like ordinary pronouns. I think that it is important to observe whether children's interpretations of reciprocals really do parallel those that they give to ordinary pronouns. Therefore I am now putting together an experiment that will look at some other aspects of children's interpretations of reciprocals. I want to find out what happens when the reciprocal pronoun is in a dependent clause that precedes the matrix sentence; and I want to see if children will go outside the bounds of a sentence to find a referent for *each other* in other cases—will they, for example, choose the subject of a preceding sentence as the referent for the reciprocal? Maybe children's versions of Reciprocal Interpretation are related to some general strategies that children use in interpreting discourse.

But what about the broader implications of the results of this experiment? There appears to be evidence that the constraints the experiment was designed to test are learned; so it appears that we must look for some other limits on the language-acquisition device.

Gold (1965, 1967) has developed a framework for the formal study of language learning. His work is important because it provides us with a basic vocabulary of concepts and results that we can use to evaluate attempts to formulate theories of language learning. Gold has shown that certain approaches to solving the problem of how a child learns a language simply cannot work, and that other approaches to the problem can work only if certain critical assumptions are made about the learner and about the kind of data available to the learner.

In Gold's framework, the problem for the learner is defined as that of selecting a given language from a class of languages. The problem facing the child is to select from the class of all possible human languages the particular language he is exposed to. It makes no sense to ask whether a particular language is learnable, then; what we want to know is whether the class of languages to which that language belongs is learnable. A child can learn any human language. Therefore, the theory of the child as a language learner must be general enough to account for this ability.

We must continue to search for some kind of constraints on universal grammar. The results of the formal study of language learning to which I refer represent, in my opinion, some of the most compelling reasons for assuming that the child comes into the world armed with some set of "assumptions" about what it is that he must set out to learn.

The proofs that Gold (1967) presents show that differences in the kinds of information given to a language learner can have profound effects on the learnability of different classes of languages. For example, he has shown that certain classes of languages that have been proposed at one time or another as models for human languages, namely, the context-sensitive languages, the context-free languages, and even the finite-state languages, are not learnable if the data received by the learner consists only of correct sentences in the language to be learned. However, with the "informant" scheme of data presentation, in which the learner gets examples of the possible instances of nonsentences, labeled as such, as well as instances of correct sentences, Gold has shown that all of the aforementioned languages as well as the set of primitively recursive languages are learnable. The class of languages computable by a Turing machine, though, is not learnable even with this very rich form of data.

This last result of Gold's has a special significance for us because Peters and Ritchie (1973) have shown that a transformational grammar that consists of a simple set of finite-state base rules coupled with a certain set of transformational rules is equivalent in computational power to a Turing machine. This means that there is no set of computable sentences that such grammars could not be used to represent, and this result, together with Gold's, makes it necessary for us to restrict the power of transformational rules, to hypothesize a greater richness in the information source, or to do both. If we do not do something, we may find ourselves with theories of language learning that predict that children cannot learn language.

Other problems arise when we consider that our theory must predict that the learner will learn a language within a psychologically plausible amount of time. It can be shown (Anderson 1976:500–501) that any learning procedure that contains no assumptions about what is to be learned and in what way the learner should go about trying to learn it will be hopelessly slow.

Perhaps there are hints in the data, and the learner expects such hints and knows how to use them. For example, the child may have access to something like Greenberg's (1963) list of language universals and could use such hints as a dominant VSO word order to predict that a language will have prepositions rather than postpositions (Greenberg's universal 3). Or, all grammars may not be equally likely, and the learner's hypotheses may move from the most likely grammars to the least likely ones. This may amount to something like the theory proposed by Chomsky that was discussed earlier. Chomsky has proposed that in language acquisition the learner has a very restricted conception of what kinds of objects constitute valid grammars.[6] He proposes, in effect, to set up an ordering scheme in which there is a set of plausible grammars, each with some nonzero probability, and a set of implausible grammars, each with zero probability. Of course, we can also imagine combinations of these two approaches in which certain hints in the data would cause the learner to narrow the hypothesis space and possibly set up a unique ordering of hypotheses as a result of a given hint. Partee (1977) has suggested that her Well-Formedness Constraint may operate in this way, reducing the range of grammars compatible with a given set of data while adding no restrictions on the size of the class of possible human languages.

The important thing to see here is that we must assume that there are some strong innate assumptions about the nature of the language-learning problem in the language-learning procedure—either explicitly stated in terms of some sort of innate "knowledge" or implicitly represented in the workings of the learning mechanism. If the child were presented with a language or, perhaps, even with a learning "situation" that did not conform to the pattern that he expected, then we would expect him either to be incapable of learning the language or to expend an inordinately large amount of time and effort in doing so. We must develop a theory that contains a hypothesis about the assumptions about language that children bring with them to the language-learning task that is "sufficiently rich to account for the acquisition of language, yet not so rich as to be inconsistent with the known diversity of language" (Chomsky 1965:58).

Roger Brown (1973) has suggested that we might look at every grammar or stage that a child goes through on the way to learning a language as an example of a possible human language. Of course, this is a perfectly obvious and trivial suggestion if we take it merely at face value: Children, presumably, are human beings, so if we find them using what appears to be a language which they have "created" for themselves, of course it must be a human language. But, what Brown's suggestion amounts to, in my opinion, is the claim that the language learner is tightly constrained from the beginning and that each guess that a child makes on the way to mastering a language can provide us with evidence for the structure of the language-learning device. Baker (1977) has suggested that those engaged in constructing theories of language learning might find it worthwhile to search for constraints on the form of rules rather than constraints on the function of rules. The idea, to simplify it somewhat, is that there may be certain kinds of rules that children would never think of hypothesizing simply because they do not have the necessary "words" in their "metalinguistic vocabulary." The conditions we set out to look for in the reciprocals experiment are conditions on the function of linguistic rules; they are general conditions that say what linguistic rules can and cannot do. Such conditions say nothing about what rules of grammar can look like. Suppose we were to start looking for constraints on the "notation" of the "language" in which children formulate their hypotheses about language. Obviously, we need constraints on the base rules and on the expressive power of transformational rules. Perhaps there are some general constraints on notation that can be found in the emerging grammars of children that can do much or all of the work that conditions like the Specified-Subject Condition and the Tensed-S Condition do.

Notes

This research was supported in part by a National Institute of Child Health and Human Development grant (PHS HD 09647–03) to S. Jay Keyser and Thomas W. Roeper. I would like to thank H. Goodluck, T. Roeper, L. Solan, and E. Williams for their valuable help and advice. Special thanks go to C. Clifton for help above and beyond the call of duty. And, finally, I would like to thank the teachers, parents, and children of the Living and Learning School, Amherst, the Congregational Church Pre-school, Amherst, and the College Church School, Northampton, where the research reported here was carried out. I, of course, take full responsibility for everything that I have said in the chapter.

1. Specifically, those modifications suggested by Bresnan (1973).

2. Chomsky has recently introduced the term "core grammar" to refer to a theory of universal grammar with highly restricted options, limited expressive power, and few parameters, which forms the basis for a kind of theory of markedness for syntax. The idea is that "Systems that fall within core grammar constitute 'the unmarked case'; we may think of them as optimal in terms of the evaluation metric. An actual language is determined by fixing the parameters of core grammar and then adding rules or rule conditions. . . ." (Chomsky and Lasnik 1977:430).

3. In earlier work, Chomsky (1973) assumed an analysis that involved a rule of *each*-Movement, which derived sentences like (3a) from sentences like *The men each like the other(s)*. For a more extensive treatment of the semantics of reciprocals, see Fiengo and Lasnik 1973 or Dougherty 1974. Notice that here we are concerned only with part of the Reciprocal rule—the part that has to do with determining the referent for the reciprocal pronoun. The rule also must say something about the reciprocality of the action expressed by the verb in reciprocal sentences.

4. In "On *Wh*-Movement" Chomsky (1977) suggests that conditions like those in (2) do not impose absolute restrictions against certain kinds of rules but that they are part of a theory of "markedness" (see also note 2 above). Rules that violate the constraints can be formulated, but they will be "marked" because they must specify the structures to which they can apply without obeying the conditions. The conditions, then, will be part of a logic of markedness that will form part of an evaluation measure for grammars. Rules that violate the conditions will be "marked" because of the additional cost involved in having to specify the structures to which they can apply.

I believe that this "relative interpretation" of the conditions on rules does not affect the hypotheses considered above if we assume the children will first consider the simplest version of a rule—that is, the unmarked case—when they start making their guesses. There are, perhaps, other equally plausible assumptions we could make, though. However, evidence from an experiment by Schane, Tranel, and Lane (1975) suggests that people are somewhat predisposed toward learning unmarked rules more easily than marked ones. They also found that errors made by subjects learning marked rules tended to be in the direction of the unmarked cases. This suggests that people may initially try out unmarked rules before moving on to try out more costly alternative analyses.

5. Twelve children (aged from 4 years to 4 years, 3 months) were excluded from the test sample for this reason.

6. Note that such restrictions as these do not necessarily put restrictions on the class of possible language, but they do put restrictions on the kinds of "machines" that can be used to generate them.

Children's Interpretation of Negation in Complex Sentences

Marianne Phinney

In the field of psycholinguistic research, there have been several studies on children's acquisition and use of negation and negative morphemes. Most of this work has been conducted with small children, generally of preschool age, using simple sentences. Little has been done to examine the types of strategies available to older children for interpreting complex syntactic structures, where negation-interpretation rules interact with other semantic and syntactic systems. This chapter will examine some of the problems presented to a child in understanding negation in complex sentences with factive matrix verbs and propose some hypotheses about processing strategies that a child might choose at various stages.

1 Negation and the Factive Verb

Klima 1964 stands as the first major analysis of negation in English within the transformational framework, and is still the most complete single work integrating both syntactic and semantic considerations. Klima's theory proposed that the semantics of negation be represented in the deep structure, as a Neg component generated in initial position as a daughter of the S. Later work, such as that of Jackendoff (1972), has proposed that negation be considered as an interpretive rule operating off the surface structure to produce the semantic representation. This proposal has been adopted in more recent versions of transformational grammar (Chomsky and Lasnik 1977; Chomsky 1978), although the semantic representation is now termed "logical form." Many of the studies of negation have been concerned with the application of negation scope and the interaction of negation and quantifier scope (Horn 1971; Lasnik 1972, 1975).

The present study is restricted to complex sentences without quantifiers, and the concern is the interpretation of propositional negation and its interaction with the matrix verb. Karttunen (1970, 1971a) discusses several categories of matrix verbs that have varying implications for their complements when negated. The best-known class of verbs is probably the factives, which are generally assumed to imply the truth of their complement whether or not the matrix verb is negated (Kiparsky and Kiparsky 1968; Karttunen 1970, 1971a, 1973; see Wilson 1972 for a dissenting view). Verbs such as *know, realize, learn,* and *remember* (with a *that* complement) all fall into this class.

Consider the following sentences.

(1) a. John knows that Carter uses Pepsodent.
    b. John doesn't know that Carter uses Pepsodent.

Sentences (1a) and (1b) both imply that Carter does indeed use Pepsodent, if the sentence is uttered in a normal discourse situation with normal intonation.[1] If in fact the complement is not true, the hearer of (1a) or (1b) might feel the utterance is inappropriate. This state of affairs, where the negation of the matrix verb still implies the truth of the complement, is not the case for nonfactive verbs. A more general case is that in which no logical implication is made about the complement when the matrix verb is negated, as in (2) and (3).

(2) The senator didn't claim that he took the bribe.
(3) Oscar didn't see the Cookie Monster eat the cookies.

Unlike (1b), sentences (2) and (3) carry no implication about the truth of their complements.

There are other classes of verbs that do carry implications about the truth of the complement. Karttunen (1971a) discusses one such class: implicatives, which imply the falsehood of the complement when they are negated. Implicatives include such verbs as *manage, remember* (with *to*), and *bother*. For example, sentence (4) implies that Kevin did not in fact get the lead:

(4) Kevin didn't manage to get the lead in the play.

Another class of verbs frequently discussed in the literature are those verbs termed "Neg-raising" verbs (Fillmore 1963; Lakoff 1969; Horn 1971). When negated, these verbs seem to imply that the complement is negated instead of the matrix verb.[2] Sentence (5a) is related to (5b), for example, in a way that (2) is not related to (6).

(5) a. Mary didn't think that the politicians were honest.

    b. Mary thought that the politicians weren't honest.

(6) The senator claimed that he didn't take the bribe.

Factives might be considered an exceptional class of verbs, because the truth of the complement does not change when the matrix verb is negated. The class of factives appears to be fairly small. Frequency analyses of children's spontaneous speech (Hart et al. 1977) show only one factive (*know*) occurring frequently. The other most commonly used verbs that could also be matrix verbs[3] are such verbs as *want, see, say, think, tell, watch, help, try,* and *ask.* Most of these verbs carry no implication about the complement when they are negated. Presumably the child must learn factivity and its implications as an exception to the general rule warranted by the majority of the verbs she uses.

Negation in the complement has never been considered to be a problem for interpretation. There are no cases where an interpretive rule has been proposed to move a negative farther up a tree than its own S. There have been proposals (Fillmore 1963; Lakoff 1969) to account for pairs like (5a) and (5b), which include a syntactic rule to move the negative to the matrix position, but this is not considered to be an interpretive rule. An interpretive account of such sentences would probably move the negative from the matrix to the complement clause to account for the relationship in a semantic representation.

The type of the complement and the direction of the embedding also appear to affect the possible interpretation. There are certain verbs that are factive with a *that* complement and implicative with a *for-to* complement, such as *remember.*

(7) Fred didn't remember that the tax bills were due today.

(8) The doctor didn't remember to call his patients.

In addition, the factive verbs do not take *for-to* complements (with the exception of *remember,* which then ceases to be factive); some will take poss-*ing* complements without losing their factivity.

(9) John didn't remember his being married yesterday.

There seems to be an intuitive sense (supported by the case of *remember*) in which the use of a *that* complement implies that the speaker is more sure of the situation represented by the sentence than would be the case if another complement type was used; that it is "more factive," if factivity can be considered as a value scale.

The direction of embedding also seems linked to the factive/non-factive distinction. Right-branching sentences utilize the distinction in the matrix verb, as discussed above. However, Karttunen (1971b) claims that left-branching *that* complements always require truth in the actual world, whereas poss-*ing* and *for-to* complements do not.

(10) a. That his friend is a forger doesn't amuse Jerry.

     b. That his friend is a forger wouldn't bother Jerry.

(11) a. His being married today didn't surprise John.

     b. His being married today wouldn't bother John.

In (10b), at least according to my intuitions, it is still asserted that Jerry's friend was a forger, but Jerry does not know about it. In (11b), there is no such assertion that "he" has been married, as there is in (11a); (11b) seems to postulate a hypothetical situation.

Karttunen's claim about left-branching *that* complements is in fact not surprising, and explains why left-branching *that* complements always take a factive matrix verb whereas the other complement types do not.

This is an apparent exception the child must learn while learning about factivity: *that* complements behave differently from other complements when they are embedded at the beginning of the sentence. One might expect this to be a later development, as sentences of this type are unusual and normally seem to be rearranged to produce right-branching structures like (12), which are more similar to nonfactive constructions.

(12) It doesn't amuse Jerry that his friend is a forger.

We have thus established three things a child must learn in order to interpret negation in complex sentences correctly: that negation normally negates the sentence it appears in (except for the Neg-raising verbs);[4] what the various verb classes are and what implications they carry about the truth value of their complements; and the difference between right- and left-branching complements and the interactions between factivity and complement type.

2 Experimental Studies and Processing Strategies

A fair amount of research on negation processing has been conducted with adults, and certain facts have been determined about negation in simple sentences and logical inference (Just and Carpenter 1971; Johnson-Laird and Tridgell 1972; Wason and Johnson-Laird 1972).

Similar studies have generally not been conducted with children because of the difficulty of the tasks, although the studies conducted by
Inhelder and Piaget (1972) shed some light on children's conception of
negation as applied to attributes like color and shape. Certain results
have been replicated consistently.

Negative sentences are almost always more difficult than affirmative
sentences (Wason and Johnson-Laird 1972), and usually take more time
to process. This holds whenever the negative sentence is given to the
subject without any situational context. Johnson-Laird and Tridgell
(1972) showed that negation is easier than affirmation only when the
sentence is denying an explicitly stated presupposition. This is, after
all, the normal context in which negation is used in natural language
(Givón 1978). In most picture-matching studies the negation is used to
support an assertion, which is more difficult than denying it.

The fact that negation often produces difficulties for adult speakers
implies that it will be at least as difficult for a child. For example, a
child may not have yet learned certain short-cuts that are possible for
adult speakers. Trabasso et al. (1971) indicated that children find binary
attributes (where *not*-X has only one possible value) more difficult to
interpret than do adults, because adults switch the attribute to the
positive complement immediately. Children treat a binary attribute the
same as a nonbinary one, using the negation as given, rather than
"translating" *not*-X into its complementary value. Since they have not
yet learned the short-cuts, the task is more difficult for them than it is
for adults; by the same token, they may give a clearer indication of the
rules they use.

True negatives are usually harder than false negatives (Wason and
Johnson-Laird 1972). Some processing models (Chase and Clark 1969;
Trabasso et al. 1971) have proposed that this results from the number of
comparisons and index changes (from true to false) necessary to match
the sentence and the situation. In normal discourse, if a negative sentence is declared true by assertion, then the presupposed situation is
generally declared false, with a result of only one index change.

Chase and Clark (1969) hypothesized a slightly different model for
processing a picture-matching task than for normal language processing. Picture matching may in fact cause more difficulty, because the
subject is being asked to do what is most difficult: match a negative
sentence to a true situation. In addition, when the picture is shown to
the subject first, it restricts the possible mental images a subject might
construct of the situation.

In general, syntactic negatives (verbs with *not*) are harder to process than semantic negatives (verbs like *deny, fail*) (Just and Carpenter 1971). A sentence with *not* in the auxiliary took longer to process than one containing a semantically negative verb, which indicates that such verbs do not seem to be decomposed into an affirmative verb plus a negative marker, as was proposed by early transformational accounts (Klima 1964). However, the claim that syntactic negatives are significantly harder than semantic negatives is somewhat controversial. A study reported by Fodor et al. (1975) found that implicit and morphological negatives (*fail* and *unable*) tended to be easier than explicit negatives (*not* + verb), but the tendency was not significant in their study.[5] Other studies with adults (Boysson-Bardies 1979, in French) have not indicated a significant difference between semantic and syntactic negatives.

Studies of negation in children have mostly been limited to observational studies, such as Bellugi (1967). There has been little done with either complex sentences, or with children over the age of 6. Boysson-Bardies (1976) reported a picture-matching study using complex sentences with performative verbs (*ask, tell*) conducted with children aged 6. The picture illustrated the complement sentence only. She found that a matrix negative was harder than an embedded negative, principally because the children tended to transfer a matrix negative to the embedded clause, as in (13).

(13) Experimenter: J'ai refusé que Pierre mette son chapeau.

Child: Ça veut dire que Pierre met pas son chapeau.

The children appeared to be treating the performative verbs as if they were implicatives, considering the matrix negative to imply that the complement is negated. In normal discourse, it is not a bad strategy. If I do not want Pierre to put on his hat, it is conceivable that Pierre will not do so, if he is in the habit of doing what I ask. (Boysson-Bardies did not consider how the child was interpreting the matrix clause, so any errors there the child might have made were not noted.)

Hopmann and Maratsos (1978) reported an interesting study in which they tested complex sentences with factive and nonfactive matrix verbs. They presented children aged 3 years, 6 months to 7 years, 1 month with sentences like (14) using both affirmative and negative versions.

(14) a. (factive)

It isn't surprising that the fish pushes the tree.

b. (nonfactive)

It isn't true that the fish pushes the tree.

The child was then asked to select one of two dolls set before him (a fish or a bunny) and to make it push the tree.

The results indicated that the knowledge of factivity increased with age; that is, as the age increased, so did the number of correct answers to the negated sentences. In addition, the percentage of responses to sentences like (14b) that chose the unmentioned doll increased with age, indicating that the children were learning the difference between factive and nonfactive verbs.

It is difficult to test factivity without using negation, and it is not clear from this study that the two factors have been separated. The indications about the developmental aspects of factivity are clear and support the findings of Bennett and Falmagne (1977), but this study cannot be considered to shed much light on the development of negation interpretation.

3 Negation Interpretation in the Adult Grammar

Having briefly discussed the facts that are necessary for a child to learn to interpret factives and negative sentences and the differences in interpretation caused by structural differences, I will now discuss a possible interpretive rule for adults and the implications for children's interpretive strategies.

Negation has always been considered a sentential operator (Klima 1964; Karttunen 1970, 1973; Jackendoff 1972). Although Klima's representation began with the negative component as sentence-initial in the deep structure, an interpretive rule could similarly represent sentential negation by adjoining the negative in the surface verb phrase to the S boundary of the sentence containing it. Sentence (15a) could be given a rough semantic representation like (15b).

(15) a. Ray didn't go to the store today.

b. [NOT [Ray went to the store today]]

This sort of representation is attractive, both because of its simplicity and because of the intuitive sense of propositional negation that is captured by the notation.[6]

It would be desirable for economy's sake to use a representation like (15b) to establish both propositional negation and scope relations. There are problems with such a representation when the subject contains a quantifier, as (16) shows.

(16) a. Someone doesn't love Mary.
   b. $_S$[[someone]$_\alpha$ $_S$[NOT $_S$[α love Mary]]]
   c. $_S$[NOT $_S$[[someone]$_\alpha$ $_S$[α love Mary]]]

The reading in (16c) should be incorrect, as *someone* should be outside the scope of the negative; ordering restrictions on the Quantifier and Negation rules would be needed. The reading of (16b) is preferred, but is misleading as an assignment of scope, as the S-attachment rule does not distinguish between subject noun phrases, which are not within negation scope, and object noun phrases, which are.

Another version of the rule would be to attach the negative to the VP. Such a rule would be easier to collapse with a scope-assignment rule and might be considered closer to the speaker's intuitions. A VP-attachment rule would yield a representation like (17).

(17) $_S$[[someone]$_\alpha$ $_S$[α $_{VP}$[NOT $_{VP}$[love Mary]]]]

Givón (1978:89) pointed out that "while in logic one most often considers negation to be a *sentential* operation, in the syntax of natural languages it is most often a *predicate-phrase* operator, excluding the subject from the scope."

The scope determination in either version of the rule would have to be constrained by hierarchical considerations such as c-command (Reinhart 1976). Although in a right-branching sentence the complement can be within the scope of negation, directionality is not the only criterion. In a left-branching sentence, such as (18), the matrix clause cannot be within the negation scope.

(18) That Henry didn't marry Hilda surprised everyone.

That *everyone* cannot be within the scope of the negative is shown by the unacceptability of (19).

(19) *That Henry didn't marry Hilda surprised anyone.

4 Hypotheses
We are now in a position to hypothesize what a child might do, given sentences with factive verbs like (20) and (21).

(20) a. Fred didn't know that Miss Piggy loves Kermit.

    b. Fred knew that Miss Piggy doesn't love Kermit.

(21) a. That those records were warped didn't surprise Pete.

    b. That those records weren't warped surprised Pete.

To interpret these sentences correctly, the child must know the domain of the negation rule,[7] the meaning of factivity, and the difference in truth values of left- and right-branching *that* complements.

4.1 The Negation Rule

The Negation Interpretation rule is described as adjoining the negative to the S or VP boundary of the sentence in which it appears to produce a partial semantic representation. Studies of the acquisition of similar rules, such as those needed to interpret quantifiers and relative clauses (Roeper and Matthei 1975; Solan and Roeper 1978), have postulated that children initially attach nodes to the highest S node. Even structures that are clause-bound in the adult grammar, such as reciprocals, have been shown to be misinterpreted by children, who assign an antecedent from a higher clause (Matthei 1978).

A possible misinterpretation of the Negation rule for children who have a "highest-S" strategy would be to interpret sentences like (20b) exactly like (20a). The [NOT] would be attached to the highest or matrix-S boundary in both cases, deriving the same representation, shown in (22), for both.

(22) $_S$[NOT $_S$[Fred knows $_S$[that Miss Piggy loves Kermit]]]

If the child hypothesizes a VP-attachment rule, he may still opt for a highest-node principle. The initial representation might be as in (23); the predicted response remains the same, to interpret the matrix verb as negated although the negative particle appeared in the embedded verb.

(23) $_S$[Fred $_{VP}$[NOT $_{VP}$[knows $_S$[that Miss Piggy loves Kermit]]]]

Left-branching structures may allow us to distinguish between an S-attachment rule and a VP-attachment rule. Even with a highest-node strategy, an S-attachment rule will produce similar representations for both (21a) and (21b). The tree in (24) shows an approximate structure for (21b).

(24)

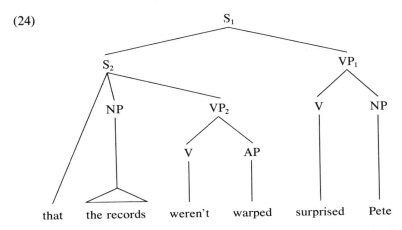

that   the records   weren't   warped   surprised   Pete

The highest S node is S_1. A negative in VP_2 normally would adjoin to S_2, producing a representation like (25).

(25) $_S[_S[NOT _S[$that the records were warped$]]$ surprised Pete$]$

If the negation interpretation rule attaches the negative leftward, a VP-attachment rule will not result in equivalent interpretations for (21a) and (21b). In (21a) the negative would be attached to VP_1, containing *surprise*. In (21b) it would have to be attached to VP_2, containing *were*. Sentence (21a) would yield a representation like (26) and (21b) would yield (27).

(26) $_S[_S[$that the records are warped$] _{VP}[NOT _{VP}[$surprised Pete$]]]$
(27) $_S[_S[$that the records $_{VP}[NOT _{VP}[$were warped$]]]$ surprised Pete$]$

The highest-node strategy and the two possible negation interpretation rules proposed indicate simple and clear predictions:

1. If the child hypothesizes a rule of S-attachment,
   a. A negative in the matrix verb should produce more correct responses than an embedded negative;
   b. There will appear to be a "transfer" of negation upward to the matrix verb from the embedded verb;
   c. There will be no difference between left- and right-branching complements.
2. If the child hypothesizes a VP-attachment rule,
   a. Left-branching complements will produce more correct responses than right-branching complements;

b. Matrix and complement negation could be distinguished sooner in left-branching sentences than in right-branching sentences;

c. Right-branching sentences should still show transfer of negation to the matrix from the embedded clause.

4.2 The Meaning of Factivity

In addition to learning that negation, like reflexives, is clause-bound, the child must learn that negation is treated in a particular way when factives are involved. Until the child learns that factives carry certain implications for the complement sentence, a negation in the matrix of a sentence like (20a) might affect the interpretation of the complement, perhaps on analogy with verbs like implicatives (see the responses of Boysson-Bardies' (1976) subjects to performatives). Studies of factives (Bennett and Falmagne 1977; Hopmann and Maratsos 1978) have shown that factivity increases as children get older and that not all verbs that are factive for adults are factive for children.

4.3 The Influence of Structure

Some of the consequences of the differences between right- and left-branching sentences were discussed in section 4.1. Another fact that the child must consider is that left-branching *that* complements are always implied to be true (Karttunen 1971b). As the matrix verbs for these types of sentences all seem to be factive, the influence of the direction of branching cannot be separated from the rule system or from the problem of factivity. As the child learns about factivity, he should also learn that the verbs that can take these complements are also factive.

5 Children's Interpretation of Negation

A pilot study I conducted with preschool and first-grade children (Phinney 1977), using sentences like (20a) and (20b), confirmed some of the hypotheses discussed in the previous section. The matrix verbs used were *see* and *watch*. The sentences were read to the child, who was then asked to select one of four pictures (see table 6.1 for example sentences and picture descriptions). At least some of the children appeared to be using a highest-S strategy; they selected the picture illustrating (28a) for sentence (28b).

(28) a. Eeyore can't see that Pooh is eating honey.

b. Eeyore can see that Pooh is not eating honey.

Table 6.1
Examples of Sentences and Pictures Used in Pilot Study

i. Eeyore can see that Pooh is eating honey. (In picture, Pooh is sitting on the ground eating from a jar of honey; Eeyore is standing in front of Pooh and watching him.)

ii. Eeyore cannot see that Pooh is eating honey. (In picture, Pooh is sitting on the ground behind a tree eating honey; Eeyore is on the other side of the tree, positioned so that he cannot see Pooh.)

iii. Eeyore can see that Pooh is not eating honey. (In picture, Pooh is looking at a flower and is not eating honey; Eeyore is looking at him.)

iv. Eeyore cannot see that Pooh is not eating honey. (In picture, Pooh is behind a tree talking with Piglet; Eeyore is on the other side of the tree eating grass and cannot see Pooh.)

This strategy was most prevalent among the 6½- to 7½-year-olds. The youngest children (3½ to 5½ years) showed a predominant strategy of selecting picture (iv), in which both clauses were negated. This result may have stemmed from the request to select the "best" picture; the younger children could have felt that the picture in which both propositions did not occur was the best choice for any negation.

Although the various factors of complement type and verb type were not as well controlled in the pilot as they might have been, and the use of a picture-matching task restricted the use of matrix verbs to those that could be represented in a drawn image, the results clearly indicated that the children were not interpreting these types of sentences as an adult would, and that further research was needed.

5.1 Negation with Factives

A more detailed study was designed to test negation in complex sentences in a more natural context (a short story), and was designed to control for sentence structure, placement of negation, and complement type. A questionnaire was used which contained 16 three-line stories, with the test sentence as the third line. The test sentences used were two-clause sentences of the type shown in (20)–(21), along with sentences of both structural types that did not contain negation. All the matrix verbs used were factives, because of the consistency of adult responses to sentences containing factives and negation. A sample story is shown in (29).

Table 6.2
Examples of Stories and Questions Used in Second Study

i. John likes Irene very much.
   Dave likes Irene too.
   Dave didn't know that John kissed Irene.
   1. Did John kiss Irene?
   2. Did Dave know what happened?

ii. Mary and John are having a party.
   John wrote the invitations.
   Mary remembered that John didn't write to Nancy.
   1. Did Mary remember what happened?
   2. Did John write to Nancy?

iii. The pig is very affectionate.
   She loves everybody.
   That the pig kissed the cow didn't please the dog.
   1. Did the pig kiss the cow?
   2. Was the dog pleased by what happened?

iv. John likes to run and jump.
   Dave plays with him.
   That John didn't jump over the fence surprised Dave.
   1. Was Dave surprised at what happened?
   2. Did John jump over the fence?

(29) Bill likes to run and jump
    Dave watches him sometimes.
    Dave knew that Bill jumped over the fence.
    1. Did Dave know what happened?   Yes   No
    2. Did Bill jump over the fence?   Yes   No

(See table 6.2 for other samples.) After each story, there were two
questions (one about each clause), to which the child was directed to
answer either *yes* or *no*. Four different questionnaires were used, all of
similar construction, with the stories presented in different orders. The
order of presentation in each questionnaire was randomized.

Factive verbs were originally chosen because they would provide the
clearest evidence on the misuse of the Negation-Interpretation rule,
since the complement should be implied to be true, and because adult
judgments on these sentences are very clear. The verbs chosen were
shown by Bennett and Falmagne (1977) to be relatively factive for
third-graders.

The subjects were 45 elementary-school children, ages 5 years, 10
months to 9 years, 2 months (5,10–9,2), in grades 1 through 3 at the

Ashby Elementary School in Ashby, Massachusetts. Two subjects
were later eliminated because they failed to complete the questionnaire. The experimenter read the questionnaire to the children, who
were tested in groups of five. The children were encouraged to read
along with the experimenter if they could. The test took 15–20 minutes
for each group.

The predictions were those discussed in section 4. Matrix negatives
in general were expected to produce more correct responses than embedded negatives. Negatives in an embedded clause were expected to
produce a response that would be equivalent to that which an adult
would give to a matrix negative. An additional possibility was that
left-branching sentences might produce more correct responses than
right-branching sentences if the child had postulated a VP-attachment
rule rather than an S-attachment rule.

5.2   Results
The subjects were originally grouped by grade. However, as neither
that nor age turned out to be a significant factor (the number of errors in
each group varied widely[8]), the subjects were then grouped by total
number of errors. The highest-error group (group 1) consisted of 15
subjects, ages 5,10–8,5, with 8–12 errors (out of 16 possible responses)
and a mean of 9.6 errors. The middle group (group 2) consisted of 18
subjects, ages 5,11–9,1, with 4–7 errors and a mean of 5.06. The
lowest-error group (group 3) consisted of 10 subjects, ages 7,4–9,2,
with 0–3 errors and a mean of 1.7 errors.

This grouping appeared to indicate the use of two different strategies,
as shown in figure 6.1. The highest-error group showed a distinctive
rightward "transfer" of negation, regardless of the direction of embedding. In sentences like (20a) and (21b) a high percentage (40 percent)
responded as if the negative was in the right-hand clause. There is also
evidence of some upward transfer from a right-branching complement,
like that in (20b). Some of the responses (28 percent) indicated that
(20b) was treated as if it were (20a). As predicted in a sentence like
(21a), there is very little transfer of the negation left and down from the
matrix of a left-branching sentence. These results indicate conflicting
strategies within this highest-error group. There is an overwhelming
tendency to transfer the negation to the right-hand clause, regardless of
structural considerations. Although for normal right-branching sentences this could be accounted for by claiming the child has not learned

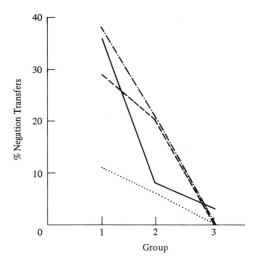

Figure 6.1
Negation-transfer strategies used by subjects. (Subjects are grouped according to number of errors—group 1: 8–12 errors; group 2: 4–7 errors; group 3: 0–3 errors.) Solid line: sentence (20a) (right branching, matrix negative). Dashed line: sentence (20b) (right-branching, embedded negative). Dotted line: sentence (21a) (left-branching, matrix negative). Dot-dash line: sentence (21b) (left-branching, embedded negative).

the difference between factives and nonfactives and is perhaps making an analogy with other verb types like implicatives or the Neg-raising verbs, it does not explain the similar reaction to left-branching sentences, where no such analogy can be made. However, Tavakolian (1977, 1978b) has proposed that children at this stage may have hypothesized flat or conjoined structures rather than hierarchical structures for complex sentences. If this is the case, then there is no reason for them to treat right- and left-branching sentences differently.

A conflicting strategy is shown by the fairly high percentage of responses indicating a transfer of negation upward in a right-branching sentence like (20b). The percentage of these responses is much higher than that of a transfer in a sentence like (21a), which is in the same direction—leftward. If this group were responding to directionality only, one might expect that the amount of leftward transfer would be the same regardless of structure. But it is not, and thus it appears that at least some of the children in this group do pay attention to hierarchical structure when the negative is in the right-hand clause. Hence, in the highest-error group, there is evidence of both a purely directional strategy, and a hierarchically based strategy, suggesting that in fact there may be two different subgroups involved.

The middle-error group (group 2) shows a shift in strategy. The predominant response here is a transfer of the negation upward to the matrix verb regardless of the relative right or left position of the negative. In other words, the group is responding to sentences like (20b) and (21b) as though they were like (20a) and (21a). These children have obviously postulated hierarchical structures for these types of sentences; as predicted by the S-attachment theory and a highest-node strategy, the matrix verb is negated rather than the embedded verb. There is little if any transfer of the negation downward from the matrix clause. There is still some evidence of right and downward transfer in sentences like (20a), which may be a continuation from the first group.

The lowest-error group (group 3) shows no distinct pattern of errors, and all error types are very low. The fact that the overall errors are low is to be expected from the makeup of the group. "Copying," or a double-negative interpretation, which occurred in the pilot study, is low for all groups, and the interaction between copying errors and sentence types is not significant.

The seeming inconsistency in the highest-error group indicated that perhaps something else was going on. The responses of these children were examined further. This highest-error group could be broken down into two subgroups of children, each showing a highly consistent unidirectional strategy. Of the 15 subjects with 8–12 errors, 46 percent evidenced only a strategy of transferring the negative rightward, with almost no leftward transfers. Thirty-three percent showed only a strategy of transferring the negative upward from an embedded clause. Three children (19 percent) showed combined strategies of right and up or left and up transfers. These children were all older children (ages 6,10, 7,3, and 8,5), although their error rates were high. Figure 6.2 shows the results for these two subgroups. The results for the "rightward" subgroup (mean errors 10.38; mean age 6,10) show a high percentage of negation transferred right and down from the matrix in sentences like (20a). Less frequent is the transfer of negation rightward from a left-branching complement like (21b), which indicates that possibly some children are treating a left-branching sentence as flat, but not the group as a whole.[9] There are few left and upward responses (4 out of 24). Note that both strategies should produce a substantial error

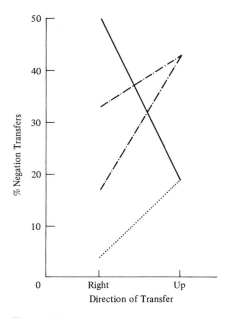

Figure 6.2
Negation-transfer data on subjects with 8–12 errors. Solid line: sentence (20a).
Dashed line: (20b). Dotted line: (21a). Dot-dash line: (21b).

rate for left-branching sentences with embedded negatives, which is just what happens.

The "upward" subgroup showed a strategy of transferring the negation upward to the matrix from the embedded clause, regardless of the left or right position of the negative. They are treating sentences like (20b) and (21b) like (20a) and (21a). This type of response is what an S-attachment rule of negation interpretation coupled with a highest-node strategy would predict.

The middle group, with 4–7 errors, also broke down into two smaller groups with different strategies. Eight subjects, or 44 percent (mean errors 4.75; mean age 7,11), showed a strategy of transferring the negative only right and upward to the matrix from a left-branching complement, treating sentences like (21b) as though they were like (21a). Six subjects (33 percent) (mean errors 4.83; mean age 7,11) showed a strategy of transferring the negation left and up from the matrix of a right-branching sentence, treating sentences like (20b) as though they were like (20a). The other four children (28 percent) showed varying

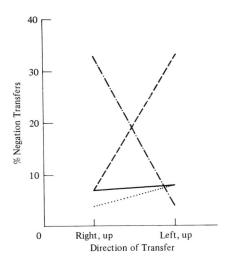

Figure 6.3
Negation-transfer data on subjects with 4–7 errors. Solid line: (20a). Dashed
line: (20b). Dotted line: (21a). Dot-dash line: (21b).

strategies. These children were assigned to one of the two subgroups on
the basis of their primary response. As figure 6.3 shows, the first subgroup is responsible for almost all the right and upward transfers, and
the second group is responsible for all the left and upward transfers.

Rather than using simply a unidirectional strategy as did the children
in the highest-error group, the children in the middle-error group appear to have constrained the situations in which they still overextended
the negation rule. As there is no substantial difference between the
right-and-up and the left-and-up subgroups in terms of mean age or
mean errors, it may be that children at this stage are selecting different
factors on which to focus, rather than that the two strategies are distinct and sequential stages.

The right-and-upward subgroup shows a significant number of errors
only on left-branching sentences with embedded negatives like (21b).
This pattern of errors cannot be explained solely by claiming that the
children have a highest-S-attachment strategy. If that were the case,
they would make errors on sentences like (20b) as well. If they have
postulated flat or conjoined structures, we would expect to see errors
on sentences like (20a) as well. Other factors must be involved. One
difference between (21b) and (20b), noted by Karttunen (1971b), is that
left-embedded *that* complements are always implied to be true. A child

just learning what factive verbs are and how they interact with the complement may have difficulties reconciling the negative with the fact that the complement is supposed to be true. Also, as the processing studies have shown, true negatives are more difficult to process correctly (Trabasso et al. 1971; Wason and Johnson-Laird 1972). These factors may conspire to produce the observed transfer of negation in sentences like (21b). There may in fact be a general reluctance to negate a complement that is implied to be true, and for these children who appear to be at the age when children learn the difference between factive and nonfactive verbs (Bennett and Falmagne 1977; Hopmann and Maratsos 1978) there appears to be a conflict between the act of negation or denial and the implications about the truth of the complement. One way for the child to resolve this conflict is to transfer the negation to the matrix verb, where the truth value of the complement will not be affected.

It appears that children who make errors only on sentences like (21b) may be sensitive to this conflict only in left-branching structures, in which the matrix verb is always factive and the complement is always implied to be true. In addition, the concept of a nonevent surprising someone, in the form of *x surprised John,* is a difficult situation to conceptualize; it is more natural to think of something that happened as the cause of surprise rather than something that did not happen. Also, because of the left-branching structure, even if there is not a highest-S strategy, there may still be confusion about which S boundary is the pertinent one, whereas there could be no such confusion in a right-branching structure, since, as we saw in (24), the boundaries for S_1 and S_2 coincide at the beginning of such sentences. A labeled bracketing of (21b), as in (30), shows this well.

(30) $_{S_1}[$ $_{S_2}[$That the records weren't warped] surprised Pete]

The fact that the left boundaries of S_1 and S_2 coincide may be a source of confusion as to which boundary the negative should attach to. A child may still attach the negative to the S_1 boundary in (30), while in (31) there could be no such confusion.

(31) $_{S_1}[$Fred knew $_{S_2}[$that Miss Piggy doesn't love Kermit]]

The left-and-upward subgroup of the middle-error group showed errors only on sentences of type (20b), which is equivalent to (31). This type of error pattern was predicted in section 5, where it was postulated that if the child hypothesized a VP-attachment rule, rather than an S-

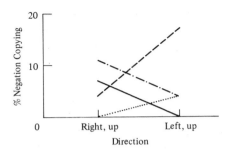

Figure 6.4
Negation-copying data on subjects with 4–7 errors. Solid line: (20a). Dashed
line: (20b). Dotted line: (21a). Dot-dash line: (21b).

attachment rule, and also used a highest-node strategy, errors should
be made on sentences like (20b) rather than those like (21b). This is the
pattern shown by the left-and-upward subgroup.

In addition, the children in this subgroup may be sensitive to an
ambiguity noted by some adult speakers. Consider a sentence like (32),
where the child was asked to respond *yes* or *no* to the questions in (33).

(32)   Mary knew that Bill didn't kick John.
(33) a. Did Bill kick John?
     b. Did Mary know what happened?

The predominant response was *yes* to (33a) and *no* to (33b).

Question (33b) is ambiguous in a sense. "What happened" can refer
either to the general situation or the specific act mentioned in the
sentence—that is, the act of Bill kicking John. In the second case, the
answer to (33b) is *yes,* Mary knew x (x being the fact that Bill did not
kick John). In the first case, however, there is a possible response of
no, in the sense that Mary couldn't know x because x is something that
didn't happen. One might expect the pattern of responses to be *no* for
both questions rather than *yes* for (33a) if that were the case. Figure 6.4
shows that in fact there was an increase in double-negative responses
on these sentences for this subgroup, although the increase was not
large.

Though it is difficult to compare the pilot study to the present study
because of the differing methodologies and sentence types, the results
are not inconsistent. There is a gap in the age groups tested in the pilot
at a crucial age, age 6, when the present study showed a purely directional response for some subjects. Both studies indicated an increase

in upward transfers of the negation at approximately the same age, around age 6,6. The results of both studies, in particular those of the more detailed study discussed here, support an S-attachment rule of negation interpretation and the use of a highest-node strategy.

6 Summary

The acquisition of a system for interpreting negation in complex sentences is not wholly dependent on any one factor, but is a coordination of a variety of structural and semantic factors. Two studies relying on different methodologies have indicated the course of this process in sentences with factive verbs. The pilot study supported the hypothesis of a negation interpretation rule that would negate a sentence, formalized by adjoining the negative to an S boundary. A highest-node principle of attachment (Solan and Roeper 1978) predicted a transfer of negation upward from the embedded clause to the matrix verb.

The second study indicated several stages that showed the interactions of the various systems. Initially there was a purely directional response of transferring the negation to the rightmost verb. It was hypothesized that these children were disregarding structural considerations because they had not hypothesized hierarchical structures for the test sentences (Tavakolian 1977, 1978b). This was followed by a stage in which hierarchical considerations took precedence, and a highest-S-attachment strategy resulted in transfer of the negation to the matrix verb. After this upward stage, it appeared that the interpretation rule was constrained further, as different groups of children seemed to choose different parts of the system on which to focus. The direction of the embedding is crucial. Two different subgroups emerged. The right-and-upward group made errors only on left-branching sentences, which indicated that they may have dropped a highest-S strategy for right-branching sentences but were still using it for left-branching sentences. It was suggested that these children were confusing the S boundary to which the negative should be attached; in addition, a possible conflict between negation and implied truth value was discussed. Another group of children, the left-and-upward group, responded according to predictions made by the hypothesis of a VP-attachment rule to interpret negation plus a highest-node principle, and some of these children appeared to be sensitive to an ambiguity that has been noted by some adult speakers. Such stages in interpretive rule application, where hierarchical criteria gradually dominate over an initial directional response, have been shown to occur in other interpretive systems as well, such as the interpretation of anaphora (Solan 1978a; Lust 1978).

The suggestion of a conflict between negation of a proposition and implied truth value of a complement clause indicates an area for further research. Although there is little experimental evidence to support this proposal, it may provide a further explanation for the difficulties observed in processing true negatives and support for the retention of the transfer strategy and overextension of the negation interpretation rule until relatively late, when most purely syntactic rules have already been learned.

The predictions that followed from the hypotheses set forth in section 4 were supported by both the pilot study and the second study. When the child is asked specifically to interpret both clauses, matrix negatives prove easier than embedded negatives. Both an S-attachment and a VP-attachment rule for negation interpretation were supported, but by different groups of subjects. Because there are no other factors to motivate one analysis rather than the other, no claim can be made about the correctness of either rule for the adult grammar.[10] The results also supported a highest-node strategy proposed by Solan and Roeper (1978); it is interesting to see that strategy applies to interpretive rules, as it was hypothesized as a strategy for syntactic transformations. The response patterns also indicated a shift in emphasis from directional to hierarchical considerations, supporting the results of Tavakolian (1977, 1978b), Lust (1978), and Solan (1978).

Notes

I gratefully acknowledge the support of the National Science Foundation and the University of Massachusetts, Amherst, during the course of this research.

I would like to thank my advisor Tom Roeper, and Chuck Clifton, Lyn Frazier, Barbara Partee, Larry Solan, and Edwin Williams, for helpful discussions during innumerable drafts of this paper.

I would also like to thank the teachers and the students of the schools who allowed me to disrupt their routines and ask strange questions: Ms. Rose Ann Jones of The Little Red School House, Amherst, Massachusetts; Ms. Mary Jane MacDonald of North Village Day Care Center, Amherst; Principal Norman May and the teachers at Spaulding Memorial School, Townsend, Massachusetts; and Principal Allan Foresman and the teachers at Ashby Elementary School, Ashby, Massachusetts.

1. Certain stressed intonations, such as an exaggerated stress on *know* in (1), can imply something else—perhaps that John is deluded in his knowledge. In

this case the truth of the complement is not implied; however, this is not the normal usage of this type of sentence.

2. There have been various analyses proposed to handle Neg-raising verbs. Initially a transformation was proposed (Fillmore 1963) to account for the synonymy of "Mary Jean didn't think Tom would ever leave" and "Mary Jean thought that Tom wouldn't ever leave" (hence the term Neg-raising). Others have rejected this view and have tried to account for the problem with semantic analyses of the particular verbs. Still others have denied that there is a problem and claimed that these two sentences are not really synonymous.

3. There is no discussion in Hart et al. 1977 about the structures in which these verbs occurred.

4. Children actually prefer an embedded negative rather than a matrix negative for these verbs, even though they prefer a matrix negative for all other complex sentences they produce (Bellugi 1967; Phinney 1977). This preference is noticeable at a fairly early age (5,6–6,6) and indicates that the children are aware that this class is different.

5. "Purely definitional negatives" (PDNs, words like *bachelor,* which supposedly contain a negative semantic feature, such as [unmarried]) were significantly easier than any of the other negative categories, indicating that PDNs were not being processed as if they contained a negative component.

6. A similar representation was briefly mentioned by May (1977:176) as a counterpart to his representation for quantifiers.

7. This type of rule has all the markings of a rule of Core Grammar (Chomsky and Lasnik 1977) and should not really have to be learned; the domain of application might have to be learned.

8. The lack of significance in grade level may have been partly the result of selecting children from different reading groups within each grade. There was a strong correlation between overall error rate and reading group within each grade level.

9. It is impossible to verify this because of the actual frequencies, which become very small because of the size of the group.

10. No claim is made here for the correctness of either rule in the adult grammar. The crucial examples are not commonly found in normal language, and it may be that the child may choose one variant or the other and never be called upon to change that choice by outside evidence (Solan 1978b).

7

Children's Grammar of Complement-Subject Interpretation

Helen Goodluck

It is widely recognized that the child's hypotheses concerning the structure and rules of the language he is acquiring are very heavily restricted.[1] As an explanation of this fact it has been proposed that the child approaches the task of language learning equipped with a set of principles for the analysis of linguistic data. These principles constitute the language-acquisition device (LAD). In this view language acquisition is a process in which a series of hypotheses are tested against the data available; the form of these hypotheses is constrained by the LAD.

The primary proposal that has been made concerning the internal organization of the LAD is that it incorporates properties of universal grammar; thus the form of the child's hypotheses about his language is held to be limited from the outset by linguistic universals. This approach to language acquisition is essentially that proposed by Chomsky (1965) and Katz (1966) and elaborated on in various ways by others (for example, McNeill 1966; Roeper 1978; Valian et al., this volume).

Chomsky (1965) distinguishes two types of universals, substantive and formal. Substantive universals are the elementary terms in which linguistic rules are formulated. For example, the categories "noun" and "verb" are substantive universals in the syntactic rules of human languages. Formal universals restrict the kinds of rules that can exist in languages, and their manner of application.

The experiments on children's grammar of complementation reported in this chapter are concerned with the empirical basis for the claim that (formal) universals constrain children's grammars. The adult grammar of the test constructions is first sketched and two candidate universals are proposed. Then evidence is presented concerning the presence of these universals in the grammar of 4–6-year-old children. The results on the whole can be interpreted as support for the hypothesis that universals limit children's grammar in the cases of the constructions tested.

1 The Adult Grammar

1.1 Constructions Studied

The study is based on three types of complement clause with a "missing subject": infinitival complements to verbs such as *tell* (as in (1)), *(in order) to* clauses (as in (2)), and participial complements introduced by a temporal preposition (*while, before,* or *after*) (as in (3)).

(1) John told Bill to grab the jewels.
(2) John hit Bill (in order) to grab the jewels.
(3) John hit Bill after grabbing the jewels.

1.2 The Referent of the Complement Subject

In the adult grammar, the subject of the complement clause in (1)–(3) must be understood as coreferential with an NP in the matrix sentence; these complement types will be referred to as obligatory-control complements. Other types of complements with missing subjects do not impose this restriction. For example, in (4), the subject of *insult* may be understood as *Bill,* but it may also be understood as referring to someone not mentioned in the sentence.

(4) To insult Mary would upset Bill.

Complements that do not require their subject to be interpreted as coreferential with an NP in the sentence will be referred to as optional-control complements.

The obligatory-control complements of (1)–(3) differ with respect to the NP in the matrix sentence that is understood as the subject of the complement. In (1), Bill is the subject of *grab;* in (2) and (3), the subject of *grab* is *John.* I will refer to the complement clause in sentences like (1) as object-controlled, and to the complement clause in sentences such as (2) and (3) as subject-controlled (and to the matrix subject and object in (1) and (2), (3), respectively, as the controller of the complement).[2]

1.3 The Syntax of Infinitival and Participial Complements

The syntactic structure in (5) will be assumed for the sentence in (1), and the syntactic structure in (6) for (2), (3). (Differences in complement morphology are disregarded here; Δ indicates an unfilled node.)

(5)

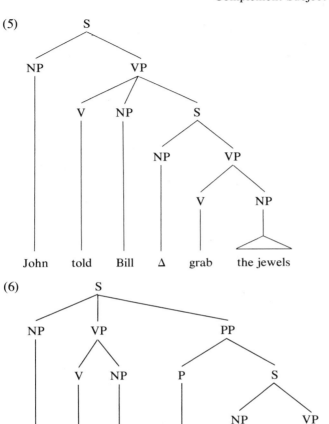

(6)

Thus, the complement in (1) is a VP constituent, whereas the complements in (2) and (3) are immediate constituents of the matrix S node.

There is some evidence to support this difference between the syntax of (1) and that of (2) and (3). First, the natural order of constituents is one in which those complements that are assumed to be S constituents follow those that are VP constituents, as shown in (7).

(7) a.   John told Bill to grab the jewels after hitting the clerk.

   b. ?John told Bill after hitting the clerk to grab the jewels.

The "unmarked" order (7a) is the one that will result automatically from the expansion of the base rules if temporal and *(in order) to* complements are generated by the phrase structure rules for S.[3] Second, temporal participials and *(in order) to* clauses are never subject to subcategorial restrictions. This is necessarily the case for S constituents, since subcategorization restricts only the occurrence of constituents that are sister to the matrix verb. By contrast, the complement type in (1) is subcategorized for (compare *John suggested to Bill to open the window* with **John suggested to Bill*). Third, temporal participials and *(in order) to* clauses can prepose, as in (8) and (9).

(8) $\left\{ \begin{array}{l} \text{(In order) to grab} \\ \text{After grabbing} \end{array} \right\}$ the jewels, John hit Bill.

(9) *To grab the jewels, John told Bill.

This difference will be accounted for if preposing cannot move complements that attach to the VP node.[4]

   Although infinitival complements such as that in (1) cannot prepose, some VP constituents can appear in initial position. Thus, for example, the PP in (10a), which is strictly subcategorized for by the matrix verb *put*, as (10b) shows, can appear in initial position, although the result is stylistically marked, as in (11).

(10) a.   John put the bread in the cupboard.

    b. *John put the bread.

(11)   In the cupboard, John put the bread.

A further argument favoring attachment of *(in order) to* and temporal participials to the S node can be made on the basis of these preposing facts. There is a distinction in the grammaticality of *wh* questions in sentences with preposed constituents, such as (12) and (13).

(12)   After grabbing the jewels, whom did John hit?

(13) *In the cupboard, what did John put?

Reinhart (1976) uses sentences such as (13) to support the claim that PPs preposed from the VP move into the COMP node, and that a different treatment is needed for preposing from S. Example (11) will have a derived structure of the form shown in (14).

(14)

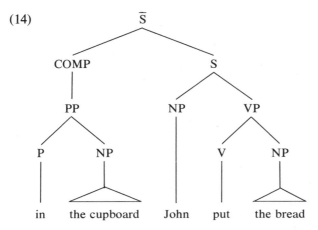

in   the cupboard   John   put   the bread

The ungrammaticality of (13) can then be explained by the presence of the *wh* word in COMP, making preposing impossible. Constituents that are preposed from S will not move into COMP, and the grammaticality of (12) can thus be accounted for.[5]

In what follows, I will assume an attachment to S analysis of the adult grammar of temporal and *in order to* complements, casting the analysis of children's development in terms of the attainment of this grammar. An S-attachment analysis has the advantage of automatically ensuring subject control of these complement types, under the condition for determining controlling NPs outlined in the next section. However, the evidence for S attachment as the sole analysis of temporals is not strong, as Reinhart (1976) has observed. In addition, it should be noted that some speakers of English permit temporals to be object-controlled (Elliot et al. 1969); such dialects require VP attachment of the complement for consistent application of the condition on control.

1.4   The Rules of Complement-Subject Interpretation
A number of different approaches have been proposed for specifying the subject of complement clauses (see, for example, Rosenbaum 1967, Jackendoff 1972, Bresnan 1977, Chomsky 1978, Solan 1978c). The approach adopted here, which essentially follows Chomsky (1978) and others, assumes that control is determined by a rule that coindexes the (lexically unfilled) complement-subject NP with the controlling NP.[6]

1.4.1   *A Syntactic Condition on Complement-Subject Interpretation.*
There is a clear correlation between the syntactic structures proposed

in section 1.3 for the complement types in (1)–(3) and the understood subject of the complement clause. The complements in (2) and (3), which are immediate constituents of the S node, are subject-controlled, while the complement in (1), which is a VP constituent, is object-controlled. Williams (1975) observes that a complement must be attached to the VP in English in order for it to be object-controlled; we will assume this restriction to be a linguistic universal.

It has been suggested in recent work (Chomsky 1978) that the identification of complement subjects for obligatory-control complements is governed by a structural principle not confined to this rule of grammar. Williams' observation that a complement must be attached to the VP for it to be object-controlled can be expressed in terms of the notion c(onstituent)-command. The definition of c-command, given in (15), derives from the work of Reinhart (1976) on pronominal reference.

(15) c-command

Node A c-commands Node B if the first branching node that dominates A also dominates B, and neither A nor B dominates the other.

The requirement that a complement must attach to the VP in order to be object-controlled will be met if the restriction given in (16) is placed on control.

(16) A controller must c-command the missing subject position.

I will refer to this as the c-command constraint on control. Thus, in (6) the NP *Bill* is not a possible controller for the complement clause, since it does not c-command the complement-subject NP (it is dominated by a branching node, VP, which does not dominate the complement subject). In (5), however, the NP *Bill* is a possible controller, since the first branching node dominating it, VP, does dominate the complement-subject position. We can assume that attachment to the VP as a prerequisite for control by the matrix object follows from c-command as a universal constraint on possible controllers.

The c-command constraint has the further consequence of automatically blocking the passive *by* phrase from controlling in (17), which has the syntactic structure (18).

(17) John was told by Bill to grab the jewels.

(18)

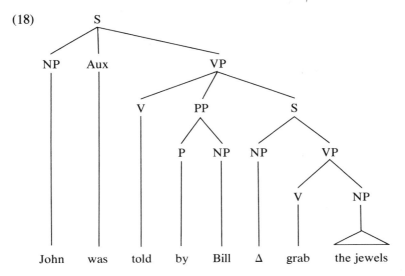

John   was   told   by   Bill   Δ   grab   the jewels

(The passive *by* phrase is assumed to be base-generated, as suggested by Bresnan (1977) and others.) In (18), the object of the *by* phrase, the NP *Bill,* does not c-command the complement-subject position, since it is dominated by a branching node (PP), which does not dominate the complement subject. The c-command constraint will in fact block control by the object of any PP of a complement not contained in that phrase. Blocking of control by the object of a preposition is, in general, correct for English, although there are exceptions.

The c-command constraint is not sufficient to specify the controller of the complement in all cases. Both the matrix subject and the matrix object c-command the complement-subject position in the structure (5); it is the matrix object that controls the infinitival complement to verbs such as *tell.* Control of a VP complement by the object NP is the general case for English. Matrix verbs that require control of an infinitival complement by the subject, such as *promise* (see (19)), are exceptions.

(19) John promised Bill to grab the jewels.

In cases where there is more than one possible controller, the controlling NP must be specified by a rule. There have been various approaches to the statement of such rules (see, for example, Rosenbaum 1967; Jackendoff 1972; Chomsky 1978). For our purposes, it will be sufficient to assume a rule that picks out the matrix direct-object NP as controller of a VP complement, with some provision for exceptional cases such as *promise*.[7]

1.4.2 *Exceptions*. As mentioned above, the block on control by the object of a preposition is not without exceptions. For example, the object of *on* controls the complement clause in (20).

(20) John relied on Bill to mow the lawn.

On Bill is a syntactic unit, as *wh*-movement shows (see (21)).

(21) On whom did John rely to mow the lawn?

Verbs such as *rely (on)* have provided some motivation for proposals that control rules should be sensitive to semantic structure. If the syntactic object of *on* is the object of the unit of semantic structure "rely on," then control of the complement of *rely on* can be unified with regular cases such as *tell;* in both cases it will be the NP filling the semantic relation of "direct object" that controls. Bresnan 1977 and Solan 1978c are recent examples of analyses in which control rules refer to the semantic structure of the matrix verb.

Cases such as *rely on* do not clearly warrant the abandonment of the c-command constraint. The requirement that a complement be attached to the VP in order for it to be object-controlled appears to be exceptionless and is captured by this condition, and in most cases the exclusion of control by the object of a preposition (as in the case of the passive prepositional phrase) is correct. We will thus continue to assume the correctness of the c-command constraint on control; it is to be hoped that future work will increase our understanding of the basis for violations of this syntactic condition.

1.4.3 *The Application of Complement-Subject Interpretation*. Given that the c-command constraint on control is a universal governing rules of complement-subject interpretation, at what level do such rules apply? The facts of English, in which complements do not prepose from the VP, do not provide clear evidence concerning the level of application of control rules under the c-command condition.[8] However, languages do permit preposing of object-controlled complements from the VP. Thus, in Swedish the direct object may be interpreted as the controller in both the preposed and sentence-final complements, as in (22).

(22) a. Jag såg Kalle sittande på gräset.
        ("I saw Kalle sitting on the grass.")
     b. Sittande på gräset såg jag Kalle.[9]

In preposed position, there is no possible structure in which the matrix object can c-command the complement-subject position, and thus consistent application of the c-command condition mandates the application of complement-subject interpretation with reference to underlying structure.

The model of Chomsky and Lasnik (1977) is an example of a model of grammar in which rules of a certain type ("rules of construal"), of which complement-subject interpretation is an example, apply with reference to underlying structure. (This will be the case regardless of whether preposing is a late stylistic rule or a member of the transformational rule component in the Chomsky-Lasnik model, given that movement transformations leave a trace of the moved constituent in the base position.) The application of rules such as complement-subject interpretation with reference to underlying rather than derived structure will be assumed to be a linguistic universal.

1.5   Summary
We have seen that the control properties of the complement types in (1)–(3) are subject to the condition that a controller must c-command the complement-subject position, and that there is evidence in favor of a theory of grammar in which rules such as complement-subject interpretation apply with reference to underlying rather than derived structure. I will assume these to be universal features of the grammar of obligatory control. A rule is necessary to select the controller from among the NPs that c-command the complement in sentences such as (1); the general case in English is for the controller of VP complements to be the direct-object NP.

In the next section, I will present experimental evidence concerning the child's grammar of complement-subject interpretation.

2   The Acquisition of Complement-Subject Interpretation
2.1   Previous Studies
In the first research carried out on children's grammar of complement-subject interpretation, C. Chomsky (1969) observed that at around 5 years *Bill* is understood as the subject of the embedded clause in both sentences like (1) ("John told Bill to grab the jewels") and sentences

with the matrix verb *promise*, such as (19) ("John promised Bill to grab the jewels"). As noted above, *promise* is an exception to the general pattern of control in English, since it requires control of a complement by the matrix subject rather than the matrix object. Chomsky proposed that at this stage children use a linear surface rule by which the NP nearest to the complement verb in the surface string is interpreted as the complement subject.[10]

Maratsos (1974) tested the interpretation of active and passive sentences with *tell* and *ask* by 4- and 5-year-old children. In his experiment, children correctly interpreted the controller of the complement as *Bill* in sentences such as (1), and as *John* in the corresponding passive sentences such as (17) ("John was told by Bill to grab the jewels"). As Maratsos observed, a simple linear-distance principle by which the NP nearest the complement verb is made controller cannot account for the success young children have in interpreting the controller of complement clauses in passive sentences. Maratsos, drawing on the linguistic work of Jackendoff (1972), suggests that his results argue that children's rules of complement-subject interpretation make reference to semantic relations such as "goal."

In section 1.4.1 it was pointed out that the *c*-command constraint in adult grammar blocks control of a complement by the object of a PP and in this way excludes the passive agent as controller. Thus, it is possible to account for Maratsos's results by assuming that the children in his experiments parsed passive sentences in the same way as an adult does, and that they knew the *c*-command constraint on control. Maratsos's claim that children's rules of complement-subject interpretation make reference to semantic terms such as "goal" is therefore not a necessary conclusion from his data.

The possibility that children at around 4 years know the block on control by the object of a preposition mandated by the *c*-command constraint also bears on the interpretation of results obtained by Tavakolian (1978b) on the acquisition of *(in order) to* clauses. Tavakolian tested children's interpretation of sentences such as (23).

(23) The cow walked around the pig to kiss the lion.

There was a very high percentage of subject control in responses to these sentences (89 percent).

The failure to overgeneralize object control in sentences such as (23) was a puzzling result to the extent that it conflicted with the results of an experiment by Goodluck and Roeper (1978) where we found that object control of participial complements, which in general only occur as VP complements with matrix verbs that are verbs of perception, was overgeneralized to nonperception verbs. That is, object control was permitted in sentences such as (25) as well as (24).

(24) John saw Bill carrying the basket.
(25) John hit Bill carrying the basket.

In Tavakolian's experiment, there was always a PP in the matrix verb phrase, as in (23). If it is the case that children block control by the object of a PP, Tavakolian's results with infinitivals do not contrast with the results of Goodluck and Roeper with participials.[11]

2.2 Experimental Evidence
Together, the experimental results reviewed above suggested that the c-command constraint might be playing a significant role in the child's rules of complement-subject interpretation, and two experiments were designed to investigate further the presence of this condition in children's grammar and to test the level of structure at which children apply rules of control.

2.2.1 *Experiment I.* This experiment was designed to extend the range of constructions for which we have evidence concerning conditions on children's grammar of control and to investigate whether children determine control with reference to underlying or derived structure.

Children were tested for their comprehension of the sentence types in (26).[12]

(26) a. Active matrix sentence with direct-object NP and a temporal participial complement
      The boy hits the girl after jumping over the fence.
   b. Active matrix sentence with a locative PP in the VP and a temporal participial complement
      The boy stands near the girl after jumping over the fence.
   c. Passive matrix sentence with a temporal participial complement
      The boy is hit by the girl after jumping over the fence.
   d. Active matrix sentence with the main verb *tell* or *ask* and an infinitival complement
      The boy tells the girl to jump over the fence.

e. Passive matrix sentence with *tell* or *ask* and an infinitival complement
   The boy is told by the girl to jump over the fence.
f. Active matrix sentence with a direct-object NP and a temporal participial complement in preposed position
   After jumping over the fence, the boy hits the girl.

For conditions (26a–e) the predictions made concerning children's interpretation of these sentence types will rest on three hypotheses. The first of these follows from a model of acquisition in which linguistic universals are not violated by the child.

1. Children's grammar is subject to the *c*-command constraint on control.

Two additional hypotheses will be made:

2. Children may attach complements that are generated as immediate constituents of the S node in adult grammar to the VP at an early stage.

3. Children have a rule that specifies that the matrix object controls a complement attached to the VP.

The second hypothesis is made on the ground that attachment of temporal clauses to the S node is an arbitrary fact about (most dialects of) English; it is not mandated by any basic principle of grammar that I am aware of, and as such may be a source of error in children's grammar.[13]

The third hypothesis is suggested by previous research (Maratsos 1974; Tavakolian 1978b; Goodluck and Roeper 1978), which has shown that by age 4 most children show a preference for interpreting the matrix object as the complement subject in the case of complements to verbs such as *tell* and *see*.

Taken together, these hypotheses lead to the following predictions about the way in which children will interpret the constructions (26a–e): First, for sentences with a direct object and a temporal participial complement (such as (26a)), it is predicted that children will interpret the complement clause as object-controlled (if participials attach only to the VP) or as either subject- or object-controlled (if participials attach freely to the VP or S node).

For sentences with the matrix verb *tell* or *ask* and a direct-object NP, such as (26d), object control is predicted, assuming that *tell* and *ask* subcategorize for an obligatory complement.

For sentence types (26b, c, e), in which there is a passive or locative PP in the VP, it is predicted that the complement clause will be controlled by the matrix subject, regardless of the position of the complement on the phrase-structure tree, since in these sentence types the only other NP in the matrix sentence is the object of a preposition, and it is blocked from controlling by the c-command constraint.

Turning to sentence type (26f), in which the complement is in preposed position, the predicted response pattern will depend on an additional hypothesis concerning the level of structure at which control is determined in children's grammar. The use of underlying rather than surface structure to determine control was proposed above as a (universal) feature of adult grammar. A model of acquisition in which putative universals shape the child's rules leads us to assume the following:

4. Children will determine control relations with reference to
   underlying rather than derived phrase structure.

If the child generates participials in final position and uses underlying structure to determine the complement subject, it is possible for the pattern of responses for the preposed condition to be the same as for the nonpreposed condition. In particular, if children are found to permit object control for nonpreposed complements this response should also be possible when the complement is in initial position, even though there is no surface structure for preposed complements in which the matrix object can c-command the complement-subject position.

However, some previous research suggested that the interpretation of preposed complements might offer special difficulties for the child and result in a different array of responses for the preposed and sentence-final conditions. The possibility that the child would make preposed complements refer to an actor not mentioned in the sentence was considered a strong one, given the evidence gathered by a number of researchers (Tavakolian 1978a; Lust in this volume; Solan in this volume) that backward pronominal and null subject anaphora is avoided by children. In both Solan's work with sentences such as (27), with a pronominal subject in a preposed temporal complement, and Tavakolian's work with sentences such as those in (28), with pronominal and null subjects of infinitival subject clauses, children aged about 5 chose an actor not mentioned in the sentence as complement subject about 60 percent of the time in acting out sentences with dolls.

(27)   After he ran around, the dog hit the pig.
(28) a. For him to kiss the pig would make the duck happy.
     b. To kiss the pig would make the duck happy.

Lust (this volume) found that children aged 2–5 made significantly more correct responses in a sentence-repetition task to sentences with forward anaphora (such as (29a)) than to sentences (such as (29b)) with backward anaphora.

(29) a. While Tom was riding the horse, he looked around.
     b. While he was outside, John saw a fire truck.

Thus, it was considered likely that children aged about 5 would tend to interpret the subject of the complement in sentences such as (26f) as referring to an actor not mentioned in the sentence; this would mean that at a certain stage children would fail to observe the adult restriction that these complements are obligatorily controlled by an NP in the matrix sentence.

A doll-manipulation paradigm was used; the experimenter read the test sentences to the subject and he or she acted out the sentences with dolls. Ten 4-year-old, ten 5-year-old, and ten 6-year-old subjects were tested. Each subject responded to four tokens of each sentence type. The matrix and subordinate verbs were varied in order to minimize the possibility of lexically biased results: Ten different matrix verbs were used in conditions (26a, c, d, and f) and eleven different matrix verb-preposition combinations (with six different matrix verbs) were used in condition (26b). Eleven subordinate verbs were used, the same for each condition. (See table 7.1 for a list of the verbs and prepositions used.) The present tense was used in all the test sentences, as in the examples in (26). The temporal prepositions *while, before,* and *after* were used in conditions a, b, c, and f, and were evenly distributed through the conditions.

Each child received a different set of sentence tokens produced by randomly combining the matrix and subordinate verbs.[14] Four different orders of presentation were used. There were two sets of dolls (a boy, a girl, and a clown; a horse, a cow, and a dog), which were switched halfway through the questionnaire, each set occurring in the first part for half the subjects. Each doll occurred with equal frequency as subject and object and with equal frequency in combination with other dolls from the set. A set of inanimate objects (a basket, a fence, a toy watch, a block, and a string of beads) were used as objects of the subordinate clause.

At the beginning of the experiment, the experimenter taught the child how to act out sentences, using conjoined sentences as examples. Three dolls were always made available to the child with which to act

Table 7.1
Verbs and Prepositions Used in Experiments I and II

Experiment I

Matrix Verbs

  Conditions c, d, e, and f

bite (A)	kiss
bump	lick (A)
hit	pat (A)
hug	punch (H)
kick	tickle

  Condition b

bump (into)	sit (by, near, on (A))
jump (on (A); over (A))	stand (by, on (A), near)
lie down (near, by)	walk (past)
run (past)	

Subordinate Verbs (all conditions)

carry (basket)	pick up (basket/beads)
climb (onto, block)	push over (fence)
hold (basket)	put on (watch/beads)
jump (over, fence/block)	stand (on, block)
hop (over, block)	wear (watch/beads)
knock down (fence)	

Experiment II

Matrix Verbs

  Conditions a and b

bite	kiss
hit	lick
hug	pat
kick	tickle

  Condition c

stand (by, next to)
run (up to)
sit down (by, near)

Subordinate Verbs

  Conditions a and b

carry (watch/basket/beads)
hop (over, fence/block)
pick up (watch/beads/basket) (Condition b only, due to error)
push over (fence)
put on (beads/watch) (Condition a only, due to error)
wear (beads/watch)

Table 7.1 (continued)
  Condition c
  climb (onto, fence/block)
  do a somersault
  knock over (fence)
  jump (over, block/fence)
  pick up (beads/basket/watch)
  roll (over (intransitive))

Note: Locative prepositions used with the matrix verbs in condition (26b), experiment I, and condition (26c), experiment II, are given in parentheses. Some subordinate verbs occurred with locative/directional PPs, and some with direct-object NPs. The prepositions used with verbs taking a PP, and the props used with each verb as direct object or object of the preposition are given in parentheses. Thus, *jump (over, fence/block)* indicates that *jump* was followed by the transitive phrase *over the fence* or *over the block,* and *wear (watch/beads)* indicates that *wear* was followed by the NP *the watch* or *the beads.* For experiment I, *H* or *A* following a verb or preposition in the matrix verb lists indicates that that verb/preposition was used only when the matrix subject and object was human or animal, respectively.

out the sentences, even though only two were mentioned in each sentence.

The subject's responses were scored according to whether the matrix subject or object or the doll not mentioned in the sentence was made the subject of the subordinate clause.[15]

The results of experiment I are summarized in table 7.2, which presents the percentage of subject control for each condition by age.[16] The percentage of object control in each condition can be obtained by subtracting the percentage of subject control from 100, with the exception that in condition f there was 8.3 percent control by an actor not mentioned in the sentence for both 4- and 5-year-olds, and in condition c there was one response of this type by a 4-year-old.

For all age groups, there was use of object control for temporal participials in condition a, in which the active matrix sentence has a direct-object NP. The hypothesis that children optionally attach temporal complements to the VP before learning that these constructions are immediate constituents of the S node is thus supported, assuming that the *c*-command condition constrains children's grammars.

There is a progression over age toward subject control of temporal complements: in condition a. At age 4, all children permitted object control to some extent, whereas three 5-year-olds and four 6-year-olds

Table 7.2
Percentage of Subject-Control Responses in Experiment I

Age	Condition					
	a (Active Temporal NP)	b (Active Temporal PP)	c (Passive Temporal)	d (Active *tell*)	e (Passive *tell*)	f (Active Temporal Preposed)
4	45.0	67.5	86.7	5.0	86.7	42.5
5	60.8	80.8	83.3	2.5	91.7	52.5
6	67.5	85.0	91.7	17.5	90.0	65.8

gave no object-controlled responses for this condition. The trend toward subject control was not significant, however ($F(2,27) = 1.273$, $P = 0.296$). It may be that some children will never reach a stage in which they block control by the matrix object, since, as mentioned above, this area is subject to dialect variation in the adult grammar. However, the data are consistent with a picture of acquisition in which a syntactic restriction on attachment of temporals to the S node begins to emerge at around age 6.

The results with active *tell* sentences (d) replicate those of Maratsos (1974) and Tavakolian (1978b) for children aged 4 and 5. Children in all three age groups did well in interpreting active sentences with *tell* and *ask;*[17] by age 4 years, the child knows that these verbs have an obligatory complement that is controlled by the matrix object.

Maratsos's results with passive *tell* sentences (e) were also replicated. At 4 years, the child understands that the matrix subject in passive sentences with verbs of speaking is the controller of the complement. The failure of the passive *by* phrase to control was equally well mastered in condition c, with a temporal participial complement, in which the matrix verb was not a verb of speaking (the difference in the percentage of subject control for this condition and the *tell* passives was not significant ($F(1,27) = 0.213$, $P = 0.648$).

In general, there was little object control in the conditions in which the NP in the matrix verb phrase was the object of a preposition. The responses to condition b, with a locative PP in the VP, show that the object of a locative as well as passive PP is not generally made controller (the difference in the percentage of subject control of participials between active sentences with a direct object and those with a locative PP (a versus b) and between active direct-object sentences and passive sentences (a versus c) was significant at the 0.001 level in both cases). This is the result predicted under the hypothesis that the c-command constraint restricts children's rules of control. However, there is some tendency, especially among the younger subjects, to permit the object of a locative PP to control. The difference in the percentage of subject control for participials between the locative condition and the passive condition approaches significance ($F(1,27)= 3.333, P = 0.079$).

Turning to children's responses to preposed complements (condition f), we see that the pattern of results lends support to the hypothesis that control relationships are determined in children's grammar with reference to underlying rather than derived structure. Object control is found for the preposed condition (f) with approximately the same frequency as for the sentence-final condition (a), and the proportion of object-controlled responses is highly correlated across these two conditions ($r(28) = 0.692, P < 0.001$). This result is consistent with a theory of acquisition in which the child determines control at underlying structure subject to the c-command constraint and preposes complements to initial position.

The results with preposed complements in this experiment contrast with those of Tavakolian (1978a) for sentences with infinitival subjects (such as (28a, b)), and those of Solan (this volume) for sentences with preposed tensed complements with pronominal subjects, such as (27). For both these sentence types, children aged about 5 were found to make the complement coreferential with an actor not mentioned in the sentence in approximately 60 percent of their responses. By contrast, this response type accounts for only 8.3 percent of the responses of 4- and 5-year-olds to the preposed condition in experiment I. It appears, therefore, that by age 4 years children sharply distinguish temporal participials from both infinitival subject clauses with null or pronominal subjects and tensed temporal complements with pronominal subjects with respect to the interpretation of the complement subject.

How can this difference be accounted for? As observed above, there are two types of missing-NP-complement constructions: obligatory-control complements, for which the complement must be interpreted as coreferential with an NP in the matrix sentence, and optional-control complements, for which the subject can be interpreted as coreferential with an NP not mentioned in the sentence. Temporal participials are obligatory-control complements, while infinitival subjects are optional-control complements. In this respect, the interpretation of infinitival subjects is similar to the interpretation of definite pronouns. Pronominal coreference is always optional in the adult grammar in sentences such as (27). Thus, in (27) the pronoun may be interpreted as referring to a person not mentioned in the sentence.

We have seen that children seem to interpret pronominal subjects of preposed tensed temporal complements similarly to missing subjects of infinitival subject clauses, and differently from the missing subject of preposed participial clauses. Thus, it may be that children are sensitive to whether coreference between the complement subject and an NP in the matrix sentence is obligatory. They look outside the sentence for a complement subject only in the cases in which coreference is optional.[18]

Lust (this volume) observes that her results with backward pronominalization sentences such as (29b) are paralleled by results with backward conjunction reduction. For example, young children characteristically reduce redundancy in conjoined constructions only in a forward direction, and they make fewer errors in repeating sentences such as (30b), with forward reduction, than they do in repeating those with backward conjunction reduction, such as (31b).

(30) a. Kittens hop and kittens run.
     b. Kittens hop and Ø run.
(31) a. Kittens hide and dogs hide.
     b. Kittens Ø and dogs hide.

Lust proposes that a single constraint governs the directionality of both pronominal and null anaphora at an early stage, and that (at least for English) backward anaphora will be blocked. I have suggested that the child restricts backward coreference only in cases of optional anaphora. It is not immediately clear that this proposal can cover the data discussed by Lust—in (31b), for example, the deleted element is obligatorily associated with a constituent in the sentence, and so anaphora is not optional in the same sense as for pronominal anaphora. Possibly the correct notion of "optional" with respect to the difficulty of backward anaphora for children refers to the possibility of an alternating structure in which a full lexical phrase can appear in place of the pronominal or null form (as in (29)–(31)).[19] Clearly, this area deserves further research.[20]

2.2.2 *Experiment II.* Experiment II tested the hypothesis that Tavakolian's (1978b) results with *(in order) to* clauses in sentences such as (23) ("The cow walked around the pig to kiss the lion"), which suggested that children rarely overgeneralized object control, reflected the child's knowledge that the object of a preposition may not be a controller.

Children were tested for their comprehension of the sentence types in (32).[21]

(32) a. Active matrix sentence with a direct-object NP and a temporal participial complement:
Daisy hits Pluto after putting on the watch.
  b. Active matrix sentence with a direct-object NP and a reduced *(in order) to* complement:
Daisy hits Pluto to put on the watch.
  c. Active matrix sentence with a locative PP in the VP and a reduced *(in order) to* complement:
Daisy stands near Pluto to do a somersault.

Under the same hypotheses that were made for experiment I—that control by the object of a preposition is blocked by the *c*-command constraint on control and that children may attach complements to the VP—overgeneralization of object control is predicted for conditions a and b, but not condition c.

As with experiment I, a toy-manipulation paradigm was used. The subjects were ten 4-year-old and ten 5-year-old children. Each subject responded to three tokens of each sentence type. Eight different matrix verbs were used in conditions a and b, and five subordinate verbs. In condition c there were five different combinations of matrix verbs and prepositions (with three different verbs) and six subordinate verbs. In selecting the matrix verbs for the experiment, care was taken to exclude any verb that subcategorized for a purpose clause, since purpose clauses are object-controlled (see note 2). Thus, the only correct adult interpretation of the *(in order) to* sentences used in experiment II was subject control of the complement. A complete list of the verbs used is given in table 7.1. The present tense was used in all the test sentences. Each child responded to one sentence with each of the prepositions *while, before,* and *after* in condition a.

Each child received a different set of sentence tokens produced by randomly combining the matrix and subordinate verbs for each condition.[22] The test sentences were presented in three blocks of one token of each condition, and three different orders of presentation were used in the questionnaires. The subject and object of the matrix sentence were two of a set of three toy animals (a horse, a cow, and a dog). Each

Table 7.3
Percentage of Subject-Control Responses in Experiment II

	Sentence Type		
Age	a (Temporal, Complement, Direct Object)	b (*In order to,* Complement, Direct Object)	c (*In order to* Complement, PP)
4	66.70	56.70	90.10
5	63.40	63.40	90.10
Mean	65.05	60.05	90.10

toy was used with equal frequency as subject and object in each condition, and occurred an equal number of times in combination with the other toys. To block a relative-clause interpretation of the sentences with *(in order) to* complements, the toy animals used in the experiment were given names (Daisy, Champion, and Pluto), which were used in the test sentences (a proper name may not head a relative clause in English). A number of inanimate objects (a basket, a block, a fence, a toy watch, and a string of beads) were used as objects in the subordinate clause.

Before the experiment began, the experimenter taught the subject the names used for the toy animals in the experiment. As the children had just completed another toy-manipulation experiment (not reported here), no further training was necessary.

The results of experiment II are summarized in table 7.3, which presents the percentage of subject control for each condition by age. The predictions made for experiment II are borne out by the results. Object control was overgeneralized in the case of both temporal and *(in order) to* complements when there was a direct object in the matrix verb phrase. When the NP in the matrix verb phrase was the object of a locative PP, however, object control was not overgeneralized for *(in order) to* complements. (The difference in the percentage of object control for conditions b and c is highly significant ($F(1,18) = 17.320$, $P = 0.001$); the difference for conditions a and b is not significant ($F(1,18) = 0.564$, $P = 0.462$).)

The distinction between the direct object and PP conditions with respect to object control for *(in order) to* clauses in this experiment supports the hypothesis that the lack of overgeneralization of object control in Tavakolian's results with *(in order) to* complements can be accounted for as a block on control by the object of a preposition. As noted above, Tavakolian's test sentences all had the syntactic structure in (23) ("The cow walked around the pig to kiss the lion"), with a PP rather than a direct object in the matrix VP.

3 Conclusions

The experiments reported here were designed to test the presence of two putative linguistic universals in children's grammar: First, the c-command condition on control, which requires that the complement clause be attached to the VP in order for it to be controlled by a direct object and which blocks control of a complement by the object of a preposition unless the complement is itself a constituent of the PP, and second, the application of rules of control with reference to underlying rather than derived structure.

It was found that children's interpretations of participial and *(in order) to* complements at age 4 are compatible with the c-command condition, provided that it is hypothesized that children may attach these complement types, which modify the S node in adult grammar, to the VP. Children permitted both subject and object control of the complement in sentences such as *The girl hits the boy after jumping over the fence,* but did not on the whole permit control of a complement by the object of a preposition—children avoided making *the boy* the subject of *jump* in *The girl stands near the boy after jumping over the fence* and *The girl is hit by the boy after jumping over the fence.*

In this picture of the child's grammar, the fact that children permit the direct object to be controller in preposed as well as in sentence-final complements (*After jumping over the fence, the boy hits the girl*) was interpreted as support for the presence in the child's grammar of the second of the candidate universals: the application of control rules with reference to underlying structure.

To the extent that the data are consistent with principles governing adult grammar, the results of these experiments can be interpreted as support for a model of language acquisition in which the child's hypotheses about the structure of his language are limited by universal grammar.

Results of this kind can also be viewed from another perspective. Acquisition data may be regarded as one kind of evidence in linguistic theory. The grammar of complement-subject interpretation has held a prominent place in the work of linguists for a number of years and has been approached from several theoretical standpoints. The degree to which the particular lingustic theories drawn on here have proved adequate for the description of children's grammar can be interpreted as a measure of support for those theories. That the c-command constraint on control and the interpretation of complement subjects at a level prior to the surface appear to govern children's grammars lends credence to the assumption that these conditions are universals.

In addition, given that certain clear-cut distinctions in the adult grammar are reflected in children's language, it appears reasonable to look to acquisition evidence for pointers in areas where the grammar of the adult language has proved more intractable. For example, cases such as *rely on* appear to be counterexamples to the syntactic c-command condition on control, and provide motivation for theories of control that make reference to semantic as well as syntactic structure. In the results of the first experiment, there was some tendency among younger subjects to permit control by the object of a locative PP. To the extent that this trend in the data parallels cases such as *rely on* in adult language, it provides support for theories of grammar that attempt to treat *rely on* and similar examples as more than arbitrary exceptions.

To give another example, a distinction was drawn between obligatory-control complements (such as temporal participials and the infinitival complement of *tell*), which require that the complement subject be interpreted as coreferential with a c-commanding NP, and free-control complements (such as infinitival subject clauses), which are not subject to the same condition. In experiment I, children almost invariably chose one of the NPs in the matrix sentence as the subject of a participial complement, regardless of whether the complement was in preposed or sentence-final position. By contrast, in experiments with infinitival subject complements (Tavakolian 1978b), children showed a preference for choosing an NP not mentioned in the sentence as complement subject. The fact that children distinguish between these complement types in their selection of complement subjects can be taken as support for linguistic analyses in which they are treated differently, even though linguists' attempts to establish criteria for distinguishing obligatory and free control complements have not been entirely successful.[19]

Just as acquisition evidence may be used to support aspects of the theory of grammar based on analysis of the adult language, it may lead us to question the generality of other principles. Some conditions governing the adult grammar are not observed by children—such results are found in Matthei's study (in this volume) of sentences containing reciprocals. As the body of evidence in favor of the presence of some types of universals in child language accrues, such negative cases deserve to be taken all the more seriously with respect to their implications for the status in the theory of grammar of the principles under investigation.

In sum, the hypothesis that universals limit the child's grammar is at present the best explanation of the fact that children's analyses of the input data are in general heavily restricted. Candidate universals offer a rich source of predictions concerning the organization of children's grammar, and confirmation of these predictions provides evidence concerning both the structure of the LAD and the status of putative universals in linguistic theory.[23]

The presence of universals in children's grammar limits the range of possible grammars that the child may form on the path to adult mastery of the language; it does not, however, necessarily tell us anything about the way in which the child selects a particular grammar or moves from one preadult stage to the next. For example, on what basis does the child reject the hypothesis that a temporal participial complement can be object-controlled? The child will hear sentences whose context and grammar support a subject-controlled reading (*The dog bit the boy after shaking itself*), but will never receive input that forces him to revise his grammar to eliminate the option of object control (for relevant discussion see Baker 1977). The problem of how the child revises his grammar to conform with the adult grammar is a pressing one for acquisition theory. With respect to the constructions studied in this chapter, the development of subject control for temporal and *(in order) to* clauses might follow from a simplicity criterion operating in conjunction with the c-command condition. Adoption of an S-attachment analysis reduces the number of possible controllers in the sentence down to the subject, and no special control rule is needed for these constructions.

Notes

I wish to thank Charles Clifton, Barbara Hall Partee, Edwin Williams, and especially Tom Roeper for essential advice and help in the course of the research. I have also benefited from many discussions on this work with Larry Solan and Susan Tavakolian, and from helpful comments from Elisabet Engdahl, Paul Hirschbühler, and Steve Lapointe. The experimental work was carried out with the cooperation of the staff and children of the following schools: The Little Red School House, Amherst, Massachusetts; The Living and Learning School, Amherst; South Hadley Child Care Center, South Hadley, Massachusetts; Tiny Tots Day Care Center, Chicopee Falls, Massachusetts; Wildwood School, Amherst. I am grateful to these schools for their help and interest, and also to Lori Taft for assisting me in administering experiment I. This work was supported in part by NIH Grant HD90647–03 to Thomas Roeper and S. Jay Keyser, and in part by a PEO International Peace Scholarship to the author. An earlier version of the chapter was presented at the University of Massachusetts Language Acquisition Conference, April 1978.

1. For discussion, see, for example, Chomsky 1975b: ch. 1.

2. *(In order) to* clauses must be distinguished from purpose clauses, such as the complement to *choose* in *John chose Bill to mow the lawn.* Purpose clauses are object-controlled, and exhibit different syntactic behavior than *(in order) to* clauses. Purpose clauses will not be dealt with in this study.

3. Sentence (7a) is ambiguous between *John* and *Bill* as the subject of *hit.* This ambiguity results from attachment of the participial complement to either the matrix S node or the S complement to *tell.* The point concerning the unmarked order of clauses holds under either reading.

4. The above tests are derived from Williams 1975; as the reader can verify, they indicate that purpose clauses (note 2) are VP rather than S constituents.

5. As Reinhart (1976) notes, it is possible that constituents "preposed" from S are base-generated in initial position, along the lines of some recent analyses of topicalized and presentential constituents. I will talk here in terms of a preposing rule, assuming that even if sentence-initial temporal PPs are base-generated the discussion of initial and final complements could be restated in terms of rules at some level of grammar at which these constructions are treated as equivalent.

6. This approach contrasts with earlier analyses within a transformational framework (see, for example, Rosenbaum 1967) in which the complement-subject position is filled by a full NP in deep structure that is deleted by a transformation (Equi-NP-deletion). The difference between these analyses is not crucial to the purpose of this chapter.

7. Complements to passive sentences will be referred to as subject-controlled, since their subject is interpreted as referring to the matrix subject. However, it should be noted that their derivation may involve the control rule applying with reference to the trace of the direct-object NP (under a movement analysis of passive sentences, as in, for example, Chomsky 1978).

8. Even if constituents preposed from S attach to $\overline{S}$, this node may not block the matrix-subject NP from c-commanding the complement-subject position, since the definition of c-command may be refined to make a node and a branching node of the same type that it immediately dominates ($\overline{S}$ and S in this case) count as equivalent to a single node (see Reinhart 1976).

9. These sentences were supplied by E. Engdahl.

10. Chomsky called this rule for interpreting complement subjects the Minimum Distance Principle, a term adopted from Rosenbaum (1967), who used the term with reference to a structural principle of node counting.

11. Tavakolian suggested that her results with *(in order) to* clauses be interpreted as evidence that children build up subcategorization frames on the basis of verb class semantics. *Tell* and other verbs of speaking would be subcategorized for an infinitive complement in the VP, but verbs from other semantic classes would not have this subcategorization frame; hence the failure to overgeneralize object control in her results with *(in order) to* clauses would be explained, given that a complement must attach to (be subcategorized for) the VP to be object-controlled. Roeper and I, by contrast, proposed that children under 5 do not restrict subcategorization frames in terms of verb-class semantics. The results of the present experiment are consistent with a theory of language acquisition in which subcategorization frames are subject to overgeneralization.

12. In addition to the structures listed in (26), children in this experiment also responded to sentences with subject-relative clauses modifying the object NP (such as *The boy hits the girl that jumps over the fence*) and sentences with the main verb *promise* (for example, *The boy promises the girl to jump over the fence*). In general, children performed much better in interpreting the relative-clause sentences than had been anticipated on the basis of some previous research (Sheldon 1974; Tavakolian, this volume), with 87, 65, and 85 percent correct responses for 4-, 5-, and 6-year-olds, respectively. This result is discussed in some detail in Goodluck 1978 (ch. 4). With *promise,* the results replicate those of previous researchers (Maratsos 1974; Chomsky 1969; Tavakolian 1978b). At age 4 there is overgeneralization of object control to the complement of *promise* sentences in 75 percent of responses. By age 5 and 6 the proportion of incorrect responses goes down to 55 percent and 30 percent, respectively.

13. The hypothesis that children may analyze complements to the S node as VP modifiers presupposes that children have a VP node in their grammar—that is, that an NP – V – NP sequence is analyzed as $_S[NP - _{VP}[V - NP]]$ rather than simply $_S[NP - V - NP]$. If the child had no VP node, the complement could only attach to the S node, and object control would not involve violation of the *c*-command condition. Although strong evidence for a VP node is lacking in the child's earliest grammar (around age 2; see Bowerman 1973:178–83), Solan and Roeper (1978) present data that argue for the presence of a VP node in the child's grammar at around 4 years, which is the age of the youngest subjects in our experiments. Given that children by age 4 have a VP in their grammars, the assumption that temporal complements may be analyzed as VP constituents will be necessary for any cases of object control by the matrix object if the hypothesis that children will not violate the *c*-command constraint on control is to be preserved.

14. Combinations that were judged to be biased toward subject or object control (for example, *The boy sits by the girl while jumping over the fence*) were excluded, as were sentences with identical matrix and subordinate verbs. To ensure relatively natural-sounding sentences, the preposition *while* was used primarily with the subordinate verbs *wear, carry,* and *hold; before* and *after* were used with the remaining subordinate verbs.

15. The order in which the main and subordinate verbs were acted out was also scored in most cases. Overall, the order of acting out indicates that children in all age groups did pay attention to the meaning of the temporal prepositions *while*, *before*, and *after*, even though they may not have understood them correctly in every case.

16. Responses were included in the data only if the (active or passive) matrix sentence was acted out correctly. Seventeen of 236 responses to passive sentences, 3 of 359 responses to active sentences in the nonpreposed conditions, and 3 of 118 responses to the preposed condition were excluded as incorrect or unclear. Seven responses were lost through experimental error.

17. The drop in performance of 6-year-old children with this sentence type is assumed to be accidental. Five 6-year-old children made a total of seven subject-controlled responses to this sentence type.

18. It should be noted that Tavakolian (1978a) assumes the complement-subject position in sentences such as (28b) to be subject to obligatory control. That control is optional in this construction can be seen more clearly from sentences such as *To take Mary out at this hour would annoy her father,* in which the preferred reading is one in which *her father* is *not* interpreted as the complement subject.

19. It has been suggested (Partee 1975; Chomsky and Lasnik 1977; Williams 1978) that a distinguishing property of those complements for which control is obligatory in the adult grammar is that they do not permit alternation between a missing subject and a lexical NP. Optional-control complements do permit alternation of this kind. Thus, (ib) and (iib) contrast with (iiib).

(i) a.   John told Bill to grab the jewels.
    b.   *John told Bill for Tom to grab the jewels.
(ii) a.   John hit Bill after grabbing the jewels.
    b.   *John hit Bill after Sue grabbing the jewels.
(iii) a.   To have committed such a crime was abhorrent to Bill.
    b.   For Sue to have committed such a crime was abhorrent to Bill.

However, this criterion for distinguishing free- and optional-control complements does not give us the right results in all cases. It predicts that *(in order) to* complements should not be obligatory-control complements:

John hit Bill (in order) to grab the jewels.
John hit Bill (in order) for Sue to grab the jewels.

20. An alternative approach to the contrast in results for preposed temporals and the results for pronouns and infinitival subject clauses might be taken in terms of an avoidance of backwards coreference in conjunction with a distinction in the level of application for rules of control and proform interpretation: control applying with reference to underlying structure, and pronoun interpretation applying at a level nearer the surface (that is, after preposing). The interpretation of definite pronouns and other anaphoric elements with reference to surface structure has been a feature of most recent analyses of

anaphora (see, for example, Reinhart 1976), but is not without problems, at least with respect to definite-pronoun anaphora (Solan 1978).

However, experimental data I have collected since this chapter was originally written suggest that neither a distinction in level of interpretation nor one between obligatory and optional coreference is alone sufficient to account for children's responses to these sentence types, and that the results for preposed and sentence-final temporal clauses in experiment I may in part be an artifact of the experimental design. In these recent experiments, children aged 5–6 treat the different complement types and null and pronominal anaphoric elements discussed here similarly, and vary as to whether they prefer internal or external coreference of the complement-subject position when the subject precedes its (potential) antecedent in surface structure. Definite pronouns and missing NPs are distinguished to some degree, however, with internal coreference occurring more frequently in the case of missing NPs. These results suggest that the obligatory-optional distinction may be relevant in accounting for children's treatment of the different proforms, but at the level of unmarked rules in the theory of grammar rather than at the level of the particular rules of the language being acquired.

21. It was originally hypothesized that semantic bias toward subject control might have contributed to the high percentage of correct responses in Tavakolian's results. The materials for conditions (30a)–(30c) were constructed to be as neutral as possible with respect to the plausibility of the matrix subject and matrix object as controller. Children in experiment II also responded to *(in order) to* clauses with the syntactic structure of (30b) and (30c), which were semantically biased toward subject control. This semantic bias did correlate with a high percentage of subject-controlled responses for both sentence types (over 85 percent). In addition, sentences with the main verb *tell* and *ask* and an infinitive complement were included in the questionnaires as a check that children who showed a high percentage of subject control (the correct adult response) for the other test sentences did distinguish between complement types with respect to control. (There was over 85 percent object control for *tell/ask* sentences.)

22. The use of verbs and prepositions was subject to the same constraints as for experiment I (note 4).

23. This is essentially the approach to the study of language-acquisition (or, more generally, of learning in any cognitive domain) put forward by Chomsky in *Reflections on Language* (1975b:15–16).

8

The Conjoined-Clause
Analysis of Relative Clauses

Susan L. Tavakolian

A key assumption in recent theories of language is that there are universal linguistic principles and schemata that greatly limit the kinds of assumptions a child brings to the language-learning task. Universal aspects of language are assumed to result from the biological composition of the human mind, and therefore to be an innately determined set of schemata and principles that limit the set of possible grammars. The existence of such schemata and principles greatly simplifies the task of a child learning the language of his community. The child approaches the data presented to him with a predetermined set of principles that restrict the nature of the hypotheses he can make about the structure of a given language.

The existence of universal aspects of language has been widely accepted by researchers in language acquisition, but the identification of specific universals and their relationship to other areas of cognitive development are unresolved issues. One general approach to the latter problem has emphasized the independence of linguistic structure from other cognitive systems.[1] Other approaches have proposed that linguistic systems are extensions of more general cognitive properties (Sinclair 1975; Piaget 1974). The discovery of linguistic universals, regardless of their ultimate relationship to other cognitive structures, will tell us what kinds of implicit knowledge a child may rely on in learning a language.

This chapter presents evidence for the existence of one such intrinsic principle: the conjoined-clause analysis. Experimental data show that children impose a conjoined-clause structure on multiple-clause sentences.[2] I propose that this conjoined-clause analysis facilitates language learning by providing the child with a predetermined hypothesis about the structure and interpretation of multiple-clause strings.

1   The Conjoined-Clause Analysis

Consider a schematized string such as

(1) NP . . . V . . . NP . . . V . . . NP

where the ellipses indicate that material such as a relative pronoun or a conjunction (but not a noun phrase or a verb) may intervene between the noun phrase and the verb. I propose that a child's first hypothesis about the structure of such a string is that it consists of two conjoined simplex sentences. The structure shown in (2) will be assigned to string (1).

(2) $_S[_S[NP - V - NP] _S[\Delta - V - NP]]$

In (2) the string is parsed into two simplex sentences, with the first NP – V – NP sequence grouped together as a simplex sentence. The second clause is composed of the remaining V–NP sequence, plus a "missing" subject, indicated by Δ. I propose that the child postulates this phonologically null form as the subject of the second clause and interprets it as being coreferential with the subject of the first clause, as shown by the arrow.

The proposed conjoined-clause analysis consists of the following set of rules: a rule for assigning conjoined-clause structure to multiple-clause sentences, the postulation of a phonologically null subject in the second clause, and a rule for assigning an antecedent to the missing subject. I propose that the rule for assigning an antecedent to the missing subject is identical to the rule used to determine the referent of a missing subject in true conjoined clauses, as in (3).

(3) $_S[_S[\text{Max ate the sandwich}] \text{ and } _S[\Delta \text{ drank the milk}]]$

That is, children use a rule that already exists in their grammars to determine a referent for the missing subject.

It is argued that this set of rules is established in a child's grammar very early and is utilized in interpreting more difficult and unfamiliar constructions. If the linear order of noun phrases and verbs in a multiple-clause sentence varies from the order specified in the conjoined-clause analysis, the sentence type will be eliminated from the conjoined-clause analysis earlier than sentences that do have the same order of elements as conjoined clauses. In the latter case, where the linear order of elements in a sentence is the same as the order in conjoined sentences, children will continue to use the conjoined-clause analysis to assign clausal structure to the sentence and to interpret missing elements. Until the child has mastered the adult system, he will continue to use the conjoined-clause analysis even when this results in an incorrect interpretation of the sentence.

The evidence I will present from children's responses to relative clauses supports the proposal that children utilize a conjoined-clause analysis to interpret multiple-clause sentences that their grammar does not yet generate and also indicates that the conjoined-clause analysis is a very widely used set of rules.

2   An Experiment on Relative Clauses

Relative clauses are a particularly difficult construction for children to produce (Menyuk 1969; Limber 1973), comprehend (Gaer 1969; H. D. Brown 1971; Sheldon 1974; Legum 1975), and imitate (C. Smith 1970; Slobin and Welsh 1973; M. Smith 1974). For this reason they offer a rich source of data on children's rules for comprehending sentences that their grammars do not yet generate. An underlying assumption of this study is that children will rely on the grammatical rules they already possess in an attempt to process difficult or unfamiliar constructions, even though these already existing rules may be inappropriate for the data at hand.

Four types of relative clauses will be analyzed; they are distinguished by the functional role of the head NP and of the relativized NP. In two types, the role of the head and of the relativized NP is the same; both are either the subject or the object of their respective clauses. In the other two types, the head NP and the relativized NP have different functions in their respective clauses. The four types are abbreviated as shown in table 8.1. The sentences shown in (4) are examples of these types.

(4) SS: The sheep that jumps over the rabbit stands on the lion.
    SO: The lion that the horse kisses knocks down the duck.
    OO: The horse hits the sheep that the duck kisses.
    OS: The duck stands on the lion that bumps into the pig.

The experiments on which this analysis is based consisted of a comprehension task involving 24 children aged 3–5 years. Eight 3-year-olds, eight 4-year-olds, and eight 5-year-olds were interviewed. The children were all nursery-school students and came from a wide variety

Table 8.1
The Four Types of Relative Clauses Analyzed

Function of Head in Main Clause	Function of Relativized NP in Relative Clause	Abbreviation[a]
subject	subject	SS
subject	object	SO
object	object	OO
object	subject	OS

a. S indicates that the NP is the subject of its own clause and O indicates that the NP is the object of its own clause.

of economic backgrounds. All were monolingual native speakers of standard English and without any known mental or language impairments.

The experiment consisted of four questionnaires. Each questionnaire was constructed by randomly assigning six animal names (*lion, pig, horse, sheep, duck, rabbit*) to the NP slots in each relative-clause type and also randomizing the eight verbals used (*bump into, jump over, walk around, kiss, hit, stand on, knock down, kick*). The only restriction was that no verb or animal was repeated within the same sentence. The list of sentences obtained in this way was then randomized. Each questionnaire contained three tokens of each sentence type; that is, there were three SS relative clauses, three SO relatives, three OO relatives, and three OS relatives. In addition each questionnaire contained three simple active declarative sentences, for a total of 15 sentences on each questionnaire. The four questionnaires were distributed among the three age groups so that two 3-year-olds, two 4-year-olds, and two 5-year-olds responded to each questionnaire.

The test situation consisted of small toy animals that the child manipulated to act out the test sentences. The questionnaire was administered to each child individually. Each child named the animals and acted out two trial sentences to make sure that he understood the nature of the task. Three animals were placed in front of the child for each sentence. The children easily comprehended the task and enjoyed moving the animals.

The conjoined-clause analysis predicts that children will structurally analyze each of the different types of relative clauses shown in (4) as consisting of conjoined simplex sentences. It also predicts that when a noun phrase is "missing" in surface structure, children will posit a

Table 8.2
General Scheme of Imposition of Conjoined-Clause Analysis on the
Four Types of Relative Clauses Analyzed

Conjoined-Clause Schema	$_S[\ _S[NP - V - NP]\ _S[\Delta - V - NP]]$
SS Relative Clauses	
Children's parsing	$_S[\ _S[NP - \mathit{that} - V - NP]\ _S[\Delta - V - NP]]$
Adult parsing	$_S[NP\ _S[\mathit{that} - V - NP] - V - NP]$
OS Relative Clauses	
Children's parsing	$_S[\ _S[NP - V - NP]\ \mathit{that}\ _S[\Delta - V - NP]]$
Adult parsing	$_S[NP - V - NP\ _S[\mathit{that} - V - NP]]$
SO Relative Clauses	
Children's parsing	$_S[\ _S[NP\ \mathit{that}\ NP - V]\ _S[\Delta - V - NP]]$
	or
	$_S[\ _S[NP\ \mathit{that}\ NP - V]\ _S[\Delta - V - NP]]$
Adult parsing	$_S[NP\ _S[\mathit{that}\ NP - V] - V - NP]$
OO Relative Clauses	
Children's parsing	$_S[\ _S[NP - V - NP]\ \mathit{that}\ _S[\Delta\ _{VP}[NP - V]]$
Adult parsing	$_S[NP - V - NP\ _S[\mathit{that}\ NP - V]]$

missing subject NP in the second clause and will interpret it as being
coreferential with the subject of the first clause. Table 8.2 indicates in
general schematic form how the conjoined clause analysis is imposed
on each relative clause type. Adult parsings of clausal boundaries are
also indicated for comparison.

In each case the first two NPs and the first verb are grouped together
as a simplex sentence. The remaining noun phrase and verb plus a
postulated missing subject constitute the second clause. The missing
subject is interpreted as being coreferential with the subject of the first
clause.

Consider now in greater detail the exact interpretation proposed for
each type of relative clause. In SS relatives the first NP–V–NP se-

Table 8.3
Distribution of Responses to SS Relative Clauses

$$\text{The }\overset{1}{\text{sheep that knocks down the }}\overset{2}{\text{rabbit stands on the }}\overset{3}{\text{lion.}}$$

Age	Response Categories				
	12,13 Correct	12,23	21,23	12,32	Other
3 years	18	2	1	0	3
4 years	16	5	1	0	2
5 years	22	0	0	2	0
Total	56	7	2	2	5
Percentage	78%	10%	3%	3%	7%

Table 8.4
Distribution of Responses to SO Relative Clauses

$$\text{The }\overset{1}{\text{lion that the }}\overset{2}{\text{horse kisses knocks down the }}\overset{3}{\text{duck.}}$$

Age	Response Categories						
	21,13 Correct	21,23	12,13	13,23	21,32	31,13	Other
3 years	5	4	5	4	0	0	6
4 years	6	5	8	0	2	1	2
5 years	4	6	9	1	0	1	3
Total	15	15	22	5	2	2	11
Percentage	21%	21%	31%	7%	3%	3%	15%

quence is parsed as a simplex sentence. This leaves a V–NP sequence remaining for the second clause. Positing a phonologically null subject will fill the gap in the second clause, and the missing subject can be assigned an antecedent by using the same rule in true conjoined clauses. Under this analysis a child would analyze an SS relative as shown in (5).

(5) $_S$[$_S$[the sheep that jumps over the rabbit] $_S$[Δ stands on the lion]]

Table 8.5
Distribution of Responses to OO Relative Clauses

    1   2   3
The horse hits the sheep that the duck kisses.

Age	Response Categories						
	12,32 Correct	12,13	12,31	12,12	31,32	12,23	Other
3 years	8	4	5	2	1	0	4
4 years	9	5	6	0	1	1	2
5 years	10	5	5	1	0	2	1
Total	27	14	16	3	2	3	7
Percentage	38%	19%	22%	4%	3%	4%	10%

The subject of the second clause is interpreted as being coreferential with the subject of the first clause. This interpretation is indistinguishable from the correct interpretation of true restrictive SS relatives when both are acted out with toy animals, as was the case in this study. Therefore, one would expect there to be a high percentage of correct responses to this relative-clause type, not only because some children correctly analyze the sentence, but also because application of the conjoined-clause analysis results in the correct response. This expectation is confirmed by children's comprehension of SS relatives. Seventy-eight percent of the responses to SS relatives received a correct response. The other 22 percent of the responses were distributed across eight different response categories. The preponderance of responses follow the pattern predicted by the conjoined-clause analysis.

See tables 8.3–8.7 for a complete distribution of responses to each relative clause type. The coded responses in each table refer to the occurrence of the NP in the linear order of the string. This coding system is adopted from Sheldon 1972. The number 1 refers to the first NP in the string, number 2 to the second NP, and number 3 to the third NP. The first number in each two-number sequence indicates the noun phrase functioning as the subject of the first verb, and the second number designates the noun phrase functioning as the object of the first verb. Each sentence has two double-number sequences. The first two numbers indicate the noun phrase functioning as subject and object of the first verb, and the second two numbers indicate the noun phrases

Table 8.6
Distribution of Responses to OS Relative Clauses

1	2	3

The lion stands on the duck that bumps into the pig.

Age	Response Categories					
	12,23 Correct	12,13	12,31	12,32	21,23	Other
3 years	1	17	1	2	1	2
4 years	4	15	3	1	0	1
5 years	9	13	1	0	1	0
Total	14	45	5	3	2	3
Percentage	19%	63%	7%	4%	3%	4%

Table 8.7
Percentage of Responses for which Each Response Category Accounts

Response Category	Relative-Clause Type				
	SS	OS	SO	OO	All Types Combined
12,13	78%[a]	63%	31%	20%	48%
12,32	3%	4%	1%	38%[a]	11%
12,23	10%	19%[a]	1%	4%	9%
21,13	1%	0	21%[a]	1%	6%
21,23	3%	3%	21%	0	6%
12,31	1%	7%	0	22%	8%
The other 19 response categories	4%	4%	21%	15%	12%
Total	100%	100%	100%	100%	100%

a. (Correct response.)

functioning as subject and object of the second verb. For example, the
response 12,13 to the OS relative clause (6)

     1   2   3
(6) The rabbit kisses the horse that jumps over the lion.

indicates that the first NP, *the rabbit,* is the subject of the first verb,
kisses, and that the second NP, *the horse,* is the object of *kiss.* The
second two numbers indicate that the first NP is also the subject of the
second verb, *jumps,* and that the third NP is the object of *jump.*

The "other" category in each table gives the number of unique responses to each relative clause. This is the number of response categories that had only one response in them.

The high percentage of correct responses to SS relative clauses
would be quite unusual if we assumed that the responses indicate a true
restrictive relative clause interpretation by children. Menyuk (1969:16)
reports that even by age 7 children rarely produce utterances in which
the matrix subject is relativized.[3] If the correct responses to SS relatives indicated a true restrictive relative-clause interpretation, the gap
between correct comprehension at 3–5 years and spontaneous production at age 7 or later would be 2–4 years. This is quite a large difference, and it seems unlikely that production lags so far behind
comprehension. A more plausible explanation of the difference lies in
the present proposal that many children derive the correct response to
SS relatives by utilizing the conjoined-clause analysis, which also happens to provide the correct response.

Consider now OS relatives such as (7).

(7) The sheep jumps over the rabbit that stands on the lion.

As with SS relatives, the initial NP–V–NP sequence forms a simplex
sentence. The second clause consists of the remaining V–NP sequence
and an inserted phonologically null subject. The subject is then interpreted as being coreferential with the subject of the first clause, using
the same rule necessary for missing subject interpretation in actual
conjoined clauses. The OS relative clause in (7) would be interpreted as
shown in (8).

(8) $_S$[$_S$[the sheep jumps over the rabbit] that $_S$[Δ stands on the lion]]

This predicted response is given to 63 percent of the OS relatives.[4]
Approximately half of the remaining 37 percent were correct re-

sponses, and the rest were distributed over six different response categories. As with SS relatives the predicted response accounts for the preponderance of children's responses. The high percentage of conjoined-clause responses to OS relatives, which is an incorrect adult response, indicates that children have a set of rules that are easily applicable to OS relatives to provide an interpretation, even though the interpretation is incorrect. It also shows that many children do not have an adult restrictive relative-clause interpretation of these sentences, since in this case the conjoined-clause analysis results in an incorrect response to the relatives. This provides further support for the contention that children's correct responses to SS relatives are not due primarily to a restrictive relative-clause interpretation, but instead reflect utilization of the conjoined-clause analysis.

The percentage of predicted responses to OS relatives is nearly as high as the percentage of predicted responses to SS relatives, and the difference between them is not statistically significant ($t = 1.157$, $df = 23, P > 0.2$). This is the result we would expect if children treat OS and SS relatives as though they were structurally identical; that is, if they analyze both strings as consisting of conjoined clauses with a missing subject in the second clause.

Consider now the third type of relative clause: the SO relative such as (9).

(9) The sheep that the rabbit jumps over stands on the lion.

The conjoined-clause analysis predicts two response types to SO relatives, depending on which NP is selected as the subject of the first clause. In both the predicted children's parsings of SO relatives the initial NP – NP – V sequence is grouped as a simplex sentence, and the second clause consists of a missing subject plus the remaining V – NP sequence. Also in both cases, the missing subject is interpreted as being coreferential with the subject of the first clause. The difference between the two responses lies in the choice of subject in the first clause. The sentence-initial noun phrase is the subject in the response shown in (10a) and the second NP in the string is the subject of the first clause in (10b).

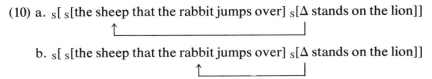

(10) a. ₛ[ₛ[the sheep that the rabbit jumps over] ₛ[Δ stands on the lion]]

b. ₛ[ₛ[the sheep that the rabbit jumps over] ₛ[Δ stands on the lion]]

This difference in the choice of subject does not bear directly on the arguments for children's use of the conjoined-clause analysis. The response shown in (10a) accounts for 31 percent of the responses to SO relatives, and the response in (10b) accounts for 21 percent of the responses. So 52 percent of the total number of responses to SO relatives can be accounted for by the conjoined-clause analysis. This percentage of predicted responses is not as high as the percentages for SS and OS relatives, but it is much higher than the percentage of responses accounted for by any other category of SO responses.

The final relative clauses to consider are the OO relatives such as (11).

(11) The sheep jumps over the rabbit that the lion stands on.

The first NP – V – NP sequence is grouped together as a simplex sentence. The second clause is analyzed as lacking a subject, even though one is present in the string, and the postulated missing subject is interpreted as being coreferential with the subject of the first clause. The preverbal NP in the second clause is analyzed as the object of the second verb. Children acted out these relatives as shown in (12), by having the toy sheep both jump over the rabbit and stand on the lion.

(12) $_S$[$_S$[the sheep jumps over the rabbit] that $_S$[Δ $_{VP}$[the lion stands on]]]

The linear structure of noun phrases and verbs in OO relatives makes them less suitable for interpretation by conjoined-clause analysis than the other types of relative-clause analysis. This difficulty in imposing the conjoined-clause analysis on OO relatives is reflected in the much smaller percentage of conjoined-clause responses. Nineteen percent of the OO relatives received the conjoined-clause response, compared with 78 percent for SS relatives, 63 percent for OS relatives, and 52 percent for SO relatives. This difference in the application of the conjoined-clause analysis may be attributed to the structure of the second clause of OO relatives. All the other relative-clause types have a postverbal NP in the second clause of the predicted children's responses, but OO relatives have only a preverbal NP in the second clause. I argue elsewhere (Tavakolian 1977) that children utilize this fact to reject the conjoined-clause analysis for OO relatives earlier than for the other relative-clause types.[5] The conjoined-clause response accounts for a smaller percentage of responses to OO relatives than is the case for the other three relative-clause types, but it is still one of the three main response categories for OO relatives.

I have argued that children's responses to relative clauses provide support for the conjoined-clause analysis. The conjoined-clause response accounts for the greatest percentage of errors to relative clauses.[6] It was the only response used consistently on all four types of relative clauses and accounts for 48 percent of the total number of responses. I have argued that the conjoined-clause analysis underlies correct responses to SS relatives and that it is utilized for the other three relative-clause types as well. In contrast, the rules underlying the correct responses to OO, SO, and OS relative clauses were not utilized in responding to other relative-clause types. A correct response to OO relatives, for example, was not used as a response to other relative clauses, and similarly for a correct response to OS and to SO relatives. But, as can be seen from the above data, a correct response to SS relatives and to conjoined sentences was used as a common response to all the other relative clauses. This further supports the argument that the rules making up the conjoined-clause response to SS relatives and to conjoined sentences represents a productive set of rules that is utilized to analyze other multiple-clause constructions.

A small number of response types account for nearly all of the relative-clause responses (see table 8.7). Although the total number of actually occurring response types was rather large (25), six different responses account for 88 percent of the total number of responses to all four types of relative clauses. The remainder of the responses are distributed among 19 different types of responses, with an average of 1.8 responses in each category. In contrast, these six categories had an average of 42.2 responses per category; they are clearly the most frequently used responses. Four of these six responses were correct responses to the relative clauses. Of these correct responses, the conjoined-clause response, which produces a correct response to SS relatives, was also the most consistently occurring incorrect response to the other relative-clause types.

There were two response types that were not correct for any relative-clause type and that were frequent errors for particular relative clauses. One of these incorrect responses has already been discussed: the conjoined-clause response to SO relatives, shown in (10b).

The sixth predominant response was given primarily to OO relatives (16 of 22 responses were given to OO relatives). It can be accounted for by the conjoined-clause analysis if the postulated null form is an object instead of a subject. Given an OO relative such as (13), many children acted it out by having the sheep jump over the rabbit and then incorrectly having the lion stand on the sheep.

(13) $_S[$ $_S[$the sheep jumps over the rabbit that] $_S[$the lion stands on $\Delta]]$

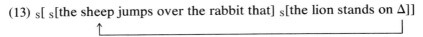

The sentence is still analyzed as consisting of conjoined clauses, but the missing noun phrase is the object instead of the subject. The rule for determining the referent of a null subject in actual conjoined clauses relates the missing subject of the second clause to the subject of the first clause. In (13) the missing form is an object, but it is still related to the subject of the first clause. Children already have a rule that will anaphorically relate missing forms, namely subjects, to the subject of an initial clause. The only modification needed to account for interpretations such as (13) is to suppose that the rule may apply to null objects as well as null subjects.

The small number of predominant responses and the fact that they can be accounted for either as instances of correct relative-clause interpretation or as cases of utilization of the conjoined-clause analysis makes it clear that children are not just randomly associating noun phrases and verbs to assign a meaning to those relative clauses they do not fully comprehend. The patterned nature of the responses provides evidence that rules are being utilized to arrive at an interpretation of the sentences. As mentioned, the conjoined-clause analysis accounts for 48 percent of the total number of responses. This figure is much higher than for any of the other predominant response categories and supports the claim that the conjoined-clause analysis is an early hypothesis that children make about the structure and interpretation of multiple-clause sentences.

As we would expect, conjoined sentences themselves are quite easy for children to correctly interpret. In a separate experiment with preschoolers aged 3–5 years, the children correctly responded to 96 percent of the sentences with two conjuncts in which the subject of the second conjunct was missing. Both imitation and production data also indicate that conjunction is an easy operation for children to acquire and imitate (Menyuk 1969; Beilin and Lust 1973; Brown 1973; Limber 1973; Slobin and Welsh 1973). Since conjunctions are mastered early in a child's language development, the rules underlying their production and comprehension are in existence at an early stage. Thus the rules constituting the conjoined-clause analysis (the structural analysis of multiple-clause strings as conjoined simplex sentences, the postulation of a phonologically null subject in the second clause, and the interpretation of the missing subject as being coreferential with the subject of the first clause) are part of the child's grammar at an early point in language development. We find evidence of their existence and generalization in the high percentage of correct responses to conjoined sentences and in children's conjoined-clause responses to relative clauses.

It might be argued that children are utilizing a nonstructural strategy to interpret relative clauses. Such a strategy could be formulated as "Interpret the subject of the first verb as the subject of all subsequent verbs." This kind of strategy would be independent of the actual structure assigned to the string. The exclusive utilization of such a strategy would vitiate the arguments for the proposed structural analysis of multiple-clause strings.

Solan and Roeper (1978) provide experimental evidence that children are indeed utilizing structure in interpreting relative clauses. Their data indicate that children's responses are structure-dependent and cannot be due solely to a nonstructural strategy. This is not to say that such a strategy does not exist at all; it is quite possible that a certain percentage of the conjoined-clause responses are the product of such a strategy. However, their data indicate that such a strategy cannot account for the total number of conjoined-clause responses. Solan and Roeper examined children's comprehension of relative clauses containing either *put* or *push* as the matrix verbal. The verb *put* subcategorizes for both a noun phrase and a prepositional phrase. Sentence (14a) is grammatical, but (14b) is not.

(14) a.   The boy put the glass on the table.
     b. *The boy put the glass.

If the object NP is modified by a relative clause, we have a sentence such as (15).

(15) The cat put the cow that kicked the dog in the barn.

The relative clause is interposed between the verb *put* and the obligatory prepositional phrase. An analysis of the sentence into conjoined clauses requires one of two interpretations: crossing lines in the tree, as shown in (16),[7] which automatically excludes a structure as ill-formed,

(16)

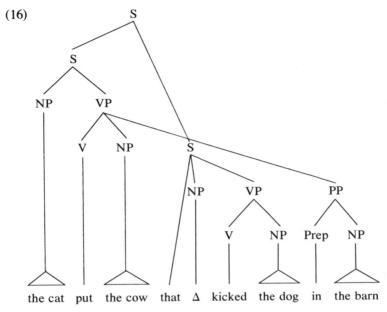

the cat   put   the cow   that   Δ   kicked   the dog   in   the barn

or ignoring the subcategorization restriction and attaching the prepositional phrase to the VP of the relative clause, as shown in (17).

(17)

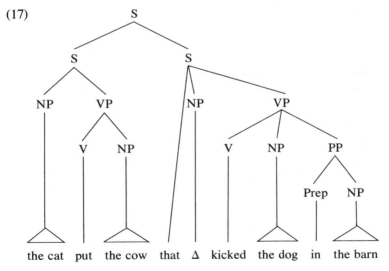

the cat   put   the cow   that   Δ   kicked   the dog   in   the barn

These sentences bear crucially on the claim that the conjoined-clause
responses might be due to a structure-independent strategy. If children
really are using a strategy that says "interpret the subject of the first

Table 8.8
Distribution of Errors According to Syntactic Structure (Modified from
Solan and Roeper 1978)

	Conjoined-Clause Responses	Failure to Interpret Relative Clause
Sentences with *put*	0	42 (80% of errors)
Sentences with *push*	40 (63% of errors)	6 (10% of errors)

verb as the subject of all subsequent verbs," then the structural configurations of the tree are irrelevant to utilization of this strategy. We
would expect children to interpret the relative clause in sentences such
as (15) as modifying the subject, and to ignore the fact that such an
interpretation creates crossed lines in the tree.

Children were pretested on sentences containing *put* to determine
whether they correctly subcategorized it for a prepositional phrase.
Those children who responded correctly were then given sentences in
which the matrix verb was *put*, such as (18a), and control sentences
with the matrix verb *push*, such as (18b), which does not subcategorize
for a prepositional phrase.

(18) a. The cat put the cow that kicked the dog in the barn.
     b. The cat pushed the cow that kicked the dog in the barn.

The responses to the sentences with *put* are striking (see table 8.8).
There were no responses in which the relative clause was interpreted as
modifying the subject of the first clause. In the sentences containing
put, 80 percent of the errors were a failure to act out the relative clause.
Children did not have the correct relative-clause interpretation available, and rather than give an interpretation that creates crossed lines in
a tree they simply left the relative clause uninterpreted. In contrast, 63
percent of the errors to sentences containing *push* are conjoined-clause
responses. Thus, whether a child gives a conjoined-clause response or
not depends critically on the structure of the sentence, which is contrary to the prediction made by a structure-independent strategy.
Where the conjoined-clause analysis is possible, it is the predominant
error; where it is structurally impossible, it never occurs.

The evidence indicates that the most prevalent interpretation of
these sentences for 3–5-year-olds is as conjoined clauses with a missing

subject in the second conjunct. The results of the Solan-Roeper experiment strengthen this analysis by showing that the response depends crucially on the structure of the relative clause and cannot be due solely to a structure-independent strategy.

3 Verbal Complements

An extension of the conjoined-clause analysis to verbal complements was tested in a separate experiment. Sentences containing either *tell* or *promise* as a matrix verbal were used. *Tell* and *promise* both take sentential complements that require interpretation of a missing subject in the complement clause, as shown in (19).

(19) a. Martha told John to paint the house red.

   b. Martha promised John to paint the house red.

An adult interpretation of (19a) requires the complement subject to be interpreted as coreferential with the object of the matrix sentence, *John*. In (19b), the complement subject must be related to the matrix subject, *Martha*.[8]

   Use of the conjoined-clause analysis to interpret these sentences would impose the interpretations shown in (20).

(20) a. $_S$[$_S$[Martha told John] $_S$[Δ to paint the house red]]

   b. $_S$[$_S$[Martha promised John] $_S$[Δ to paint the house red]]

In each case, the sentence is parsed into two conjoined sentences, a missing subject is postulated, and the missing subject is interpreted as being coreferential to the subject of the first clause. A conjoined-clause response to these sentences results in an incorrect interpretation of (20a) and a correct interpretation of (20b).

   Children aged 3–5 years were given a toy-moving task identical to the one described for the relative-clause experiment. In addition to the verb *tell*, the verbals *shout at* and *whisper to* were used for variety. The same eight verbs were used in the complement clause as were used for the relative clauses, and the test sentences were prepared in the same way. The only difference was that the matrix verbal in this experiment was either *promise* or one of *tell*, *whisper to*, and *shout at*. Each child received three tokens of *promise* sentences and three of *tell* sentences. (The experiment also contained other sentence types not relevant to the present discussion.)

The results of the experiment are as predicted by the conjoined-clause analysis. One-third of the children (8 of 24) gave conjoined-clause responses to both *tell* and *promise* sentences. They selected the subject of the first clause as the antecedent of the missing subject in the second clause, as shown in (20a) and (20b).

The conjoined-clause responses are a surprising departure of the facts from the commonly held assumption that children use a Minimum Distance Strategy[9] to determine the referent of an embedded complement subject very early in language development. C. Chomsky (1969) found in her seminal work on children's responses to verbal complements that children interpreted *tell* and *promise* sentences in the same way. However, the children in her study selected the matrix indirect object as the NP coreferential with the missing complement subject, as shown in (21).

(21) a. $_s$[the horse promises the pig $_s$[Δ to bump into the sheep]]

b. $_s$[the horse tells the pig $_s$[Δ to bump into the sheep]]

In the present study one-third of the children also gave this pattern of responses.[10] The children giving conjoined-clause responses were younger than those giving responses such as (21), although the difference in age was not statistically significant. The mean age of the former group was 4 years, 0 months, and for the latter group it was 4 years, 5 months. The children in Chomsky's study were older than the ones in this study; 5 years was the lower age limit in her study and the upper age limit in mine. Chomsky found that the 5-year-olds correctly interpreted *tell* complements, and this was also true of most of the 5-year-olds in my study (six of eight 5-year-olds responded correctly).

The results of the two studies suggest a developmental sequence in the acquisition of verbal complements. Children first utilize the conjoined-clause analysis. This results in the same interpretation for both *tell* and *promise* sentences; in each case the missing complement subject is interpreted as coreferential with the matrix subject. In the next stage children again interpret *tell* and *promise* sentences in the same way, but now the antecedent of the missing complement subject is the indirect object of the matrix clause. The final stage is an adult interpretation of both complements.

4   Conclusion

In summary, children's responses indicate that they utilize the conjoined-clause analysis to interpret relative clauses and verbal complements at an early stage of language development. Other multiple-clause
structures may be analyzed in the same way, subject to interaction with
other restrictions present in the grammar (Goodluck 1978).

One of the implications of the conjoined-clause analysis is that the
language-acquisition device is quite narrowly restricted in the early
stages of development. It seems plausible that the conjoined-clause
analysis is a universal feature of language acquisition. The value of
such a restriction in language development is that it greatly limits the
number and kind of possible hypotheses a child must entertain in constructing a grammar for his language.

A second implication of the conjoined-clause analysis is that it suggests an order of development for recursive rules in the grammar.
Initially, recursion in a child's grammar occurs through iteration rather
than embedding. The first recursive rule, which introduces sentences,
would be (22),

(22) $S \rightarrow S^*$

which would be structurally realized as (23).

(23)

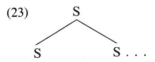

When a child's grammar begins to generate multiple-clause sentences,
they are generated by rule (22) and have the structure of (23). This
proposal is consistent with various data (Menyuk 1969, 1971; Brown
1973; Limber 1973) concerning children's early production of multiple-
clause sentences, and is also corroborated by the evidence presented in
this study.

Developmental priority of iterative rules would constrain the kinds of
assumptions a child brings to the language-learning task at an early
stage, and thus would restrict the number of possible grammars. Such a
restriction is desirable in a theory of language acquisition. Principles
that limit the number of possible grammars at a particular stage can
help account for the phenomenally rapid rate at which children learn
their language. At each stage of development children can utilize far-
reaching principles to reduce the number and kinds of hypotheses they

make about new linguistic data. Although a hypothesis such as the conjoined-clause analysis produces many incorrect interpretations in terms of an adult grammar, it is also a very powerful hypothesis with wide applicability and can be used to structurally analyze a great many strings.

Notes

An earlier version of this chapter appeared in Goodluck and Solan 1978. I am indebted to many people in the preparation of this article. A particular note of thanks goes to Tom Roeper. Also Helen Goodluck, Larry Solan, Edwin Williams, and Nancy Myers provided pertinent comments. Tom Wasow and Barbara Partee commented on the work in an early stage. I also profited from a timely statistical note by Jerry Myers and from a discussion with Melissa Bowerman and her students. The research for this chapter was supported in part by NIH grant HD 09647 to S. Jay Keyser and Thomas Roeper.

1. See Chomsky 1965 and 1975b for general discussion that laid the foundations for this approach. Many recent researchers in language acquisition have assumed this theoretical position. See other chapters in this volume for examples of language-acquisition research based on this approach.

2. This claim is no doubt too strong as it stands. Goodluck (1978) shows that children are incorporating into their grammars restrictions on the choice of a subject for a complement clause that cannot be accounted for by the conjoined-clause analysis.

3. The absence of SS relatives in spontaneous speech may not argue for a restriction on competence. See Limber (1976) for a discussion of the absence of center-embedded relatives in both child and adult speech.

4. Sheldon (1972) obtained a similarly high number of this response type to OS relatives; however, Goodluck (1978) did not replicate the results for OS relatives. A difference in the experimental materials used may account for the difference in results, and Helen Goodluck and I are now investigating this possibility.

5. Sheldon (1972) argues that children do relatively well on OO relatives because comprehension is improved when the two noun phrases share the same function. However, see deVilliers, Flusberg, Hakuta, and Cohen 1979 and Tavakolian 1977 for arguments against parallel function as an explanation of relative clause responses. Solan (1975) did find that parallel sequencing is a factor in children's interpretation of infinitival complements. Parallel sequencing differs from parallel function in that the latter refers to the deep-structure grammatical function of NPs whereas the former deals with surface-structure ordering of NPs.

6. A number of researchers have noted that the most common error children make on relative clauses is to take the first noun in the sentence as the agent of both actions (Sheldon 1972; Lahey 1974; Legum 1975).

7. The structure in (17) is somewhat different from the one proposed by Solan and Roeper. They attach the relative clause directly to the top S. This difference in structure is not relevant to the present point. Either structure results in crossed lines in the tree.

8. The proper formulation of these interpretations in an adult grammar has been the subject of much research. See Bresnan 1976 and Partee 1975 for two more recent and very different approaches. The approach adopted for an adult grammar will not affect the proposal made here for children's acquisition of language. However, the final formulation could affect the kinds of rules proposed to account for the change from a child to an adult grammar.

9. The Minimum Distance Principle was first proposed by Rosenbaum (1967) as a principle governing deletion of complement subjects in certain embedded sentences. C. Chomsky and others have used the terminology as a convenient way of referring to the recognition strategy used by children in interpreting such sentences.

10. The remaining one-third of the children consisted of five who responded correctly to both *tell* and *promise* sentences and three who did not fit into any of the three patterns discussed.

9

A "Little Linguist" Model of Syntax Learning

Virginia Valian,
Judith Winzemer,
Anne Erreich

This chapter outlines a learning theory for syntax. The underlying idea is that the child's language-acquisition mechanism is a hypothesis-testing device. We first sketch our version of such a model, then present examples of candidate hypotheses that the device tests and discuss principles that constrain the hypotheses the device can formulate. Finally, we discuss the implications of our model for linguistic theory and compare our approach with others.

To become a successful language user, the child needs to develop sophistication in a variety of interdependent areas: phonology, semantics, syntax, cognition, pragmatics, and so on. By concentrating on syntax we do not deny the importance of these related areas for language use. We claim only that syntax acquisition can be profitably studied apart from these other areas. Research in the development of these other systems supplements but does not supplant work on syntax acquisition.

A syntax-acquisition theory must specify how the child's syntax-learning mechanism acquires the rules of the syntactic component of the language. In doing so it must specify the nature of the device through which learning is effected. Chomsky (1965), Katz (1966), Fodor (1966), and others have suggested the metaphor of the child as a little linguist who tests hypotheses to discover the syntactic rules of his language. Both the child and the linguist test hypotheses in the form of candidate rules, and both use linguistic evidence to confirm or disconfirm those hypotheses. However, this is an analogy that contains several disanalogies. Whereas the linguist consciously projects hypotheses, the child's device operates unconsciously. Also, the linguist is not as efficient or successful as the child is. We propose, then, that the

acquisition device is one that tests hypotheses in a manner that is
methodologically similar to the manner in which linguists test them.

1 Outline of the Model

There are four components of a hypothesis-testing model:

1. what is learned,
2. what the innate properties of the device are,
3. what the content of the hypotheses is, and
4. how evidence confirms or disconfirms hypotheses.

Our model attempts to give substance to these four components. Like
Fodor (1966), we propose that the child learns a transformational
grammar, that the initial hypothesis space is constrained, that the child
tests hypotheses that consist of candidate rules, and that these hypotheses are confirmed or disconfirmed by data available to the child. We
specify the four components of the model as follows.

1. In acquiring the syntactic component of a transformational grammar, what the child learns must include phrase-structure rules (which
generate deep-structure representations) and transformational rules
(which map deep-structure representations into surface structure). (We
do not assume that the child's grammar and linguists' current candidate
grammars are identical. We assume only that the child learns a transformational grammar, the exact form of which has yet to be specified.)

2. The innate portion of the language-acquisition device contains
principles expressing the linguistic universals. These provide, among
other things, the set of elements and operations for constructing syntactic rules and constraints on the form and function of those rules.

3. The hypotheses that the device tests are expressed as candidate
rules (either phrase-structure or transformational rules).

4. Correctly or incorrectly analyzed utterances that the child hears
serve as the evidence against which hypotheses are tested. The child's
hypotheses are confirmed if they predict evidence. The child will not
entertain hypotheses that predict no data. The utterances presented to
the child may receive a correct or an incorrect analysis, depending on
the adequacy of his rule system at that time. We assume that the child
receives examples of the major constructions of his language, but that
frequency of utterance type is not a major independent variable. Both
assumptions are supported by the literature (Brown 1973; Newport et
al. 1977).

2 Origin of Hypotheses

Where do the child's initial hypotheses come from? Candidate rules derive from linguistic universals (though they will also be constrained by already existing rules and incoming data). The child assumes that the grammar of his language is organized like a transformational grammar. The child will not consider the possibility that a phrase-structure grammar could be adequate to express the rules of his language, even though his first guess about any particular structure may be that it is base-generated. The child knows that transformations will be required, but not which ones.

The child will only formulate rules that follow the definitions of rule types and that observe the constraints on rule formulation and operation that obtain in transformational grammars. Phrase-structure rules will expand only one category at a time; transformations will be structure-dependent; all deletions will be recoverable. The abbreviatory conventions that obtain in transformational grammar, such as the collapsing of phrase-structure rules through the use of parentheses and brackets, will also obtain in the child's rule system, thereby allowing the child to capture more generalizations. Finally, the child will formulate syntactic hypotheses only in terms of the syntactic categories and relations that are valid for natural languages (categories such as noun and verb, relations such as subject and object), and not in terms of semantic categories like *round object, movement,* and so on.

2.1 Some Candidate Hypotheses

The syntax-acquisition device must determine the correct formulation of transformational and phrase-structure rules; the device does this by projecting and testing candidate rules. In Mayer et al. 1978 we presented errors from the speech of two children; we claimed that the errors reflected incorrectly formulated rules that were, for some period of time, part of these children's grammars. The data presented there are relevant to two transformational rules: Tense-Hopping and Subject-Auxiliary Inversion. The errors represent early hypotheses of the children's devices about how these two rules should be formulated.

Transformations are standardly divided into three parts: first, the structural description (SD), or the string of abstract syntactic elements that is input to the transformation; second, the basic operations, or the operation or combination of operations that the rule performs—that is, whether it copies, deletes, or inserts elements; third, the structural change (SC), or the string that is the output of the transformation. In

order to learn transformational rules, the device must determine the
correct SD, the correct set of basic operations, and the correct SC for
every transformation. Incorrect hypotheses on the part of the child's
device about the SD, the SC, or the basic operations of any transformation should result in characteristic errors in child speech.

We will focus on incorrect hypotheses about basic operations. Although linguistic universals specify the stock of basic operations, they
do not determine the particular set of operations for any given rule.
Thus, one source of error in the device's formulation of candidate rules
lies in its choice of basic operations for a rule. One type of basic-
operations error is the failure to include one or more of the operations
specified in the adult version of the rule. The data from two children
presented below provide evidence for this kind of misformulation:
Each child has a transformational rule—Tense-Hopping in one case,
Subject-Aux Inversion in the other—incorrectly formulated, in that
the device has omitted one of the basic operations that is included in
the adult formulation of the rule.

The first set of data comes from R, age 2 years, 4 months (2,4).
During the period in which he was observed, R produced the following
utterances:

I did broke it
I did rode my bike
Jenni did left with Daddy

We propose that these errors result from an incorrectly formulated rule
of Tense-Hopping.[1] The correct rule (Akmajian and Heny 1975) is as
follows.

Tense-Hopping:

SD:	X	Tense	V	Y
	1	2	3	4
SC:	1	$\emptyset$	3#2	4

R seems to have an incorrectly formulated Tense-Hopping rule, since
the correct rule fails to derive his incorrect sentences. R's rule is incorrectly formulated as Tense-Copying:

Tense-Copying:

SD:	X	Tense	V	Y
	1	2	3	4
SC:	1	2	3#2	4

R's rule correctly copies the tense element that originates to the left of
the verb around to the right of the verb, but incorrectly fails to delete it
from its original position; we thus call it a tense-copying rule. Whereas
the adult rule calls for copying and deletion, R's rule is incorrectly
formulated as copying without deletion. The incorrect rule derives R's
utterances, such as *I did broke it,* as shown in diagrams (1)–(4).

(1) Base structure:

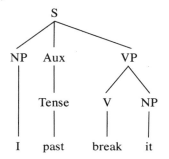

(2) Tense-Copying:

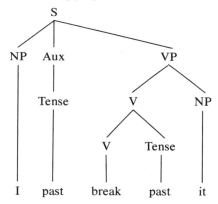

(3) *do*-Insertion:

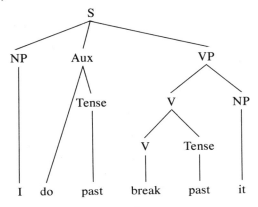

(4) Morphophonemic rules:

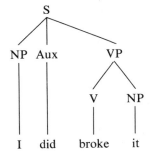

Another child, E, observed between the ages of 1,10 and 2,6 (Hurford 1975), produced the following incorrect questions:

Did you came home?
What's that is?
What's this is?
Whose is that is?
What did you bought?
What did you did?

These errors are due to a misformulated rule of Subject-Aux Inversion. The correct rule[2] (Akmajian and Heny 1975) is as follows.

Subject-Auxiliary Inversion:

$$
\text{SD:}\quad Q\qquad NP\qquad \text{Tense}\qquad \left(\left\{\begin{matrix}\text{Modal}\\\text{Have}\\\text{Be}\end{matrix}\right\}\right)\qquad X
$$

	1	2	3	4
	1	3+2	∅	4

SC:

Like Tense-Hopping, Subject-Aux Inversion involves two basic operations, copying and deletion. The correct rule derives questions like *Did you come home?* as shown in diagrams (5)–(8).

(5) Base structure:

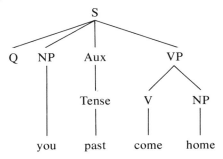

(6) Subject-Aux Inversion:

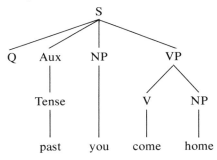

(7) *do*-Insertion:

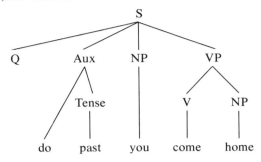

(8) Morphophonemic rules:

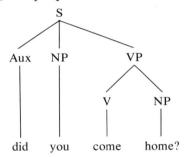

E seems to have an incorrectly formulated Subject-Aux Inversion rule, since the correct rule fails to derive her incorrect questions.

E's rule is incorrectly formulated as follows:

Aux-Copying (after Hurford 1975):

SD:	Q	NP	Tense	$\left(\begin{bmatrix} \text{Modal} \\ \left\{ \text{Have} \right\} \\ \text{Be} \end{bmatrix} \right)$	X
	1	2	3		4
SC:	1	3+2	3		4

This rule copies the tense marker and any optional elements into presubject position but fails to delete them from their original postsubject position. We thus call the rule Aux-Copying, after Hurford (1975). The incorrect rule derives E's questions, such as *Did you came home?*, as shown in diagrams (9)–(13).

(9) Base structure:

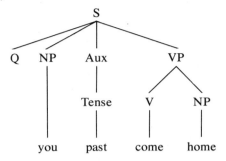

(10) Aux-Copying:

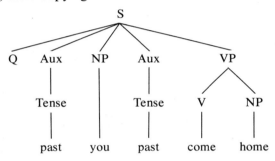

(11) Tense-Hopping:

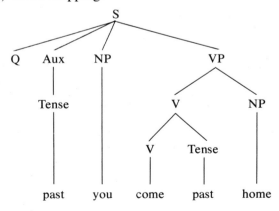

(12) *do*-Insertion:

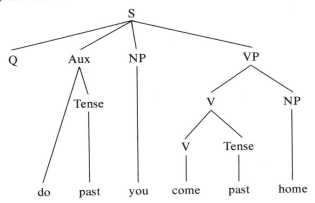

(13) Morphophonemic rules:

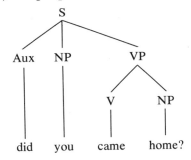

We have presented examples of misformulations of Tense-Hopping and Subject-Aux Inversion. In the adult grammar these rules involve copying and deletion. Each child's incorrectly formulated rule involves copying alone, without accompanying deletion. Thus, each child's rule lacks one of the operations specified in the adult formulation.

The children's grammars differ in terms of which rule is incorrectly formulated. R acquired the adult rule of Subject-Aux Inversion before he acquired Tense-Hopping,[3] whereas E acquired the adult rule of Tense-Hopping before she acquired Subject-Aux Inversion. From the point of view of when the two rules were acquired, the children differ. This superficial difference in order of rule acquisition, we argue, should not obscure the important underlying similarity between children in the manner of rule acquisition. In the present case, the important similarity between the two children is that each is constructing a transformation out of basic operations.

Table 9.1
Errors Predicted on Basis of Basic-Operations Statement

Transformation	Error
Tense-Hopping	I did broke it. (Mayer et al. 1978)
Subject-Aux Inversion	What shall we shall have? (Bellugi 1971)
Particle Movement	The barber cut off his hair off. (Menyuk 1969)
Dative Movement	Could you get me a banana for me? (Fay 1975)
wh-Movement	What did I see what? (not observed)
ing-Hopping	I being going to the store. (not observed)
Negative Placement	What not can't I do? (not observed)

On the basis of our analysis of the children's errors we make a general statement about one kind of hypothesis the language-acquisition device should entertain, namely, hypotheses in which the content is a projection about the basic operations of a rule. The basic-operations statement predicts that for any transformation composed of more than one basic operation, there will be errors in child speech correctly analyzed as the result of failure to apply one (or more) of the operations specified in the adult formulation of the rule.[4]

The basic-operations statement predicts the copying without deletion errors presented above. It further predicts that for any movement transformation there will be errors that result from copying without deletion, all other things being equal. Thus, it predicts the errors shown in table 9.1. Failure to find copying without deletion errors for all movement transformations will constitute disconfirmation of the model unless the errors are ruled out on other grounds. The following sorts of grounds would rule out copying without deletion errors resulting from rule misformulation. (See also Valian et al. 1979 for more discussion of grounds for ruling out errors.)

• If the rule that is being learned is not in fact a movement transformation, errors of copying without deletion errors would not be expected. Stevens (1978) argues that there is no rule of *wh*-Movement, and that, rather, *wh* is generated in place (sentence-initially) by the phrase-structure rules. If this is the correct analysis of *wh* constructions, then *wh*-copying should not occur. Conversely, errors that we have explained as copying without deletion errors only provide confirming evidence for the basic-operations statement if the rules being learned are in fact movement rules. Goodluck and Solan (1979), following Lapointe, argue that Tense-Hopping and *ing*-Hopping are not movement transformations, that verb affixes are handled by lexical subcategorization of verbs. If their analysis is correct, the errors we have cited are not confirmation of the basic-operations statement.

• If there is no linguistic evidence that the rule predicts, there will be no support for the incorrectly formulated rule. This is discussed in the section on linguistic evidence.

• If an incorrectly formulated rule were to violate a universal or a principle of derived constituent structure it would not be formulated.

3   Constraints on the Device

What constrains the device's formulation and maintenance of hypotheses? Linguistic universals, Occam's razor, and linguistic evidence. Linguistic universals and Occam's razor constrain the class of hypotheses that the device can formulate. Linguistic evidence determines which of the possible hypotheses will be retained by the device. The role of linguistic universals, as stated earlier, is to limit the initial hypothesis space by setting conditions on the form and function of syntactic rules.

3.1   Occam's Razor

Occam's razor states that entities are not to be multiplied beyond necessity. Just as linguists and scientists use Occam's razor in formulating and evaluating hypotheses, so, we claim, does the child's language-acquisition device. Only by employing Occam's razor can the child rule out certain "absurd" hypotheses. One example of the role of Occam's razor here concerns our prior presentation of a formulation of the tense-copying rule. This rule was analyzed as containing one basic operation, copying. If Occam's razor were not employed, the rule could also be formulated as two rules: one rule that copies tense into the new position and deletes it from its original position, and a second rule that recopies tense into the original position. This formulation involves three basic operations: copying, deletion, and copying again. Occam's razor rules out this formulation because it involves more operations and rules than are necessary to achieve the desired output. Occam's razor guarantees that the minimum number of operations will be used to get from the structural description to the structural change, and that the minimum number of rules will be used to effect any change.

3.2 Linguistic Evidence

In order for the device to maintain a hypothesis, it must predict some portion of the incoming data. Predicted data confirm the hypothesis; inconsistent data disconfirm it. In the case of correct hypotheses, it is clear that the data will be accurately predicted; therefore, the hypotheses will be retained; but in the case of incorrect hypotheses, what sort of data would be predicted such that the device would retain the hypotheses for some period of time? For example, why would a child retain, even for a short period, a tense-copying rule rather than a tense-hopping rule? The tense-copying rule generates sentences like *I did broke it,* which the child never hears. Further, all declarative sentences such as *I liked it* contain only one tensed verb and thus provide evidence against the rule.

There are, however, classes of data that the tense-copying rule predicts. Two assumptions must be made for our argument here to be correct. The first is that the utterances the child hears are a representative sample of the language; otherwise he will not be exposed to the classes of data that will provide misleading data. We know of no research that contradicts our assumption, which is also shared by Wexler, Culicover, and Hamburger (1975) and Wexler (1978).

The second assumption is that an incorrect rule will assign an incorrect surface structure to grammatical utterances. When a child hears an utterance, he must preanalyze it before applying syntactic rules, because syntactic rules operate on a sequence of abstract categories, not on a sequence of sounds. The preanalysis is dependent on the rules that the device is currently using. For example, if the device formulates a tense-copying rule it might misanalyze present-tense emphatics like *I do like it* as having the surface structure shown in (14).

(14)   I   do   like   it

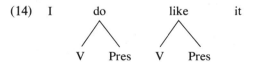

Under this misanalysis there are two identical tenses in the sentence, in precisely those places predicted by the tense-copying rule. The untensed main verbs in sentences like *I do like it* can consistently be misinterpreted as tensed forms, except in the third-person singular. In fact, all verbs but *be* have a present-tense form identical to their untensed form, except in the third-person singular.

As diagrams (15)–(17) show, there are other classes of data which the tense-copying rule predicts (again, on the assumption that the device misanalyzes their surface structure). In all cases, the main verb can be misanalyzed as verb + tense instead of just verb.

(15) Present-tense negatives (except in third-person singular):[5]

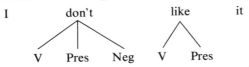

(16) Negative imperatives (except with *be*):[6]

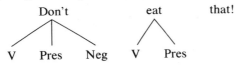

(17) Positive emphatic imperatives (except with *be*):

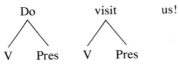

Thus there are several classes of data that provide evidence for the tense-copying rule under the misanalysis that the rule makes likely. Similarly, there exist classes of data that the Aux-Copying rule predicts, again on the assumption of a misanalysis of surface structure. For example, the main verbs in questions like *Do you like it?* and *Do you want some?*, if misanalyzed as verb + present tense, provide evidence for the Aux-Copying rule. In questions involving *do*-Insertion, as in present-tense emphatics, the untensed main verb can consistently be misinterpreted as a tensed form, thus providing support for the Aux-Copying rule.

We have shown that there are classes of sentences that provide confirming evidence for the incorrect rules, if the rules assign an incorrect surface structure. All the confirming evidence presented, however, has been in the present tense. In order for the child to produce errors in the past tense, like *I did broke it* (which R produced) and *Did you came home?* (which E produced), the device must overgeneralize the rule from cases that it predicts to cases where the data are inconsistent with the rule. It remains to be demonstrated that such behavior is typical of the language-acquisition device.

What causes the device to give up incorrect hypotheses? As evidence contradictory to an incorrect rule mounts, the device will abandon the incorrect rule in favor of the correct one. For example, in the case of tense-copying, the device will abandon it in favor of the correct hopping rule because the hopping rule predicts both the data predicted by the copying rule and the data the copying rule cannot handle.

The reformulation of the tense-copying rule also forces a reanalysis of the surface structure of main verbs in those sentences which had previously been misanalyzed. In those cases where the main verb had been analyzed as verb + present tense, it will now be analyzed simply as verb. In general, as rules change, so will surface-structure analyses. Conversely, as correct surface assignments are established, they will serve to limit future hypotheses about rules.

4   Competing Rules

Our discussion of evidence implies that the child should occasionally entertain competing rules. For example, the child may simultaneously entertain a tense-copying and a tense-hopping rule. This situation can arise if more than one formulation of a rule could generate the sentences in a class of data. This is the case with sentences like *Do you like it?;* these sentences could be generated with either a subject-aux-inversion or an aux-copying rule. The data are predictable by more than one rule; they fit both hypotheses.

The child, like a scientist, may be slow to see that all the data can be subsumed under one of two competing hypotheses. As evidence mounts, the incorrect rule or rules will be relinquished in favor of the correct rule, because the correct rule will eventually be seen to predict all the data, rendering the incorrect rule or rules unnecessary. Occam's razor dictates the removal of the incorrect rule. It follows from our analysis that the correct rule cannot precede the incorrect rule in acquisition: If the child already has a correct hypothesis that accounts for all the data there is no reason to entertain a competing one.

A formal statement of the necessary and sufficient conditions for two rules to be competing rules can now be offered: A necessary condition for two transformations to be in competition is that both rules have the same structural description but different structural changes. For phrase-structure rules, a necessary condition is that both rules have the same left-hand side but different right-hand sides.

For transformational and phrase-structure rules there must also be a class of grammatical sentences that could be generated by both of the rules. These conditions are each necessary but only jointly sufficient for two rules to be competing. Our definition of a competing rule may be quite restrictive in that there may be few possibilities that will meet the joint conditions. Hence, it may be necessary to define a broader class of conflicting rules, in which either condition may be relaxed, in order to describe more of the child's rules.

5 Relevance of Language-Acquisition Data to Linguistic Theory

How do language-acquisition data and linguistic theory interrelate? With respect to particular grammar, we claim that there is no formal relevance, only heuristic relevance, for language-acquisition theory. (By formal relevance we refer to the situation in which a feature of X implies a similar feature in Y. By heuristic relevance we refer to a situation in which a feature of X is a source of ideas about Y.) With respect to universal grammar, we claim that there is limited formal relevance.

We consider particular grammar first. The grammar of English has heuristic relevance because it gives us ideas about where to look for mistakes in the child's hypotheses. We know that the child has to learn how to form questions, assign tense, and so on. Knowing something about what the child has to learn gives us hints about how the child can get it wrong. However, we cannot conclude from the adult form of a particular rule that the child must have either that rule or a particular deformation of that rule. Nor can we conclude from the child's possession of a particular rule that the adult must have a rule of a particular form.

For example, the child may have a rule of *do*-Insertion, which is later abandoned in favor of *do*-Deletion. For the same reasons that linguists argue about whether *do* is transformationally inserted or deleted, the child may initially opt for either possibility, later replacing it with the other one. Even if we could be sure that the adult formulation is *do*-Deletion, we could not be sure that the child formulation was *do*-Deletion. Conversely, even if we could be sure that the child version was *do*-Insertion, we could not be sure that the adult formulation was *do*-Insertion.

Thus, in our assumption that R and E both have a rule of *do*-Insertion we may be incorrect, but nothing about the adult grammar can settle that. However, even if our assumption is incorrect, our theoretical framework is still intact. We will have misdescribed at least one of the child's rules, but the framework will allow a correct redescription. Similarly, the rules we use for heuristic purposes are drawn from standard texts adopting variants of the standard theory (Akmajian and Heny 1975; Culicover 1976; Baker 1978) and could be incorrect. We use the rules because they are the most widely known, not because we are arguing for their correctness. Were another system shown to be correct ("trace" theory, say), the errors could be redescribed within that system. Copying without deletion, for example, could be redescribed as mistaken phonological spelling out of the trace left by the moved element. The conclusion of our remarks about particular grammar, then, is that it and language-acquisition data are not formally relevant to each other.

The situation is somewhat different with universal grammar. Universal grammar posits basic operations, and our theory crucially incorporates the notion of basic operations. Our theory claims that the child uses basic operations as the building blocks for constructing transformations. If basic operations did not exist, our theory would be fundamentally mistaken. However, to the extent that we are successful in building a language-acquisition theory that uses the notion of basic operations, we provide support for them as linguistic universals. Conversely, to the extent that linguistic theory relies on such notions, it provides support for them as important in acquisition theory.

It is important to distinguish here between the notion of basic operations and the question of exactly what the basic operations are. Our work provides support for the notion that there are basic operations, but it provides no support for the existence of any particular set of basic operations. For example, we have assumed that movement is copying plus deletion, and have analyzed the children's errors in those terms. It could be, however, that movement is a basic operation (that is, is not itself decomposable). The children's errors could be redescribed as movement plus insertion (assuming copying was not a basic operation) or as movement plus copying (assuming copying was a basic operation). Since, by definition, any set of basic operations will be sufficient to describe the alteration from structural description to structural change, they will also be sufficient to describe any basic-operations error. The conclusion of our remarks about universal grammar, then, is that it and language-acquisition data are only partially formally relevant to each other.

6   Our Approach Compared with Others

There are two levels on which our theoretical approach can be compared with other views of syntax acquisition. The first level concerns general features: What kind of theory is being proposed? What is the domain of the theory? What sort of analogy does the theory make use of? The second level concerns particular features: How does the theory handle various phenomena? What specific predictions does it make? In this section we compare our approach with others at the first level; see Mayer et al. 1978 and Erreich, Valian, and Mayer 1980 for comparisons at the second level.

Our model proposes that the child learns a transformational grammar (of which current candidates are only approximations), and that the way the child learns a grammar is analogous to the way a scientist constructs a theory. Transformational grammar characterizes what the child learns; hypothesis testing characterizes how the child learns. In terms of the four components of the model, our concentration is on the content of the hypotheses and how the hypotheses interact with evidence. The domain of our theory is the mechanism by which the child acquires the syntax of his language; the domain is not linguistic theory or particular grammar (except as mentioned at the end of section 5). Our theory is a learning theory, not a linguistic theory. If it is incorrect, it is incorrect primarily as a characterization of how learning takes place. It may also be incorrect in its assumption that a transformational grammar characterizes adults' knowledge, but the evidence for that will not come from language-acquisition studies.

We emphasize the difference between what the child learns and how the child learns because of its importance in correctly evaluating the usefulness of transformational grammar to psycholinguistics. In our view, much of the criticism against "transformational" syntax acquisition is due to the heavy concentration in that literature on what is learned. The criticism frequently takes the following form: Transformational grammar is a useless, unmotivated, gratuitous component in a theory of language acquisition and should be omitted. We now explore the source of such a criticism, and its validity.

The bulk of studies in transformational syntax acquisition have concentrated on whether and when a particular aspect of grammar forms part of the child's knowledge. Such studies are commonly considered (at least by their authors) to be theoretically motivated, the theory being supplied by transformational grammar. But it is asking too much of transformational grammar to be a theory of either acquisition or use. Although it is essential to know what is learned (at least in broad outline), a theory of what is learned does not and cannot provide a theory of how learning takes place.

There is, then, an appropriate criticism to be leveled against investigators of transformational syntax acquisition: We have not learned very much about how syntax is acquired, even if we have learned something about what is acquired by what point. This correct criticism, however, is often invalidly extended to a criticism of transformational grammar as a model of what is learned, or as a component of an acquisition or use theory. The correctness of the statement that transformational grammar is not an acquisition or use theory has no bearing on whether transformational grammar correctly characterizes what is acquired and used.

Consider the following analogy. You want to build a rocket. All the books you find that are titularly on rocket building turn out not to tell you how to build a rocket. Instead they tell you some of the abstract physical principles you will need to know in order to build a rocket. A correct criticism of those books is that they fail to tell you how to build a rocket. If the books represent the state of knowledge about rocket building, a valid inference is that the theory of rocket building is pitifully inadequate. An invalid inference is that, to build a rocket, you can do without the abstract physical principles claimed to be involved. A further invalid inference is that the principles themselves are incorrect.

We are not here claiming the correctness of some variety of transformational grammar as a model of what is learned. Perhaps no variety is.[7] The point is that you cannot determine its incorrectness or irrelevance from the absence of an explanatory theory of language acquisition, any more than you could determine the incorrectness or irrelevance of physical theory from the absence of a theory of rocket building. (See Valian 1979 for more discussion.)

Thus, much of the current criticism of transformational grammar's value to psycholinguistic theory seems misdirected. It is, however, a criticism some developmental psycholinguists have invited either by neglecting the question of how learning takes place, or by conflating an answer to what is learned with an answer to how learning occurs. Our theory expressly addresses the question of how learning takes place. Incorporated in the theory is some variety of transformational grammar as a model of what is learned, because no other model seems to fit the linguistic and psycholinguistic facts as well. We are agnostic about what variety most closely approximates the true grammar of English. We use an *Aspects* variety purely for convenience.

We now compare our approach with three other current approaches. The first approach concentrates on the first component of a learning theory, namely what is learned, rather than on how learning takes place (Lust 1977b; Roeper 1978; Tavakolian 1978b; Solan 1978d; Goodluck 1978; Valian and Caplan 1979). Although how learning takes place is seen as an important question it is not addressed directly. In this approach there is often considerable interest in implications for linguistic theory and particular grammar, contrary to our view of the limited reciprocal relevance of grammar and language acquisition (see section 5).

The second approach concentrates on the second component of a learning theory, namely what is innate. Wexler and his colleagues (Wexler 1976, 1978; Wexler, Culicover, and Hamburger, 1975; Culicover 1976) are concerned with constraining the class of possible languages made available by linguistic theory, in particular by restricting them to the class that is learnable by a procedure or device that has certain characteristics. Their predictions are not about how rules are acquired, but about the existence of constraints on rules (such as the binary principle and the freezing principle) that would thereby serve to limit possible languages. Their theory says little about how the mechanism operates in the actual acquisition of a rule, and some of the assumptions they make about the character of the language-acquisition device—such as that it forgets all previous data, that it changes only one rule at a time, and that the deep structure of an utterance is inferable from its surface structure plus the context in which it occurs— seem unrealistic from the standpoint of actual language acquisition. In contrast, our theory is not directed at developing restrictions on the class of languages permitted by linguistic theory; it is concerned with characterizing how the device learns any particular language.

The third approach has the same domain as our model, namely the mechanism by which syntax is learned. However, a different kind of mechanism is suggested. This approach views the child as an inductive generalizer who is sensitive to distributional regularities in the utterances he hears (Maratsos 1977, 1979; Maratsos and Kuczaj 1978; Kuczaj 1976; Prideaux 1976). Categories and rules are abstracted from experience.[8] In contrast, our model proposes that the child makes use of distributional regularities (Erreich et al. 1980), but primarily to test hypotheses made available by the linguistic universals. A secondary area of contrast is in what assumptions are made about what is learned; investigators who take this approach generally think that the child learns something less than a full transformational grammar.

Our model has something in common with each of the three approaches to syntax acquisition mentioned, but it is also substantively different from each of them. Our model proposes a rich view of what the child learns, shared by the first and second approaches; its goal is the specification of how the child learns, shared by the third approach. Our model explicitly proposes that learning takes place through hypothesis testing.

Notes

The order of authors' names is random. We thank J. J. Katz for helpful discussion and criticism of this manuscript.

1. In the adult grammar tense may not be treated apart from other affixes, but in R's grammar it apparently is. We assume here that Tense-Hopping is a transformational rule (a rule that maps a phrase marker into another phrase marker), leaving open whether the rule is at the syntactic or morphological level.

2. There are many different versions of Subject-Aux Inversion, most notably one in which the category Aux is inverted, the contents of Aux being appropriately limited by other rules. We adopt the present formulation only for convenience.

3. R's question data are not presented here; he did correctly form questions. See Mayer, Erreich, and Valian 1978 for a fuller presentation of R's data and rules.

4. This kind of error—leaving out an operation—is not the only kind of basic-operations error that could occur. The device could also project a rule that contains an extra operation or the wrong operation.

5. This error analysis also assumes that the tense-copying rule is formulated such that it has an SD incorrectly containing an optional Neg marker.

6. See note 5.

7. There are, however, no language-acquisition data that demonstrate that transformational grammar is not a model of what is learned, nor any adult psycholinguistic data that demonstrate that it does not form part of adult knowledge, whereas there are data from both areas indicating that aspects of transformational grammar are learned. Further, the relative success of transformational grammar compared to weaker approaches in characterizing natural language presents evidence that some such powerful system will be necessary to characterize speakers' knowledge.

8. This approach is therefore empiricist and subject to the standard criticisms of induction as a source of abstract knowledge. See, for example, Hempel 1965:5–6 and Katz 1966, 1971.

References

Aaronson, D., and Rieber, R. 1979. *Psycholinguistic Research*. Hillsdale, N.J.: Erlbaum.

Akmajian, A., and Heny, F. 1975. *Introduction to the Principles of Transformational Syntax*. Cambridge, Mass.: MIT Press.

Anderson, J. 1976. *Language, Memory, and Thought*. Hillsdale, N.J.: Erlbaum.

Anderson, S., and Kiparsky, P., eds. 1973. *A Festschrift for Morris Halle*. New York: Holt, Rinehart and Winston.

Aronoff, M. 1976. *Word Formation in Generative Grammar*. Cambridge, Mass.: MIT Press.

Bach, E., and Harms, R. T. 1968. *Universals in Linguistic Theory*. New York: Holt, Rinehart and Winston.

Baker, C. L. 1977. "Comments on the paper by Culicover and Wexler." In P. Culicover, T. Wasow, and A. Akmajian, eds. 1977. *Formal Syntax*. New York: Academic.

Baker, C. L. 1978. *Introduction to Generative-Transformational Syntax*. Englewood Cliffs, N.J.: Prentice-Hall.

Beilin, H., ed. 1975. *Studies in the Cognitive Basis of Language Development*. New York: Academic.

Beilin, H., and Lust, B. 1975. "A study of the development of logical and linguistic connectives. In Beilin, H., ed. 1975. *Studies in the Cognitive Basis of Language Development*. New York: Academic.

Bellugi, U. 1967. Acquisition of Negation. Doctoral dissertation, Harvard University.

Bellugi, U. 1971. "Simplification in children's language." In R. Huxley and E. Ingram, eds. 1971. *Language Acquisition: Models and Methods*. London: Academic.

Bennett, S., and Falmagne, R. J. 1977. "A study of children's linguistic intuitions about factive presuppositions." Presented at Boston University Conference on Language Development.

Bever, T. 1970. "The cognitive basis for linguistic structures." In J. Hayes, ed. 1970. *Cognition and the Development of Language*. New York: Wiley.

Bierwisch, M., and Heidolph, K. E., eds. 1968. *Progress in Linguistics*. The Hague: Mouton.

Bowerman, M. 1973. *Early Syntactic Development, A Cross Linguistic Study with Special Reference to Finnish*. London: Cambridge University Press.

Boysson-Bardies, B. de. 1976. *Négation et Performance Linguistique*. The Hague: Mouton.

Brame, M. 1978. "The base hypothesis and the spelling prohibition." *Linguistic Analysis* 4:1–30.

Bresnan, J. 1973. "Sentence stress and syntactic transformations." In J. Hintikka, J. M. E. Moravcsik, and P. Suppes, eds. 1973. *Approaches to Natural Language*. Dordrecht, Holland: Reidel.

Bresnan, J. 1976a. "On the form and functioning of transformations." *Linguistic Inquiry* 7.1:3–40.

Bresnan, J. 1976b. "Towards a realistic model of transformational grammar." Paper presented at the Bell Telephone Centennial Symposium on Language and Communication, MIT.

Bresnan, J. 1978. "A realistic transformational grammar." In M. Halle, J. Bresnan, and G. Miller, eds. *Linguistic Theory and Psychological Reality*. Cambridge, Mass.: MIT Press.

Brown, H. 1971. "Children's comprehension of relativized English sentences." *Child Development* 42:1923–1936.

Brown, R. 1968. "The development of Wh questions in child speech." *Journal of Verbal Learning and Verbal Behavior* 7:279–290.

Brown, R. 1970. *Psycholinguistics: Selected Papers by Roger Brown*. New York: Free Press.

Brown, R. 1973. *A First Language: The Early Stages*. Cambridge, Mass.: Harvard University Press.

Brown, R., and Hanlon, C. 1970. "Derivational complexity and order of acquisition in child speech." In J. Hayes, ed. 1970. *Cognition and the Development of Language*. New York: Wiley.

Bruner, J., Caudill, E., and Ninio, A. In press. *Language and Experience*. London: Routledge and Kegan Paul.

Chase, W., and Clark, H. 1969. "Mental operations in the comparison of sentences and pictures." In L. Gregy, ed. 1969. *Cognition in Learning and Memory*. New York: Wiley.

Chomsky, C. 1969. *The Acquisition of Syntax in Children from 5 to 10*. Cambridge, Mass.: MIT Press.

Chomsky, N. 1964. "On the notion 'rule' of grammar. In J. A. Fodor and J. Katz, eds. 1964. *The Structure of Language*. Englewood Cliffs, N.J.: Prentice-Hall.

Chomsky, N. 1965. *Aspects of the Theory of Syntax*. Cambridge, Mass.: MIT Press.

Chomsky, N. 1970. "Remarks on nominalization." In R. Jacobs and P. Rosenbaum, eds. 1970. *Readings in English Transformational Grammar*. Waltham, Mass.: Ginn.

Chomsky, N. 1973. "Conditions on transformations." In S. Anderson and P. Kiparsky, eds. 1973. *A Festschrift for Morris Halle*. New York: Holt, Rinehart and Winston.

Chomsky, N. 1975a. "Conditions on rules of grammar." Mimeographed, MIT.

Chomsky, N. 1975b. *Reflections on Language*. New York: Pantheon.

Chomsky, N. 1976. *The Logical Structure of Linguistic Theory*. New York: Plenum.

Chomsky, N. 1977. "On Wh-movement." In P. Culicover, T. Wasow, and A. Akmajian, eds. 1977. *Formal Syntax*. New York: Academic.

Chomsky, N. 1980. "On binding." *Linguistic Inquiry* 11.1:1–46.

Chomsky, N., and Halle, M. 1968. *The Sound Pattern of English*. New York: Harper & Row.

Chomsky, N., and Lasnik, H. 1977. "Filters and control." *Linguistic Inquiry* 8:425–504.

Clark, E. 1970. "How children describe events in time." In G. D'Arcais and W. Levelt, eds. 1970. *Advances in Psycholinguistics*. New York: American Elsevier.

Clark, H. 1973. "The language-as-fixed-effect fallacy: A critique of language statistics in psychological research." *Journal of Verbal Learning and Verbal Behavior* 12:335–359.

Cole, P., ed. 1978. *Syntax and Semantics*. Vol. 9: *Pragmatics*. New York: Academic.

Cooper, W., and Walker, E., eds. 1979. *Sentence Processing: Psycholinguistic Studies Presented to Merrill Garrett*. Hillsdale, N.J.: Erlbaum.

Culicover, P. 1976. *Syntax*. New York: Academic.

Culicover, P., Wasow, T., and Akmajian, A., eds. 1977. *Formal Syntax*. New York: Academic.

D'Arcais, G., and Levelt, W., eds. 1970. *Advances in Psycholinguistics*. New York: American Elsevier.

Davidson, D., and Harmon, G., eds. 1972. *Semantics of Natural Language*. Dordrecht, Holland: Reidel.

Davis, J., Hockney, D., and Wilson, W., eds. 1975. *Contemporary Research in Philosophical Logic and Linguistic Semantics*. Dordrecht, Holland: Reidel.

deVilliers, J., Flusberg, H. Trager, and Hakuta, K. 1976. "The roots of coordination in child speech." Paper presented at Boston University Conference on Language Development.

deVilliers, J., Flusberg, H. Trager, Hakuta, K., and Cohen, M. 1979. "Children's comprehension of relative clauses." *Journal of Psycholinguistic Research* 8.5:499–518.

Dougherty, R. 1974. "The syntax and semantics of *each other* constructions." *Foundations of Language* 12:1–47.

Echeverria, M. 1975. Late Stages in the Acquisition of Spanish Syntax. Doctoral dissertation, University of Washington.

Eckman, F., and Hastings, A. 1979. *Studies in First and Second Language Acquisition*. Rowley, Mass.: Newbury House.

Elliott, D., Legum, S., and Thompson, S. 1969. "Syntactic variation as linguistic data." In *Papers from the Fifth Regional Meeting, Chicago Linguistic Society*. Chicago: Chicago Linguistic Society.

Erreich, A., Valian, V., and Winzemer, J. 1980. "Aspects of a theory of language acquisition." *Journal of Child Language* 7.1:157–179.

Ervin-Tripp, S., and Miller, W. 1977. "Early discourse: some questions about questions." In M. Lewis and L. Rosenblum, eds. 1977. *Interaction, Conversation, and the Development of Language*. New York: Wiley.

Fay, D. 1975. "Simplification in children's speech and the formulation of movement rules." *Texas Linguistic Forum* 2:97–102.

Ferguson, C., and Slobin, D., eds. 1973. *Studies of Child Language Development*. New York: Holt, Rinehart and Winston.

Fiengo, R., and Lasnik, H. 1973. "The logical structure of reciprocal sentences." *Foundations of Language* 9:447–468.

Fillmore, C. 1963. "The position of embedding transformations in a grammar." *Word* 19:208–231.

Fillmore, C. 1968. "The case for case." In E. Bach and R. T. Harms, eds. 1968. *Universals in Linguistic Theory*. New York: Holt, Rinehart and Winston.

Fodor, J. A. 1966. "How to learn to talk: Some simple ways." In F. Smith and G. Miller, eds. 1966. *The Genesis of Language*. Cambridge, Mass.: MIT Press.

Fodor, J. A., Bever, T., and Garrett, M. 1974. *The Psychology of Language*. New York: McGraw-Hill.

Fodor, J. A., and Katz, J., eds. 1964. *The Structure of Language*. Englewood Cliffs, N.J.: Prentice-Hall.

Fodor, J. D., Fodor, J. A., and Garrett, M. 1975. "The psychological unreality of semantic representations." *Linguistic Inquiry* 6:515–531.

Gaer, E. 1969. "Children's understanding and production of sentences." *Journal of Verbal Learning and Verbal Behavior* 8:289–294.

Givón, T. 1978. "Negation in English: pragmatics, function, ontology." In P. Cole, ed. 1978. *Syntax and Semantics*. Vol. 9: *Pragmatics*. New York: Academic.

Gold, E. 1965. "Limiting recursion." *The Journal of Symbolic Logic* 30:28–48.

Gold, E. 1967. "Language identification in the limit." *Information and Control* 10:447–474.

Goodluck, H. 1978. Linguistic Principles in Children's Grammar of Complement Interpretation. Doctoral dissertation, University of Massachusetts, Amherst. Reproduced by the Graduate Linguistic Student Association, Department of Linguistics, University of Massachusetts, Amherst.

Goodluck, H., and Roeper, T. 1978. "The acquisition of perception verb complements." In H. Goodluck and L. Solan, eds. 1978. *Papers in the Structure and Development of Child Language*. University of Massachusetts Occasional Papers in Linguistics, vol. 4.

Goodluck, H., and Solan, L., eds. 1978. *Papers in the Structure and Development of Child Language*. University of Massachusetts Occasional Papers in Linguistics, vol. 4.

Goodluck, H., and Solan, L. 1979. "A re-evaluation of the basic-operations hypothesis." *Cognition* 7:85–91.

Greenberg, J. 1963. "Some universals of grammar with particular reference to the order of meaningful elements." In J. Greenberg, ed. 1963. *Universals of Language*. Cambridge, Mass.: MIT Press.

Greenberg, J. 1963. *Universals of Language*. Cambridge, Mass.: MIT Press.

Gregy, L., ed. 1969. *Cognition in Learning and Memory*. New York: Wiley.

Halle, M., Bresnan, J., and Miller, G., eds. 1976. *Linguistic Theory and Psychological Reality*. Cambridge, Mass.: MIT Press.

Hamburger, H., and Wexler, K. 1975. "A mathematical theory of learning transformational grammar." *Journal of Mathematical Psychology* 12:137–177.

Hammerton, M. 1970. "Disputed interpretation of a pronoun." *Nature* 226.

Hankamer, J. 1971. Constraints on Deletion in Syntax. Doctoral dissertation, Yale University.

Hankamer, J., and Sag, I. 1976. "Deep and Surface Anaphora." *Linguistic Inquiry* 7:391–428.

Harries, H. 1973. Coordination reduction. Stanford University Working Papers on Language Universals, no. 11.

Hart, N., Walker, R., and Gray, B. 1977. *The Language of Children: A Key to Literacy*. Reading, Mass.: Addison-Wesley.

Hayes, J., ed. 1970. *Cognition and the Development of Language*. New York: Wiley.

Hintikka, J., Moravcsik, J. M. E., and Suppes, P., eds. 1973. *Approaches to Natural Language*. Dordrecht, Holland: Reidel.

Hopmann, M., and Maratsos, M. 1978. "A developmental study of factivity and negation in complex syntax." *Journal of Child Language* 5:295–309.

Horn, L. 1971. "Negative transportation: unsafe at any speed?" *Papers from the Eighth Regional Meeting, Chicago Linguistic Society*. Chicago Linguistic Society.

Hurford, J. 1975. "A child and the English question formation rule." *Journal of Child Language* 2:299–301.

Hust, J., and Brame, M. 1976. "Jackendoff on interpretive semantics." *Linguistic Analysis* 2:243–277.

Huxley, R., and Ingram, E., eds. 1971. *Language Acquisition: Models and Methods*. London: Academic.

Inhelder, B., and Piaget, J. 1969. *The Early Growth of Logic in the Child*. New York: Norton.

Jackendoff, R. 1972. *Semantic Interpretation in Generative Grammar*. Cambridge, Mass.: MIT Press.

Jackendoff, R. 1977. *$\bar{X}$ Syntax: A Study of Phrase Structure*. Linguistic Inquiry Monograph 2. Cambridge, Mass.: MIT Press.

Jacobs, R., and Rosenbaum, P., eds. 1970. *Readings in English Transformational Grammar*. Waltham, Mass.: Ginn.

Johnson-Laird, P., and Tridgell, J. 1972. "When negation is easier than affirmation." *Quarterly Journal of Experimental Psychology* 24:87–91.

Just, M., and Carpenter, P. 1971. "Comprehension of negation with quantifiers." *Journal of Verbal Learning and Verbal Behavior* 10:244–253.

Karttunen, L. 1970. "On the semantics of complement sentences." *Papers from the Sixth Regional Meeting, Chicago Linguistic Society*. Chicago: Chicago Linguistic Society.

Karttunen, L. 1971a. "Implicatives." *Language* 47:340–358.

Karttunen, L. 1971b. "Some observations on factivity." *Papers in Linguistics* 3:55–69.

Karttunen, L. 1973. "Presuppositions of compound sentences." *Linguistic Inquiry* 4:169–193.

Katz, J. 1966. *The Philosophy of Language*. New York: Harper & Row.

Katz, J. 1971. *The Underlying Reality of Language and Its Philosophical Import*. New York: Harper & Row.

Keenan, E., ed. 1975. *Formal Semantics of Natural Language*. Cambridge University Press.

Kempson, R. 1977. *Semantic Theory*. Cambridge University Press.

Kimball, J., ed. 1975. *Syntax and Semantics*. Vol. 4. New York: Academic.

Kiparsky, P., and Kiparsky, C. 1968. "Fact." In M. Bierwisch and K. E. Heidolph, eds. 1968. *Progress in Linguistics*. The Hague: Mouton.

Klima, E. 1964. "Negation in English." In J. A. Fodor and J. Katz, eds. 1964. *The Structure of Language*. Englewood Cliffs, N.J.: Prentice-Hall.

Kornfeld, J. 1973. "Clause boundary and dominance effects on sentence perception." *Research Laboratory of Electronics Quarterly Progress Report*, No. 110, MIT.

Koster, J. 1978. "Conditions, empty nodes, and markedness." *Linguistic Inquiry* 9:551–593.

Kuczaj, S. 1976. "Arguments against Hurford's 'Aux copying rule'." *Journal of Child Language* 3:423–427.

Kuno, S. 1972. "Functional sentence perspective." *Linguistic Inquiry* 3:269–320.

Kuno, S. 1973. *The Structure of the Japanese Language*. Cambridge, Mass.: MIT Press.

Lahey, M. 1974. "Use of prosody and syntactic markers in children's comprehension of spoken sentences." *Journal of Speech and Hearing Research* 17:656–668.

Langacker, R. 1969. "On pronominalization and the chain of command." In D. Reibel and R. Schane, eds. 1969. *Modern Studies in English*. Englewood Cliffs, N.J.: Prentice-Hall.

Langendoen, D. 1973. Review of Burt, *From Deep to Surface Structure*. *Language* 49:714–725.

Lapointe, S. 1977. "A lexical reanalysis of the English auxiliary system." Unpublished ms., University of Massachusetts, Amherst.

Lasnik, H. 1972. Analyses of Negation in English. Doctoral dissertation, MIT. Reproduced by the Indiana University Linguistics Club, Bloomington.

Lasnik, H. 1975. "On the semantics of negation." In J. Davis, D. Hockney, and W. Wilson, eds. 1975. *Contemporary Research in Philosophical Logic and Linguistic Semantics*. Dordrecht, Holland: Reidel.

Lasnik, H. 1976. "Remarks on coreference." *Linguistic Analysis* 2:1–22.

Legum, S. 1975. "Strategies in the acquisition of relative clauses." Southwest Regional Laboratory Technical Note TN 2–75–10.

Lenneberg, E., ed. 1964. *New Directions in the Study of Language*. Cambridge, Mass.: MIT Press.

Lenneberg, E., and Lenneberg, E. 1975. *Foundations of Language Development*. New York: Academic.

Levin, H., and Kaplan, E. 1970. "Grammatical structure in reading." In H. Levin and R. Williams, eds. 1970. *Basic Studies in Reading*. New York: Basic Books.

Levin, H., and Williams, R., eds. 1970. *Basic Studies in Reading*. New York: Basic Books.

Lewis, M., and Rosenblum, L., eds. 1977. *Interaction, Conversation, and the Development of Language*. New York: Wiley.

Limber, J. 1973. "The genesis of complex sentences." In T. Moore, ed. 1973. *Cognitive Development and the Acquisition of Language*. New York: Academic.

Limber, J. 1976. "Unravelling competence, performance and pragmatics in the speech of young children." *Journal of Child Language* 3:309–318.

Lust, B. 1977a. "Constraint on anaphora in early child language." Paper presented at Boston University Conference on Language Development.

Lust, B. 1977b. "Conjunction reduction in child language." *Journal of Child Language* 4:257–287.

Lust, B. 1978. "Constraint on anaphora in child language: A study of 6 languages." Unpublished ms., Cornell University.

Lust, B., and Barazangi, N. 1978. "The structure of coordination in children's first language acquisition of Syrian Arabic." Paper presented at Linguistic Society of America Summer Meeting, University of Illinois, Urbana.

Lust, B., and Clifford. T. In preparation. "The 3D Study: Effects of depth, distance and directionality on children's acquisition of anaphora."

Lust, B., and Mervis, C. 1980. "Coordination in the natural speech of young children." *Journal of Child Language* 7.2:1–26.

Lust, B., Loveland, K., and Kornet, R. 1980. "The development of coreference and anaphora in first language: syntactic and pragmatic constraints." *Linguistic Analysis* 6.2:217–249.

Lust B., and Wakayama, T. 1979. "The structure of coordination in children's first language acquisition in Japanese." In P. Eckman and A. Hastings, eds. 1979. *Studies in First and Second Language Acquisition*. Rowley, Mass.: Newbury House.

Lyons, J., and Wales, R., eds. 1966. *Psycholinguistic Papers*. University of Edinburgh Press.

Maling, J. 1972. "On gapping and the order of constituents." *Linguistic Inquiry* 3:101–108.

Maratsos, M. 1974. "How preschool children understand missing complement subjects." *Child Development* 45:700–706.

Maratsos, M. 1978. "New models in linguistics and language acquisition." In M. Halle, J. Bresnan, and G. Miller, eds. 1976. *Linguistic Theory and Psychological Reality*. Cambridge, Mass.: MIT Press.

Maratsos, M. 1979. "How to get from words to sentences." In D. Aaronson and R. Rieber, eds. *Psycholinguistic Research*. Hillsdale, N.J.: Erlbaum.

Maratsos, M., and Abramovitch, R. 1975. "How children understand full, truncated, and anomalous passives." *Journal of Verbal Learning and Verbal Behavior* 14:145–147.

Maratsos, M., and Kuczaj, S. 1978. "Against a transformationalist account: A simpler analysis of auxiliary overmarkings." *Journal of Child Language* 5: 337–346.

May, R. 1977. The Grammar of Quantification. Doctoral dissertation, MIT.

Mayer, J., Erreich, A., and Valian, V. 1978. "Transformations, basic operations and language acquisition." *Cognition* 6:1–13.

McNeill, D. 1966. "Developmental psycholinguistics." In F. Smith and G. Miller, eds. 1966. *The Genesis of Language*. Cambridge, Mass.: MIT Press.

Menyuk, P. 1969. *Sentences Children Use*. Cambridge, Mass.: MIT Press.

Menyuk, P. 1971. *The Acquisition and Development of Language*. Englewood Cliffs, N.J.: Prentice-Hall.

Milsark, G. 1974. *Existential Sentences in English*. Doctoral dissertation, MIT.

Montague, R. 1974. In Thomason, R., ed. *Formal Philosophy: Selected Papers of Richard Montague*. New Haven, Conn.: Yale University Press.

Moore, T., ed. 1973. *Cognitive Development and the Acquisition of Language*. New York: Academic.

Nakai, S. 1976. "Anaphoric relations in Japanese." Unpublished ms., University of Massachusetts, Amherst.

Newport, E., Gleitman, H., and Gleitman, L. 1977. "Mother, please, I'd rather do it myself: Some effects and non-effects of maternal speech style." In C. Snow and C. Ferguson, eds. 1977. *Talking to Children: Language Input and Acquisition*. Cambridge University Press.

O'Brien, R., ed. 1971. *22nd Annual Roundtable*. Monograph Series on Languages and Linguistics. Washington, D.C.: Georgetown University Press.

Partee, B. 1975. "Deletion and variable binding." In E. Keenan, ed. 1975. *Formal Semantics of Natural Language*. Cambridge University Press.

Partee, B., ed. 1976. *Montague Grammar*. New York: Academic.

Partee, B. 1977. "The well-formedness constraint." Unpublished ms., University of Massachusetts, Amherst.

Peters, S., ed. 1972. *Goals of Linguistic Theory*. Englewood Cliffs, N.J.: Prentice-Hall.

Peters, S., and Ritchie, R. 1973. "Nonfiltering and local-filtering transformational grammars." In J. Hintikka, J. M. E. Moravcsik, and P. Suppes, eds. *Approaches to Natural Language*. Dordrecht, Holland: Reidel.

Phinney, M. 1977. "Interpretation of negation in complex sentences." Unpublished ms., University of Massachusetts, Amherst.

Piaget, J. 1974. *The Language and Thought of the Child*. New York: New American Library.

Postal, P. 1971. *Cross-Over Phenomena*. New York: Holt, Rinehart and Winston.

Prideaux, G. 1976. "A functional analysis of English question acquisition: A response to Hurford." *Journal of Child Language* 3:417–422.

Read, C., and Hare, V. 1977. "Children's interpretation of reflexive pronouns in English." Paper presented at the Sixth Annual University of Wisconsin–Milwaukee Linguistics Symposium.

Reed, C., ed. 1971. *The Learning of Language*. New York: Scribner's.

Reibel, D., and Shane, R., eds. 1969. *Modern Studies in English*. Englewood Cliffs, N.J.: Prentice-Hall.

Reinhart, T. 1974. "Syntax and reference." Paper presented at Fifth Annual Meeting of the Northeastern Linguistic Society, Harvard University.

Reinhart, T. 1976. The Syntactic Domain of Anaphora. Doctoral dissertation, MIT.

Roeper, R. 1973. "Theoretical implications of word order: topicalization and inflections in German language acquisition." In C. Ferguson and D. Slobin, eds. 1973. *Studies of Child Language Development*. New York: Holt, Rinehart and Winston.

Roeper, T. 1978. "Linguistic universals and the acquisition of gerunds." In H. Goodluck and L. Solan, eds. 1978. *Papers in the Structure and Development of Child Language*. University of Massachusetts Occasional Papers in Linguistics, vol. 4.

Roeper, T. In press. "A lexical approach to language acquisition." Paper presented at "State of the Art in Language Acquisition" conference, University of Pennsylvania, May, 1978. To appear in the proceedings, L. Gleitman and E. Wanner, eds. Cambridge, Mass.: Harvard University Press.

Roeper, T., Bing, J., Lapointe, S., and Tavakolian, S. In preparation. "A lexical approach to language acquisition. II: -able and verbal compounds."

Roeper, T., and Mattei, E. 1975. "On the acquisition of *all* and *some*." *Papers and Reports on Child Language Development*. Stanford, Calif.: Stanford University Committee on Linguistics.

Roeper, T., and Siegel, M. 1978. "A lexical transformation for verbal compounds." *Linguistic Inquiry* 9:199–260.

Rosenbaum, P. 1967. *The Grammar of English Predicate Complement Constructions*. Cambridge, Mass.: MIT Press.

Ross, J. 1967. Constraints on Variables in Syntax. Doctoral dissertation, MIT.

Saenz, R., ed. 1978. University of Massachusetts Occasional Papers in Linguistics, vol. 3.

Schane, S., Tranel, B., and Lane, H. 1975. "On the psychological reality of a natural rule of syllable structure." *Cognition* 3:351–358.

Sheldon, A. 1972. The Acquisition of Relative Clauses in English. Doctoral dissertation, University of Texas. Reproduced by the Indiana University Linguistics Club, Bloomington.

Sheldon, A. 1974. "The role of parallel function in the acquisition of relative clauses in English." *Journal of Verbal Learning and Verbal Behavior* 13:272–281.

Sinclair, A., Jarvella, R., and Levelt, W. 1978. *The Child's Conception of Language*. Berlin: Springer-Verlag.

Sinclair, H. 1975. "The role of cognitive structures in language acquisition." In E. Lenneberg and E. Lenneberg, eds. 1975. *Foundations of Language Development*. New York: Academic.

Slobin, D. 1973. "Cognitive prerequisites for the development of grammar." In C. Ferguson and D. Slobin, eds. 1973. *Studies of Child Language Development*. New York: Holt, Rinehart and Winston.

Slobin, D., and Welsh, C. 1973. "Elicited imitation as a research tool in developmental psycholinguistics." In C. Ferguson and D. Slobin, eds. 1973. *Studies of Child Language Development*. New York: Holt, Rinehart and Winston.

Smith, F., and Miller, G., eds. 1966. *The Genesis of Language*. Cambridge, Mass.: MIT Press.

Smith, M. 1974. "The adequacy and reality of underlying representations: relative clause formation." *Papers from the Tenth Regional Meeting of the Chicago Linguistic Society*. Chicago Linguistic Society.

Snow, C., and Ferguson, C., eds. 1977. *Talking to Children: Language Input and Acquisition*. Cambridge University Press.

Solan, L. 1975. "The acquisition of infinitival complements." Unpublished ms., University of Massachusetts, Amherst.

Solan, L. 1978a. Anaphora in Child Language. Doctoral dissertation, University of Massachusetts, Amherst.

Solan, L. 1978b. "Language acquisition and speakers' variation in restrictions on anaphora." Paper presented at the meetings of the Northeastern Linguistics Society, New York.

Solan, L. 1978c. "On interpreting missing complement NPs." In R. Saenz, ed. 1978. University of Massachusetts Occasional Papers in Linguistics, vol. 3.

Solan, L. 1978d. "The acquisition of tough movement." In H. Goodluck and L. Solan, eds. 1978. *Papers in the Structure and Development of Child Language*. University of Massachusetts Occasional Papers in Linguistics, vol. 4.

Solan, L., and Roeper, T. 1978. "Children's use of syntactic structure in interpreting relative clauses." In H. Goodluck and L. Solan, eds. 1978. *Papers in the Structure and Development of Child Language*. University of Massachusetts Occasional Papers in Linguistics, vol. 4.

Stenning, K. 1978. "Anaphora as an approach to pragmatics." In M. Halle, J. Bresnan, and G. Miller, eds. 1976. *Linguistic Theory and Psychological Reality*. Cambridge, Mass.: MIT Press.

Stevens, M. 1978. "A re-analysis of *Wh*-question formation in child language." Paper presented at the Northeastern Linguistics Society, New York.

Tavakolian, S. 1977. Structural Principles in the Acquisition of Complex Sentences. Doctoral dissertation, University of Massachusetts, Amherst.

Tavakolian, S. 1978a. "Children's comprehension of pronominal subjects and missing subjects in complicated sentences." In H. Goodluck and L. Solan, eds. 1978. *Papers in the Structure and Development of Child Language*. University of Massachusetts Occasional Papers in Linguistics, vol. 4.

Tavakolian, S. 1978b. "The conjoined clause analysis of relative clauses and other structures." In H. Goodluck and L. Solan, eds. 1978. *Papers in the Structure and Development of Child Language*. University of Massachusetts Occasional Papers in Linguistics, vol. 4.

Trabasso, T., Rollings, H., and Shaughnessy, E. 1971. "Storage and verification stages in processing concepts." *Cognitive Psychology* 2:239–289.

Valian, V. 1979. "The wherefores and therefores of the competence-performance distinction." In W. Cooper and E. Walker, eds. 1979. *Sentence Processing: Psycholinguistic Studies Presented to Merrill Garrett*. Hillsdale, N.J.: Erlbaum.

Valian, V., and Caplan, J. 1979. "What children say when asked "What?": A study of the use of syntactic knowledge." *Journal of Experimental Child Psychology* 28:424–444.

Valian, V., Erreich, A., and Mayer, J. 1979. "From where do speech errors come from?" Unpublished ms., City University of New York Graduate Center.

Vergnaud, J.-R. 1973. "Formal properties of lexical derivations." *Quarterly Progress Report* No. 108, 280–287, Research Laboratory of Electronics, MIT.

Wanner, E., and Maratsos, M. 1974. "An ATN approach to comprehension." Unpublished ms., Harvard University.

Wason, P., and Johnson-Laird, P. 1972. *Psychology of Reasoning*. Cambridge, Mass.: Harvard University Press.

Wasow, T. 1972. Anaphoric Relations in English. Doctoral dissertation, MIT.

Wasow, T. 1977. "Transformations and the lexicon." In P. Culicover, T. Wasow, and A. Akmajian, eds. 1977. *Formal Syntax*. New York: Academic.

Wattman, J. 1977. "On the acquisition of the active-stative distinction." Unpublished ms., Hampshire College, Amherst, Mass.

Wexler, K. 1976. "Empirical questions about developmental psycholinguistics raised by a theory of language acquisition." Paper presented at the Psychology of Language Conference, Stirling, Scotland.

Wexler, K. 1978. "A principle theory for language acquisition." Paper presented at "State of the Art in Language Acquisition" conference, University of Pennsylvania. To appear in the proceedings, L. Gleitman and E. Wanner, eds. Cambridge, Mass.: Harvard University Press.

Wexler, K., and Culicover, P. 1980. *Formal Principles of Language Acquisition*. Cambridge, Mass.: MIT Press.

Wexler, K., Culicover, P., and Hamburger, H. 1975. "Learning-theoretic foundations of linguistic universals." *Theoretical Linguistics* 2:213–253.

Williams, E. 1970. "Small clauses in English." In J. Kimball, ed. 1975. *Syntax and Semantics,* vol. 4. New York: Academic.

Williams, E. 1974. Rule Ordering in Syntax. Doctoral dissertation, MIT.

Williams, E. 1977a. "Discourse and logical form." *Linguistic Inquiry* 8:101–139.

Williams, E. 1977b. "On deep and surface anaphora." *Linguistic Inquiry* 8:692–696.

Wilson, D. 1972. "Presuppositions on factives." *Linguistic Inquiry* 3:405–410.

Contributors

Edwin S. Williams, Department of Linguistics, University of Massachusetts, Amherst

Thomas Roeper, Department of Linguistics, University of Massachusetts, Amherst

Steven Lapointe, Department of Psychology, Johns Hopkins University

Janet Bing, Department of English, University of New Hampshire, Durham

Lawrence Solan, Department of Human Development and Family Studies, Cornell University, Ithaca, New York

Barbara Lust, Department of Human Development and Family Studies, Cornell University, Ithaca, New York

Edward H. Matthei, School of Social Sciences, University of California at Irvine

Marianne Phinney, Department of Linguistics, University of Massachusetts, Amherst

Helen Goodluck, Department of Linguistics, University of Wisconsin

Susan L. Tavakolian, Department of Linguistics, Ohio State University, Columbus

Virginia Valian, Department of Psychology, Columbia University

Judith Winzemer, Department of Psychology, Fairleigh Dickinson University

Anne Erreich, Children's Hospital, Boston

Index